# How to Do the Work

# How to Do the Work

## Recognize Your Patterns, Heal from Your Past, and Create Your Self

Dr. Nicole LePera

HARPER WAVE
*An Imprint of* HarperCollins*Publishers*

FIRST EDITION

*Designed by Nancy Singer*

Library of Congress Cataloging-in-Publication Data

Names: LePera, Nicole, author.
Title: How to do the work : recognize your patterns, heal from your past, and create your self / Dr. Nicole LePera.
Identifiers: LCCN 2020042773 (print) | LCCN 2020042774 (ebook) | ISBN 9780063012097 (hardback) | ISBN 9780063012103 (epub)
Subjects: LCSH: Mind and body. | Healing—Psychological aspects. | Self-help techniques.
Classification: LCC BF161 .L4345 2021 (print) | LCC BF161 (ebook) | DDC 128/.2—dc23
LC record available at https://lccn.loc.gov/2020042773
LC ebook record available at https://lccn.loc.gov/2020042774

21 22 23 24 25 LSC 10 9 8 7

For Lolly, who saw me before even I could.

To each of you, I see you.

As above, so below, as within, so without, to perform the miracles of one only thing.

—Hermes Trismegistus, *The Great Work*

The evolution of man is the evolution of his consciousness. With objective consciousness it is possible to see and feel the unity of everything. Attempts to connect these phenomena into some sort of system in a scientific or philosophical way lead to nothing because man cannot reconstruct the idea of the whole starting from separate facts.

—George Gurdjieff, *The Fourth Way*

Not everything that is faced can be changed, but nothing can be changed until it is faced.

—James Baldwin, *Remember This House*
(inspiration for the film *I Am Not Your Negro*)

Very truly I tell you, no one can enter the kingdom of God unless . . . we become illuminated and enlightened to the Truth of who we are and where we are going . . . to the light while we live through love.

—Jesus, about *The Great Work*

# Contents

# A note on *doing the work*

A long, rich tradition of *the work* of transcending our human experience has been passed down by different messengers throughout the ages. The ancient Hermetic traditions spoke of mysterious alchemy, while modern mystics, such as George Gurdjieff, urged seekers to engage more deeply in the world by attaining higher levels of consciousness. We see similar language used in the required knowledge for antiracism training and the necessary dismantling of systemic oppression, as well as in substance use recovery models, like twelve-step programs. What all of these iterations of *the work* share—and what this book will foster and continue—is the pursuit of insight into the Self and our place in our community. The goal of *my* work is to provide you with the tools to understand and harness the complex interconnectedness of your mind, body, and soul. This will foster deeper, more authentic, more meaningful relationships with yourself, with others, and within the greater society. What follows is my journey, and I hope that it inspires you to find your own version of *the work*.

# Preface

# Dark Night of the Soul

Poets and mystics always seem to have their transcendental awakenings somewhere divine—on a mountaintop, while staring off into the open sea, by a babbling brook, next to a burning bush. Mine happened in a log cabin in the middle of the woods, where I found myself sobbing uncontrollably into a bowl of oatmeal.

I was in upstate New York with my partner, Lolly, on what was supposed to be a vacation, a retreat from the stress of city life in Philadelphia.

As I ate my breakfast, I pored through the pages of another psychologist's book, my version of a "beach read." The topic? Emotionally unavailable mothers. As I read it—for professional enrichment, or so I believed—the words activated an unexpected, and confusing, emotional response.

"You're burnt out," my partner, Lolly, offered. "You need to take a step back. Try to relax."

I brushed her off. I didn't believe that I was in any way unique in my general feelings and experiences. I heard similar complaints from so many of my clients and friends. *Who doesn't get out of bed in the morning dreading the day ahead? Who doesn't feel distracted at work? Who doesn't feel distanced from the people they love? Who in the world can honestly say that they aren't living each day for their vacation? Isn't this just what happens when you get older?*

I had recently "celebrated" my thirtieth birthday and thought to myself, *Is this it?* Even though I'd already checked off so many of the boxes that I'd dreamed of since I was a child—living in a city of my choosing, running my own private therapy practice, finding a loving partner—I still felt like there was something essential in my being that was lost or missing or had never been there in the first place. After years of being in relationships yet feeling emotionally alone, I had finally met a person who felt *right* because she was so different from me. Whereas I was hesitant and often disengaged, Lolly was passionate and headstrong. She often challenged me in ways that I felt were exciting. I should have been happy, or, at the very least, content. Instead I felt outside myself, detached, emotionless. I felt *nothing*.

On top of it all, I was experiencing physical issues that had become so acute that I could no longer ignore them. There was the brain fog, which would cloud me so thoroughly that I sometimes not only forgot words or phrases but entered a complete state of blankness. This was particularly upsetting, especially during the few times when it happened in session with clients. Persistent gut issues, which had plagued me for years, now made me feel heavy and constantly weighed down. Then one day I fainted out of the blue—full-on passed out at a friend's house, which terrified everyone.

Sitting in the rocking chair with my bowl of oatmeal in such a serene setting, I suddenly felt how hollowed out my life had become. I was energetically drained, in the clutches of existential despair, frustrated by my clients' inability to make progress, angered at my own limitations in the pursuit of their care and my own, and deeply constricted by a free-floating sluggishness and dissatisfaction that made me question the point of everything. Back at home in the hustle and bustle of city life, I could mask these troubling feelings by channeling all of these energies into action: cleaning the kitchen, walking the dog, making endless plans. Moving, moving, moving. If you didn't look too closely you might admire my type A efficiency. But dig in just a little bit, and you'd realize that I was moving my body to distract myself from some deeply rooted unresolved feelings. In the middle of the woods, without a thing to do but read about the lasting effects of childhood trauma, I could no longer escape myself. The book exposed so many of the feelings about my mother and my family that I had long repressed. It was like looking into a mirror. There I was, naked, no distractions, and very uncomfortable with what I saw.

When I did look more honestly at myself overall, it was hard not to notice that many of the issues I was having closely mirrored those I saw in my mother's own struggles; in particular my mother's own relationship with her body and emotions. I watched her struggle in many ways with near constant physical pain in her knees and back, and frequent anxiety and worry. As I grew up there were, of course, many ways I was different from my mom. I was physically active, making it a priority to take care of my body by exercising and eating healthy. In my twenties, I even became a vegetarian after befriending a cow at an animal sanctuary, making it impossible for me to imagine eating any animal ever again. Sure, the bulk of my diet revolved around hyperprocessed fake meat and vegan junk food (vegan Philly cheesesteaks were a particular favorite), but at least I cared about what I put into my body. With the exception of alcohol, which I still overindulged in, I sometimes took that caring to an extreme, restricting myself and eating joylessly.

I always thought that I was *nothing like my mom*, but as these emotional and now physical issues erupted, spilling into all aspects of my life, I realized it was time to start questioning things. And that realization sent me sobbing into a pile of hot mush. Contained in this sad, somewhat pathetic picture was a message. This outpouring of emotion was so unusual, so outside the realm of my typical personality, that I couldn't ignore this soul signal. Something was screaming out for me to pay attention, and there was nothing for me to hide behind in the middle of the woods. It was time to come face-to-face with my suffering, my pain, my trauma, and ultimately my true Self.

Today I call that incident my dark night of the soul, my rock bottom. Hitting rock bottom is like a death, and for some of us, it can literally bring us close to death. Death, of course, enables rebirth, and I emerged determined to figure out what was wrong. That painful moment brought the light in, revealing so much of myself that I buried. Suddenly, clarity hit: *I need to find change.* I had no idea that this insight would lead to a physical, psychological, and spiritual awakening and eventually become an international movement.

Initially, I focused on what I felt was most pressing: my body. I assessed myself physically: How was I sick, and where was this sickness manifesting? I knew intuitively that the way back would start with nutrition and movement. I enlisted Lolly, who I call my Energizer Bunny of self-improvement, to help keep me on the path to honestly dealing with how I was mistreating my vessel. She kicked me out of bed in the morning, shoved dumbbells into my hands, and forced us to consciously move our bodies several times a day. We dug into nutrition research and found that many of our ideas about what was "healthy" were debatable. We began a morning ritual incorporating breathwork and meditation—again, every day. Though I participated somewhat begrudgingly at first and there were missed days, tears, sore muscles, aching souls, and threats of quitting, after many months a routine took hold. I began to crave this new routine, and I felt stronger physically and mentally than I had in my entire life.

As my body began to heal, I began to question so many other truths that I had once felt were self-evident. I learned new ways of thinking about mental wellness. I realized that a disconnect among mind, body, and soul can manifest as sickness and dysregulation. I discovered that our genes are not destiny and that in order to change, we have to become consciously aware of our thought patterns and habits, which have been shaped by the people we care for, and have been cared for by, the most. I discovered a new, wider definition of trauma, one that takes into account the profound spiritual effects that stress and adverse experiences in childhood have on the body's nervous system. I realized that I had unresolved traumas from my childhood that continued to affect me every single day.

The more I learned, the more I integrated what I was learning into the new daily choices I was consistently making. Over time, I adapted to those changes and began to transform. Once my physiology began to heal, I went deeper, harnessing some of the insights I'd learned in my diverse range of clinical experience and applying them to the knowledge I was building about the integration of the whole person—our physical, psychological, and spiritual Selves. I met my inner child, learned how to reparent her, examined the trauma bonds that were holding me hostage, learned how to set boundaries, and began to engage with the world with an emotional maturity that I had never before known was possible, as it had been an entirely unknown state to me. I realized that this inner work didn't stop inside me but extended beyond myself into each and every relationship and into the greater community at large. This revelatory understanding of mind-body-soul wellness is encapsulated in the pages that follow, which set forth the basic tenets of Holistic Psychology.

I write to you today from a place of continued healing. My symptoms of anxiety and panic have largely disappeared. I no longer relate to the world from a reactive place, and I am able to access more awareness and compassion. I feel connected to and present with my loved ones—and I am able to set boundaries with those who are not active participants in my journey. I am conscious for the first time in my adult life. I didn't see it when I hit rock bottom. I didn't see it a year later. Today I know that I would not be here writing this book if I had not accessed the depths of my despair.

I launched The Holistic Psychologist in 2018 after deciding that I wanted to share the tools I'd discovered with others. I *had* to share. Soon after I began sharing my story on Instagram, letters of trauma, healing, and emotional resilience began pouring into my inbox. My messages of holistic healing had resonated in the collective mind, crossing age and cultural lines. Today more than three million people follow my account and have taken on the identity of #SelfHealers—active participants in their mental, physical, and spiritual wellness. Supporting this community has become my life's work.

I honored the one-year anniversary of The Holistic Psychologist by hosting a West Coast inner child meditation to thank my community for their support and to give an opportunity to connect in real life and celebrate our shared journeys. Days before, I googled "Venice Beach locations" and haphazardly picked a meetup spot. I offered free tickets on Instagram and crossed my fingers that people would be interested. Within a few hours, three thousand people had signed up. I couldn't believe it.

As I sat under the hot sun in the middle of the wide expanse of Venice Beach, joggers and various characters from southern California bobbed by. I set my sights on the waves lapping against the shore. The warm sand under my toes and the chilly wetness of my ocean-soaked hair made me acutely aware of my body in space and time. I felt so present, so alive as I lifted my hands in prayer, imagining the various life paths that had brought each and every one of the remarkable humans around me to the beach that morning. I scanned the crowd and briefly felt overwhelmed by the sheer number of eyes on me, a person who has always hated being the center of attention. Then I began:

> Something brought you here. Something inside of you came here with a deep longing to heal. A longing to be the highest version of yourself. This is something to celebrate. We all have a childhood that is creating our current reality, and today we've chosen to heal from our past in order to create a new future.
>
> The part of you that knows this to be true is your intuition. It has always been there. We have simply developed a habit of not listening to or trusting what it says. Being here today is a step in healing that broken trust within ourselves.

As I said those words, I locked eyes with a stranger in the crowd. She smiled at me and touched her heart, as if to say "Thank you." Suddenly, tears filled my eyes. I was crying—and these were not the same tears that I had shed into my oatmeal all those years before.

These were tears of love, of acceptance, of joy. These were tears of healing.

I'm a living testament to this truth: Awakenings are not mystical experiences that are reserved only for monks, mystics, and poets. They are not only for "spiritual" people. They are for each and every one of us who wants to change—who aches to heal, to thrive, to shine.

With your awareness awakened, anything is possible.

# Introduction

# A Primer on Holistic Psychology

*How to Do the Work* is the testament of a revolutionary approach to mental, physical, and spiritual wellness called Holistic Psychology. It's a movement of empowerment that's committed to the daily practice of creating your own wellness by breaking negative patterns, healing from your past, and creating your conscious Self.

Holistic Psychology focuses on the mind, body, and soul in the service of rebalancing the body and nervous system and healing unresolved emotional wounds. This work gives you the power to transform yourself into the person you've always been at your core. It tells a new, exciting story, where physical and psychological symptoms are *messages*, not lifelong diagnoses that can only be managed. It's a story that gets to the root of chronic pain, stress, fatigue, anxiety, gut dysregulation, and nervous system imbalances that have long been dismissed or ignored by traditional Western medicine. It helps explain why so many of us feel stuck, detached, or lost. It offers practical tools that will enable you to create new habits for yourself, understand the behavior of others, and release the idea that your worth is determined by any person or thing outside yourself. If you commit to doing *the work* every day, there will come a time when you will look in the mirror and feel awestruck by the person looking back at you.

These holistic methods—exercises that harness the power of the physical (with breathwork and bodywork), the psychological (by changing your relationship to your thoughts and past experiences), and the spiritual (by connecting to our authentic Self and to the greater collective)—are effective because the body, mind, and soul are *connected*. They work because they are both based in the science of epigenetics and the reality that we have far more impact over our mental wellness than we may think. Healing is a conscious process that can be lived daily through changes in our habits and patterns.

So many of us exist in a state of unconsciousness. We navigate through the world running on blind autopilot, carrying out automatic, habitual behaviors that don't serve us or reflect who we fundamentally are and what we deeply desire. The practice of Holistic Psychology helps us reconnect to our inner guidance system, which conditioned patterns learned in early childhood have taught us to disconnect from. Holistic Psychology helps us find that intuitive voice, to trust it, and to let go of the "personality" that has been modeled and shaped by parent-figures, friends, teachers, and society at large, allowing us to bring consciousness to our unconscious selves.

In these pages you will find a new paradigm for an integrative approach to healing that incorporates the mind, body, and soul. Please note that I am not advocating for a tearing down of the old model; I'm not suggesting that the tools of conventional psychotherapy and other therapeutic models don't have value. Instead, I'm proposing an approach that embraces aspects of various modalities—from psychology and neuroscience to mindfulness and spirituality practices—in an effort to cultivate what I believe are the most effective and integrative techniques for healing and wellness. I have incorporated lessons and insights from traditional models like cognitive behavioral therapy (CBT) and psychoanalysis, while also bringing in holistic aspects that are (as of this writing) not entirely embraced by mainstream psychology. It's important to understand that the practice of Holistic Psychology is rooted in freedom, choice, and ultimately empowerment. Some things will resonate, others won't; the objective is to use the tools that work best for *you*. Just the act of choosing will help you connect more deeply to your intuition and your authentic Self.

Learning to heal yourself—SelfHealing—is an act of self-empowerment. SelfHealing is not only possible, it is our reality as human beings, because no one outside of us can truly know what is best for each of us in our uniqueness. Problematically, for far too many of us, quality health care, especially mental health care, is out of reach. We live in a world where there are gross inequities in access according to where we live, what we look like, and who we are. Even those of us who are privileged enough to afford the type of care we need often encounter the eye-opening truth that not all care is created equal. And if we are lucky enough to find a truly helpful provider, we are confined by the limited amount of face-to-face time we get with that person. This book offers a self-directed learning model that contains the information and prompts that will enable *you* to do *the work* of healing yourself each and every day. Truly comprehending your past, listening to it, witnessing it, learning from it, is a process that enables deep change. Change that lasts. It enables true transformation.

*How to Do the Work* is presented in three parts. The first part provides the foundation as we become aware of our conscious Self, the power of our thoughts, and the influence of stress and childhood trauma on all the systems of our bodies. It allows us to understand how physical dysregulation in our bodily systems keeps us from moving forward mentally and emotionally. In the second part, we will peel back a layer and enter "the mind." We will explore the workings of the conscious and subconscious, learning how powerful conditioning from our parent-figures shaped our worlds, creating thought and behavior patterns that persist today. We will then dive a bit deeper into our mind and meet our inner child. We will learn about the ego stories that protect us and keep us repeating relationship patterns we began experiencing in childhood. In the final part, which I consider to be the essence of *the work*, we will learn how to apply the knowledge we've gained to achieve the emotional maturity that allows you to connect more authentically with others. No person is an island. We are social creatures, and it is not until we are able to truly embody our authentic Self that we become able to connect deeply with the people we love. This creates the foundation from which to cultivate a sense of oneness with the collective "we," or something greater than ourselves. Along the way, I've included prompts and tools intended to meet you wherever you are on your journey.

All you need to begin this transformation is your conscious Self, a desire to dig deep, and an understanding that change is not easy and the road ahead will sometimes be rough. There are no quick fixes here, which is a difficult fact to come to terms with especially for the many of us who have been conditioned to believe in the illusion of the magic bullet solution. I will be the first to say that *the work* is just that: work. There are no shortcuts, and no one else can do it for you. It can feel uncomfortable or even downright scary to become an active participant in your own healing. Ultimately, learning who you are and what you are capable of is not only empowering and transformative, but one of the most profound experiences we can have.

Some people who follow my work tell me that I deliver truths wrapped up in nice, comfy blankets. I take that as a compliment, and I'm going to get real for a second: There is such a thing as getting *too* comfortable. Healing rarely comes *without* difficulty. It's painful at times and terrifying, too. It means letting go of narratives that hold you back and harm you. It means letting a part of yourself die so that another part of you can be reborn. Not everyone wants to get better. And that's okay. Some people have an identity tied to sickness. Others fear true wellness because it is the unknown and the unknown is unpredictable. There is comfort in knowing exactly what your life will look like, even if that reality is making you sick. Our minds are familiarity-seeking machines. The familiar feels safe; that is, until we teach ourselves that discomfort is temporary and a necessary part of transformation.

You will know when you're ready to begin this journey. Then you'll second-guess yourself and want to quit. This is when it's the most important to stay committed and keep repeating the practice until it becomes a discipline. Eventually, that discipline becomes confidence, and confidence becomes change, and change becomes transformation. The real work has nothing to do with anything "out there." It has everything to do with what's in you. It comes *from* you.

The first step, a surprisingly challenging one, is to begin to imagine a future that looks different from the present. Close your eyes. Once you are able to envision a reality alternate to the one you're living, you're ready to move forward. And if you can't yet envision that reality, you're far from alone. There's a reason for this mental block. Stick with me; this book is written for you, as I was that person.

Let's get started.

# How to Do the Work

# 1

# You Are Your Own Best Healer

This scenario will likely feel familiar: You decide that today is the day that you'll change your life. You'll start going to the gym, eat less processed food, take a break from social media, cut ties with a problematic ex. You're determined that *this time* these changes will stick. Later—maybe it's a few hours, maybe a few days or even weeks—mental resistance enters. You start to feel physically unable to avoid sugary soda. You can't muster up the energy to go to the gym, and you feel compelled to send a certain ex a quick text message to check in. The mind starts to scream at you with convincing stories to keep you in your familiar life with pleas like, "You deserve a break." The body joins the mind with feelings of exhaustion and heaviness. The overwhelming message becomes: "You *can't* do this."

Over my decade of work as a researcher and clinical psychologist, "stuck" was the word most commonly used by my clients to describe the way they felt. Every client came to therapy because they wanted to change. Some wanted to change things about themselves by creating habits, learning new behaviors, or finding ways to stop disliking themselves. Others wanted to shift things outside themselves, like changing a problematic dynamic with a parent-figure or a spouse or a colleague. Many wanted (and needed) to make both internal and external changes. I've treated wealthy people and people living in poverty; hyperfunctional, high-powered types; and those who have been incarcerated and shunned by traditional society. Unanimously, no matter their backgrounds, every client felt stuck—stuck in bad habits, damaging behaviors, predictable and problematic patterns—and it made them feel lonely, isolated, and hopeless. Almost all of them worried about how this "stuckness" was perceived by others and often obsessed about the many ways everyone in their lives perceived them. Most shared a deep-rooted belief that their consistent inability to sustain change reflected evidence of deeper, intrinsic damage or "unworthiness"—a description used by many.

Often my clients who were more self-aware could identify their problematic behaviors and could even visualize a clear path to change. But few were able to take that first step from *knowing* to *doing*. The ones who could see a way out expressed feelings of shame about their instinctual falling back into patterns of unwanted behavior. They felt ashamed that they *knew* better and still could not *do* better, which was why they had ended up in my office.

Even my help and support were often of limited value. Fifty minutes of therapy per week did not seem sufficient to effect meaningful change for a majority of my clients. Some became so frustrated by this unfulfilling merry-go-round that they stopped seeking therapy altogether. Although many others benefited from our time together, the improvements were painfully slow to come. A session would seem highly productive, and then the same client would return the next week with stories that reflected the same predictable set of problems. Many clients expressed incredible insight in therapy, piecing together all the patterns that held them back, and would then feel unable to resist the instinctual pull toward the familiar in real life (outside of my therapy office). They could look *backward* and see the issues, yet they hadn't built the capacity to apply that insight in real time to their present life. I observed similar patterns with people who went through deeply transformative experiences—those who attended intensive retreats or mind-altering ayahuasca ceremonies—and then, over time, slid right back into the old, unwanted behaviors that had sent them looking for answers in the first place. Their inability to move forward after experiencing something so seemingly transformative threw many of my clients into crisis: *What is wrong with me? Why can't I change?*

What I came to realize is that therapy and singular transformative experiences (like ayahuasca ceremonies) can take us only so far along the path to healing. To truly actualize change, you have to engage in *the work* of making new choices every day. In order to achieve mental wellness, you must begin by being an active *daily* participant in your own healing.

The more I looked around, I saw the same frustration, even beyond my practice among my circle of friends. So many of them were taking medication for insomnia, depression, and anxiety. Some hadn't officially been diagnosed with any type of mood disorder, yet they were channeling a lot of the same symptoms into seemingly acceptable expressions, such as hyperachievement, constant traveling, and obsessive social media engagement. These people were the ones who got straight A's, who finished their assignments weeks before they were due, who ran marathons, who landed high-stress jobs and excelled in pressure cooker environments. In many ways, I was one of these people.

I knew firsthand the limits of the traditional model of mental health care. I started therapy in my twenties, when I was plagued by near-constant panic attacks while dealing with my mother's serious heart condition. Antianxiety medication helped me through, but I still felt listless, detached, tired—older than my years. I was a psychologist, someone who was supposed to help others understand their inner world, yet I continued to be a stranger to, and unable to truly help, even myself.

## MY PATH

I was born into a typical middle-class family in Philadelphia. My dad had a stable nine-to-five job, and my mom kept the home. We ate breakfast at 7:00 a.m. every morning and dinner at 5:30 p.m. every evening. The family motto was "Family is everything," and by all outside estimations that motto rang true. We were the picture of middle-class normalcy and happiness—an all-American projection that clouded the reality.

In fact, we were a sick family. My sister suffered from life-threateningly serious health issues as a child, and my mother struggled with her own phantom pains that confined her to bed for days. Though my family never talked openly about my mother's illness, I was aware. I knew that my mom was suffering. I knew that she was sick. I knew that she was not present because she was in pain. I knew that she was distracted and chronically anxious. Amid all the stress, my emotional world could understandably be forgotten.

I was the third and last child—a "happy accident," they'd say. My siblings are significantly older than I (my brother could vote by the time I came around), and they never really shared my experiences. As many of you know, even if you live in the same home, you never truly live the same childhood. My parents joked that I was their "Christ child." I slept well, hardly caused issues, and more or less kept out of trouble. I was an active kid who was filled with lots of energy and was always on the go. I learned very early on to ease any burden of my existence by being as near to perfect as possible in all of the ways I knew I had excelled.

My mother was not particularly expressive with her emotions. We were not really a "touchy" family and physical touch was minimal. To my memory, "I love yous" in childhood were very inconsistent. In fact, the first time I really remember hearing those words expressed openly was when my mother was undergoing heart surgery when I was in my early twenties. Don't get me wrong, I did have an inner knowing that my parents loved me very much. I would learn later that my mom's parents had been cold and detached in their own displays of love and affection. My mom, a wounded child herself, had never been shown the love she craved deeply. As a result, she was unable to express love to her own children, whom she did love deeply.

Overall, the family lived in a general state of emotional avoidance where anything unpleasant was merely ignored. When I started acting out (briefly dropping the Christ child pose), partying before I'd even officially become a teenager and stumbling home with red eyes and slurring my words, no one said a word to me about my behavior. This avoidance would carry on until someone's repressed emotions would bubble up, overwhelm them, and explode. That happened once when my mom read a personal note of mine, discovered evidence of my drinking, and became hysterical—throwing things, crying, and shrieking "You're going to kill me! I'm going to have a heart attack and drop dead right this moment!"

Growing up, I often felt different from others I met and, for as long as I can remember, I was drawn to understand what made people behave as they did. Not surprisingly, eventually I found myself wanting to be a psychologist. It's not only that I wanted to help people; I wanted to *understand* them. I wanted to point to research and be able to say "See! This is why you are the way you are! This is why I am the way I am!" That interest led me to Cornell University, where I studied psychology, and then to a PhD program in clinical psychology at the New School for Social Research in New York. Because of the "scientist practitioner model" the program followed, I was required to both do research and provide therapy. I was a sponge, eagerly soaking up all the information I possibly could about various approaches to therapy, knowing I wanted to practice in a way that would truly help others to understand themselves and to heal.

There I learned cognitive behavioral therapy (CBT), a standardized approach to therapy that is highly prescribed and goal oriented. During CBT sessions, clients often focus on one issue, maybe depression, anxiety in crowds, or marriage troubles. The objective of this practice is to help a patient identify the flawed thought patterns that underlie their behavior—a process that can help some find relief from consistent problematic feelings.

The CBT model is based on the premise that our thoughts affect our emotions and ultimately our behaviors. When we change our relationship with our thoughts, we change the cascade of emotions that floods our bodies and persuades us to act in certain ways, which is a cornerstone of the work in this book. CBT is often referred to as the "gold standard" in psychotherapy because its highly replicable, or repeatable, structure and format makes it great for lab study. While studying it taught me a valuable lesson about the power of our thoughts, it can be a bit rigid when applied in the real world. Eventually, in my practice with clients, it sometimes felt constraining and not really tailored to the unique individual in front of me.

During my graduate studies, I was particularly drawn to interpersonal therapy, a far more open-ended therapeutic model that uses the bond between client and practitioner as a catalyst for improving other relationships in the client's life. Most of us have problematic relationship dynamics in some part of our life—whether with family, partners, friends, or colleagues—so being able to engage in a new, healthier dynamic with a therapist can be profoundly healing. How we show up in our relationships is really emblematic of our general wellness, and often indicates *how we show up in life*, a theme we'll explore throughout this book. In the Holistic Psychology framework, we incorporate the understanding that our relationships are modeled on our earliest bonds with our parent-figures, an act of behavior modeling called conditioning, which we will learn more about in chapter 2.

Over the course of my training, I studied psychodynamic approaches, theories of the mind that suggest that people are driven by forces inside them. I studied these models—ones usually associated with the cliché of the couch and the pipe-smoking analyst—at both the New York Psychoanalytic Society & Institute and the Philadelphia School of Psychoanalysis. There I learned about the pull of the subconscious, the deeply embedded part of our psyche that holds our memories and is the source of our drives, or automatic instincts or motivations. As I started practicing therapy, the insight I gained into the role of our subconscious was profound. I kept noticing that all of my clients would realize the aspects of their lives they needed to change—using substances as distractions, flying into anger in romantic relationships, reverting to childlike behaviors in familial relationships—yet every time, they'd return to therapy with a story that reflected the same repeated subconscious cycle. I saw it in myself, too. That realization was instrumental in the creation and evolution of the philosophy of Holistic Psychology.

While I learned these new modalities, I started to research and work in the substance use recovery field. I ran outpatient and inpatient substance treatment groups and facilitated a program to help those with substance abuse issues develop the interpersonal skills to support their recovery processes. This helped me gain perspective into the actual lived experiences of those who struggle to control their substance use. Eventually these experiences led me to the conclusion that addiction isn't limited to specific substances and experiences such as alcohol, drugs, gambling, and sex; cycles of human emotions can be addicting too. Emotional addiction is particularly powerful when we habitually seek or avoid certain emotional states as a way to cope with trauma. Studying addiction showed me the inextricable link between our bodies and minds, as well as the central role of the nervous system in mental wellness, a topic that we will discuss in detail later in this book.

At various points in my postdoctoral work, I tried to incorporate outside elements into my psychology practice. I felt that mindfulness gave us tremendous opportunities for self-reflection and self-awareness. After conducting and publishing my own research on this topic,[1] I tried to convince my doctoral adviser to let me study the practice of meditation and its effect on addictive behaviors for my dissertation project. I was denied. He didn't believe that mindfulness had therapeutic value; he saw it as a fad, not something worthy of study.

Looking back now, I can see that a path was unfolding before me. My inner guide was showing me all that I needed to create a holistic model of healing. I opened my own private practice where I incorporated many aspects of all the modalities that I had studied. Though I was offering an integrative approach to therapy, several years in, I started to feel frustrated. My clients were gaining some awareness, but the changes were slow. I could feel their confidence leaving them. And simultaneously, I felt my own confidence waning.

I looked around me—really looked, as if for the first time. It's not an exaggeration to say that every single one of my clients who came to me for psychological treatment also had underlying physical symptoms. Long out of school, I started to ask new questions: Why did so many of my clients suffer from digestive issues, ranging from irritable bowel syndrome (IBS) to constipation? Why were there such high rates of autoimmune diseases? And why did almost all of us feel panicky and unsafe almost all the time?

I can say with certainty that I would not have found my path without the mainstream training I received in school. I brought so much of what I learned in the academic setting into my creation of Holistic Psychology. But the more I discovered on my own about the mind-body-soul connection, the more clearly I saw the limitations of my traditional training.

## MIND-BODY-SOUL CONNECTION

Close your eyes. Picture a lemon. See its glossy yellow skin. Hold it in your hands. Feel its ridges. Put it to your nose; imagine the clean scent hitting your nostrils. Now imagine slicing a wedge from the lemon. Watch the juice jump out as you cut through the flesh. See the oval pits. Now put that lemon wedge to your mouth. Your lips may sting on contact. Taste the acidity, the cool citrus, the freshness. Does your mouth pucker or fill up with saliva? The mere thought of a lemon can provoke an entire sensory response. You've just experienced the mind-body connection without putting down this book.

This visualization exercise is a simple but powerful way to show how mind and body are united. Unfortunately, Western medicine is constrained by the belief that the mind and body are separate entities—clinicians treat the mind (psychology or psychiatry) or the body (every other branch of medicine) and rarely incorporate treatment for both at the same time. This arbitrary separation of mind and body holds medicine back from its potential for healing and sometimes even makes us sicker in the process. Indigenous and Eastern cultures, on the other hand, have fully understood and honored the connections among the mind, body, and soul/spirit[2]—the sense of something higher than ourselves[3]—for thousands of years. They have long used ritual and ceremony to tap into the Self in order to connect with ancestors for guidance and clarity, and operated with an inner "knowing" that a whole person is made up of interconnected parts.

Mainstream Western medicine has long deemed this connection "unscientific." In the seventeenth century, the concept of "mind-body dualism,"[4,5] a literal disconnection between the mind and body, was birthed by the French philosopher René Descartes. This dichotomy persists four hundred years later. We still treat the mind as distinct from the body. If you're sick psychologically, you see one type of doctor, have one set of medical records, and end up in one type of hospital; if your symptoms are deemed "physical," the process plays out much differently. As technology advanced in the nineteenth century, we learned more about human biology and the ways in which things in our environment (viruses, bacteria) can harm us. Medicine became a field of intervention. When symptoms emerge, a physician is there to manage them, either by eradicating them (with surgery, for example) or by treating them (with prescription medicines that come with known and unknown side effects). Instead of listening to the body—after all, symptoms are its way of communicating with us—we seek to silence it. In the process of suppressing symptoms, we often suffer new harms. The idea of a whole-person approach to care has been cast aside for a symptom management approach, and it has created a vicious cycle of dependence. It's what I call the Band-Aid model, where we focus on treating individual symptoms as they arise and never look at the underlying causes.

Psychiatry once called itself "the science [or study] of the psyche or soul." Today the focus of psychiatry has become overwhelmingly biological. You're much more likely to be asked about a family history of mental illness and be given a prescription for antidepressants than to be asked about childhood trauma or given guidance about your nutrition and lifestyle. The field has fully embraced the protocol of the *Diagnostic and Statistical Manual of Mental Disorders* (DSM-5), created by the American Psychiatric Association, which catalogs symptoms as a means to a diagnosis—typically a "disorder," which is genetic or "organic" in origin, not environmental or learned. By assigning a genetic cause, we naturally imagine our sickness to be part of who we are. When we *become* a diagnosis, it decreases incentive to change or try to explore root causes. We identify with the label. *This is who I am.*

Since the turn of the twentieth century we've believed in genetic causes of diagnoses— a theory called genetic determinism. Under this model, our genes (and subsequent health) are determined at birth. We are "destined" to inherit or be exempt from certain diseases based on the blind luck or misfortune of our DNA. Genetic determinism doesn't consider the role of family backgrounds, traumas, habits, or anything else within the environment. In this dynamic we are not active participants in our own health and wellness. Why would we be? If something is predetermined, it's not necessary to look at anything beyond our DNA. But the more science has learned about the body and its interaction with the environment around it (in its myriad forms, from our nutrition to our relationships to our racially oppressive systems), the more complex the story becomes. We are not merely expressions of coding but products of remarkable arrays of interactions that are both within and outside of our control. Once we see beyond the narrative that genetics are destiny, we can take ownership of our health. This allows us to see how "choiceless" we once were and empowers us with the ability to create real and lasting change.

I saw this "choicelessness" firsthand in my training. I too was taught that psychiatric disorders are genetic; that each of us has been handed down a destiny in our DNA and there's very little, if anything, we can do about it. My job was to catalog symptoms—insomnia, weight gain, weight loss, anger, irritability, sadness—and offer a diagnosis that I then would attempt to treat by offering a supportive relationship through therapy. If that wasn't enough, I could refer the patient to a psychiatrist, who would prescribe psychotropic medication. Those were the options. There were no discussions about the body's role in what we knew as mental illness, and we were never counseled to use words like "healing" or "wellness." The idea of harnessing the power of the body to help heal the mind was dismissed as antiscience. Or, worse, New Age nonsense.

When we don't ask how we can contribute to our own wellness, we become helpless and dependent. The message we learn is this: we are totally at the whim of our bodies, and the only way to feel okay is to put our health into the hands of clinicians, who have the magic bullets that can make us better, who have all the answers, who can save us. But the reality is that we get sicker and sicker. As I started to question the status quo, I came to this realization: we find ourselves unable to change because we are not being told the whole truth about our human existence.

## THE POWER TO TRANSFORM

There is an awakening going on right this moment. No longer do we need to accept the narrative of "faulty genes" as our fate. Emerging science tells us that the genes we inherit aren't fixed; they are influenced by their environment, beginning in utero and continuing throughout our lives. The groundbreaking discovery of epigenetics tells a new story about our ability to change.

We are, of course, given a set of genes, but, like a deck of cards, to some degree we can choose which hands we want to play. We can make choices about our sleep, nutrition, relationships, and the ways we move our body that all alter gene expression.

Biologist Bruce Lipton has been spreading the gospel about the role of epigenetics for years and calls its influence "the new biology."[6] Along the way, he has been a powerful critic of genetic determinism as a gross distortion of the truth of our biology. In reality, everything—

from the amniotic fluid that surrounds us in the womb to the words we hear from our parent-figures as children to the air we breathe to the chemicals we ingest—influences our genes, causing some to switch on and others to switch off. We do have a genetic code at birth. But gene expression and repression are influenced by our environment. In other words: our life experiences alter us at the cellular level.

The science of epigenetics[7] has shifted us away from the disease management model to a new paradigm that recognizes the impact of our daily environment on our health. The result is a radically new perspective: we can be active participants in our own well-being. This goes for our "physical" health and risk for developing diseases such as diabetes and cancer as well as for our mental and emotional health. Epigenetic factors[8] play a significant role in the development of psychiatric conditions. This is shown in identical twin studies where one twin develops a serious mental illness, such as schizophrenia or bipolar disorder, and the other does not. Studies of stress (as early as in the womb) and its connection to the development of mental illnesses later in life also show the profound ways in which our environment affects every part of the body, including its most powerful organ: the brain. Addiction and trauma specialist Dr. Gabor Maté, for example, has written extensively about the deep imprints emotional stress leaves on the structure of the brain, causing many common physical and psychological illnesses.

The idea that genetics are not destiny was a profound realization for me personally. I believed that because my family was sick, I was destined to be sick, too. The epigenetic perspective gave me the tools to reframe my perception of my own body. I may have inherited certain propensities from my family, but that didn't mean I had to become them.

Studies have shown that the influence of epigenetics transcends generations. Our ancestors' lived experiences shaped their DNA, which in turn shapes ours. That means our lives don't end with us but are passed down—the good and the bad, the trauma and the joy. In studies of mice in lab settings, not only did those that were exposed to extreme diets or stress display changes in their heart and metabolism, but so did their offspring and their offspring's offspring and so forth. There is evidence that this applies to humans, too.[9,10] Studies show that the children of trauma survivors, including those who endure ongoing systemic racism, have shown health issues similar to those of their parents as well as increased rates of many diseases.

If the genes we inherited were adversely affected by the experiences of generations before us, how do we stop the cycle? Some environmental factors are out of our control—we cannot choose the circumstances of our childhoods, let alone the circumstances of our great-grandparents' childhoods—but many factors are *within* our control. We can provide ourselves with the nurturing we may not have received as children. We can learn to give ourselves secure bonds and the ability to create a sense of safety. We can change what we eat, how often we exercise, our state of consciousness, and the thoughts and beliefs we express. As Dr. Lipton put it, "This is really what the whole new biology is all about. Take us away from, 'You are the victim of life,' to introducing the fact that we are the creators of our life."[11]

We are not *only* our genetic wiring. Once we understand this, the more inadequate the traditional deterministic approach of "recircuiting" faulty wiring through interventions such as medicine and surgery seems. We can *and should* help heal our bodies and our minds to create wellness for ourselves.

## THE PLACEBO EFFECT

The more I learned about epigenetics, the more I began studying the literature of healing and transformation. I learned about the power of belief and the placebo effect, which is a term that describes the power of an inert substance (such as a sugar pill) to improve symptoms of illness. I've been obsessed throughout my life with stories of spontaneous remission and people overcoming the most debilitating illnesses, seemingly impossible without medical intervention. Even still, these stories always seemed radical. They seemed more like miracles than anything scientifically valid.

The mind can create real, measurable changes in the body—and the placebo effect is mainstream science's recognition of this fact. A significant placebo effect has been documented in conditions ranging from Parkinson's disease[12] to irritable bowel syndrome.[13] Some of the strongest responses have been observed in depression studies,[14] where participants who believe they are on antidepressants but are really taking sugar pills report feeling generally improved. You don't even need to be sick to experience the placebo effect. In a study at the University of Glasgow,[15] researchers told fifteen runners that they were being administered doping drugs and then asked them to run a race. The runners' race times increased significantly even though they were getting only saline injections.

When our body expects to get better, it sends out messages to start the healing process. Hormones, immune cells, and neurochemicals are all released. The placebo effect provides proof that when we believe we are going to get better or feel better, we often do. It's a testament to the power of the mind to affect the body with mere suggestion.

But there is a flip side to this. It's called the nocebo effect,[16,17] and it's the placebo effect's "evil twin." This occurs when our thoughts don't make us better, they make us worse. To study this effect, researchers often tell participants that the drugs they are taking have terrible side effects, when they are really only taking a sugar pill. Believing they were taking an active medication, many people actually began to experience the warned-about side effects.

One notable, and extreme, example of the dangers of the nocebo effect[18] took place outside a lab in the 1970s, when a physician accidentally told a patient who had been diagnosed with esophageal cancer that he had three months to live. When the man died a few weeks later, an autopsy revealed that he had been misdiagnosed; there was zero evidence of cancer in his esophagus. He died, it seemed, though it's impossible to say for sure, because he believed he was going to die. His doctor later said in an interview, "I thought he had cancer. He thought he had cancer. Everybody around him thought he had cancer. Did I remove hope in some way?"[19]

In another documented case of the nocebo effect from 2007,[20] a twenty-six-year-old man who was participating in a clinical trial on antidepressants was rushed to the hospital after an attempted overdose. On the heels of a fight with his girlfriend, he took twenty-nine of the pills that he'd been prescribed for the study. When he arrived at the hospital, his blood pressure dropped to dangerously low, near-death levels and he was sweating, shaking, and breathing rapidly. Once the doctors were able to stabilize him, they tested him and found no evidence of drugs in his system. When a doctor from the clinical trial arrived at the hospital, he realized that the young man had been in the placebo group, meaning that he had taken an inert, or nonactive, pill. He had, it seemed, overdosed on his own negative thoughts and wishes.

## HOLISTIC PSYCHOLOGY

Gaining this insight into the connection between mental and physical health was game changing for me. Learning that we actively participate in our mental wellness (or lack thereof) with every choice inspired me to keep learning and studying as much as I could about our potential for full-body healing.

I learned about the diffuse effects of chronic inflammation on the brain thanks to the emerging field of psychoneuroimmunology. So many great thinkers opened my eyes to the role of nutrition and its effects on the ecosystem of the gut, which talks directly to the brain. I geeked out on the new science of polyvagal theory and the role of the nervous system in mental and physical well-being (all things we will tackle later in this book). It's unbelievable what we are learning. We're in the midst of a major shift in our understanding of what makes us sick and helps us get healthy.

As I lifted my head from all the books and research papers, I realized that that knowledge was shaping my perspective on the role I played in my own health. I wanted to integrate everything I'd learned from mainstream psychology with all the new research on mind-body healing. It was from this perspective that I formulated the tenants of Holistic Psychology, which are fundamentally meant to address all aspects of the person (mind, body, and soul). The basic tenets of Holistic Psychology are as follows.

1. Healing is a daily event. You can't "go somewhere" to be healed; you must go inward to be healed. This means a daily commitment to doing *the work*. You are responsible for your healing and will be an active participant in that process. Your level of activity is directly connected to your level of healing. Small and consistent choices are the path to deep transformation.
2. Though many things are beyond our control, others are within our control. Holistic Psychology harnesses the power of choice, because choice enables healing.
3. Holistic tools are very practical and approachable. Change can and often still feels overwhelming. This is because the main function of your subconscious mind is to keep you safe, and it is threatened by change. We experience this "pull toward the familiar" in the different discomforts we often feel as we change. The practice of making consistent, small, daily choices through these push-and-pull resistances helps empower us to maintain change.
4. Taking responsibility for your mental wellness, though intimidating, can be incredibly empowering. There is a palpable shift occurring in the collective, with many people becoming increasingly frustrated with the inequities and limitations of our health care system. There is likely an intuitive part of you that knows there is more available to you, or you wouldn't have picked up this book. I will share the emerging science that illustrates the many reasons why the old model no longer works and provide you with a road map to harness this new model of mental wellness.

As I share the philosophy and tools of Holistic Psychology with a widening circle of people, I am constantly in awe of the outpourings of gratitude and stories of resilience and healing. I can't tell you how many tears I've wiped from my eyes as I learn about the incredible strength and inner power of people all over the world.

There is one story that sticks out in my mind as a truly remarkable metamorphosis, and I want to share it with you. I connected early with a woman named Ally Bazely, who recognized herself in many of my discussions about self-sabotage, especially her need for external validation and her inability to maintain new productive habits. Most of all, it was the understanding that her deepest wounds were not caused by others, but by her betraying her intuitive Self, or authentic being, that resonated deeply and enabled her to see her life more clearly. "It was like for the first time, someone was shining a light on the shadows that were causing me so much pain," she later wrote.

This was an especially difficult time, what she would consider to be her own dark night of the soul. She recently survived a terrifying adverse reaction to the medication she was taking to treat her multiple sclerosis. Her throat swelled. She weaved in and out of consciousness, watching *The Price Is Right* on her mother's couch. Her doctors told her that she would likely never be well enough to return to work. "Nobody could tell me what was happening. Not my doctor, not my neurologist, not the drug company. Nobody knew what my recovery would look like. Or if there would even be one," she wrote. She was deeply depressed, tired of living a life confined to her couch. She was desperate to change but given zero direction about what a healthy life with a chronic condition might look like—or if such a dream was even possible for her. Some people with MS live lives uncomplicated by the disease, and others can lose their ability to walk and may suffer neurological impairments. She had no idea which of those people she would or could be. In fact, her parents started looking to move her into a wheelchair-accessible condo because it seemed that she would never walk again, as her options for treatment were limited and her prognosis was "poor."

Despite that broad range of outcomes, no one advised Ally on how she could manage or better yet alleviate her symptoms, no one asked about her prior struggles with depression or traumas from her experiences as a child. No one even asked her how she could take part in her own healing, because that was not a part of the vocabulary of care used by mainstream medicine. Ally had to investigate those things herself.

During that low point, Ally was scrolling through social media on her phone when she saw my post on self-betrayal. She read about how to heal self-betrayal by rebuilding the trust you have with yourself, and was inspired to take a meaningful step forward. She decided to make and keep one small daily promise to support her health—the smaller and more sustainable, the better. She promised herself to drink one glass of water every morning before her coffee. At first, she felt silly. *How can one glass of water change my life?* Still, she set a reminder on her phone at 6:45 a.m. to drink that water and followed up dutifully.

A week in, she resisted the urge to make other changes and instead focused on that daily win of drinking her water. She paused after drinking her water to congratulate herself and reflect on how proud she was that she stuck to it. "OMG," she would say to herself, "look at you go."

Thirty days later, Ally added journaling to her morning ritual and began to follow my prompts for an exercise that I call Future Self Journaling (you can grab the whole guide for free at https://yourholisticpsychologist.com), and created for my own healing. This practice enables you to consciously create new neural pathways in the brain that will lead to new desired thoughts, feelings, and behaviors. Before Future Self Journaling, Ally always wanted to have a journaling practice but could never maintain it. It was only when she combined journaling with the glass of water, a practice that was already integrated into the rituals of her life, that she kept that promise to herself. Soon into the practice, she discovered that it felt safer to be kinder to her future self than to her current self, and her writing reflected that softer approach. The more she wrote about herself in a kinder way, the more she began to notice the constant chatter of negative self-talk running through her head all day long. The more she started to trust herself, the quieter the chatter became and the more her daily acts of self-care and self-love started to extend out into the rest of her life.

Ally calls what followed a "rebirth." She discovered the work of Dr. Terry Wahls and her namesake protocol, a nutrition and lifestyle program that helps treat symptoms of MS; she began to set boundaries; she began to practice daily meditation, yoga, and journaling; she began to interact with her environment on a whole different level; and of course, she still drank that daily glass of water. Every single day. "I feel more at home within myself today than I have in the past fourteen years," she wrote in a blog post. "The dreams that have lived with me my whole life have been reignited."

Today Ally's MS has been in remission for over a year. Once confined to a couch, she now can not only walk upstairs but has started cycling and even running, two activities she thought that her MS had forever stolen from her.

Ally's story shows us the power of choice. She learned that even when faced with a grim diagnosis, she had within her the power to make beneficial changes. This acceptance of choice in our health and well-being is the first takeaway that I hope stays with you as you continue forward on your own journey.

---

## DO THE WORK: SEE IF YOU ARE STUCK

Spend some time reflecting on the following questions about being stuck, while also exploring the reason(s) why you may feel stuck in these areas. For instance, you may be able to identify patterns in your thoughts, emotions, and behaviors that keep you repeating these unhelpful patterns. It may help to explore these as a journaling exercise.

Do you often find yourself unable to keep promises to yourself, attempting to make new choices or create new habits but always falling back on your old ones? Yes ________

Do you often find yourself reacting emotionally to events, feeling out of control, and even ashamed about your behaviors after the fact? Yes

Do you often find yourself distracted and/or disconnected from yourself and others and/or from the present moment itself, maybe lost in thought about the past or the future or feeling "somewhere else" entirely? yes

Do you often find yourself feeling overwhelmed and torn down by internal critical thoughts, making it difficult to tune in to your physical, emotional, and spiritual needs? Yes

Do you often find yourself struggling to express your wants, needs, beliefs, and/or feelings in relationships? Yes

Do you often find yourself feeling overwhelmed or unable to cope with stress or any (or all) of your feelings? Yes

Do you often find yourself repeating past experiences and patterns in your day-to-day life? Yes

---

If you answered "yes" to one or more of these questions, you are likely feeling stuck as a result of your past experiences and conditioning. It may seem as though change is not possible, but I assure you that this is not the case. The first way to create change is to begin to practice imagining a future that's different from your past and present realities.

## FUTURE SELF JOURNAL

Future Self Journaling (FSJ) is a daily practice aimed at helping you break out of your subconscious autopilot—or the daily conditioned habits that are keeping you stuck repeating your past. You can begin to move forward by consistently engaging in the following activities:

- Witnessing the ways you remain "stuck" in your past conditioning
- Setting a conscious daily intention to change
- Setting small, actionable steps that support daily choices aligned with a different future outcome
- Empowering these daily choices despite the universal experience and presence of mental resistance

To begin this new daily practice, you will want to grab a notebook. Some of you may want to spend some time personalizing or decorating your journal or creating a small ceremony around which you will honor yourself for making this choice. You may decide to spend a few moments setting an intention for how you will use this new practice and focusing on what you will gain from keeping these daily promises to yourself.

Now you are ready to begin the practice of making and keeping a small daily promise to yourself to create change in these areas. If you are someone like myself or Ally or the million other people who are struggling with self-betrayal as a result of their past experiences, know that *you are not alone*. You are now joining a movement of millions of others from around the world who are also practicing these small daily promises to themselves.

# 2

# The Conscious Self: Becoming Aware

During my first session with Jessica, I thought, "I would totally be friends with this person." She was almost exactly my age, working at a store I even shopped at myself, and dressing the part of your cool hippie friend. She seemed warm, likable, the life of the party.

She had tried therapy before, and it hadn't clicked. She decided to try again because she, too, experienced the universal feeling of stuckness and found me during a panicked search on *Psychology Today*'s website. Initially, she used our sessions to vent about her week as I nodded along. She requested little from me. She just wanted a safe space to talk—about work stuff, daily stress, annoying roommates, and always the sense that she was missing out on something.

Over the course of our work together, the facade of laid-back hippieness fell away, and I recognized her chronic anxiety and her need to please others, all of which manifested in high-achieving perfectionism. Then to numb all the anxieties and what-ifs, she'd party—drink some wine, smoke some pot, do some drugs, all to relax and quiet the inner critic. But no matter what she did or what she achieved, she never felt satisfied.

Then she met a guy. All of the anxiety and dissatisfaction that she felt in her daily life was now projected onto this new partner. *Did she really like him, or was their relationship just convenient? Should she move in with him or break up with him?* Back and forth, back and forth, from one extreme thought to the next. Over time, as their relationship hit new milestones and marriage seemed almost inevitable, she became increasingly emotionally reactive. Week after week she would repeat the same narratives about her relationship. She talked about their volatile arguments and how she would act out, name-calling or door slamming, and then afterward feel bereft and ashamed. To cope, she would binge-drink to numb herself. Then, on a loop, the drinking would amplify her emotional reactivity, beginning again the cycle of name-calling and door slamming. Round and round she went, stuck in a pattern of acting out that was causing her and her partner so much distress. The shame spirals and reactivity had become so familiar and predictable that they became a reliable part of their relationship.

Every week Jessica would tell me about her behavior, and we would identify several things she could start doing that would set her up for a better outcome the following week. After witnessing the role alcohol played in her reactivity, she decided one of those things would be limiting her use of it. When she returned to therapy without having made those changes, she would belittle herself for her lack of follow-through. "As usual," she would say, "I haven't stuck with anything I said I would."

Two years into our weekly therapy sessions, she got so frustrated that she angrily blurted out, "Maybe I should take a break from therapy. I just come here repeating myself over and over again." It wasn't the first time I heard this frustration expressed. It's hard enough experiencing disappointment alone; it's even harder to have a witness to your perceived failures. It's understandable how clients can begin to see me (or any other therapist) as a disapproving parent-figure.

The trouble was, she couldn't move forward. She was trapped—or stuck—in a cycle of her own reactivity. Every thought that crossed her mind became a belief, a communication, expressed by her core Self. She couldn't make a decision because as her thoughts switched from one extreme—*I love this guy*—to another extreme—*I hate this guy*—she followed each fully without any questioning or restraint.

The reality is this: few of us have any real connection to who we really are, yet we want others to see through all of our layers of self-betrayal and into our core selves. Like Jessica, we all want to be better versions of ourselves. But our attempts to do so have failed because we don't understand our own minds and bodies. We don't have the practical tools to understand how to create the changes we seek to make. We can't expect others to do for us what we can't do for ourselves.

## YOU ARE NOT YOUR THOUGHTS

When people hear about my whole-person approach to healing, they want to dive right in and meet their inner child, start the reparenting process, do the ego work, remove the trauma. This desire for the quick fix, emblematic of the Western culture in many ways, comes from an understandable want to end the incredible discomfort of living with these wounds. Before we can get to these deeper layers, we first have to gain the ability to witness our internal world. It may not sound sexy, but it's fundamental. Everything that follows is grounded in awakening your conscious awareness.

I was introduced to the concept of consciousness when I was least looking for it. It was a desperate time. I was in my twenties, living on my own for the first time in New York City, heavily medicated for anxiety, ordering all manner of supplements and magic potions to manage the physical and emotional agitation that seemed to follow me around. I was working a research job in midtown Manhattan to supplement my (lack of) income in my PhD program, and during lunch breaks I would take a walk, attempting to fend off an approaching anxiety attack. I gravitated to the beautiful Romanesque brick Church of Saint Michael the Archangel near the Empire State Building. I would sit outside it, breathing in and out and pleading "God, help me through this."

One day, after experiencing one of these panic-attack walks ironically enough on my way to school, I found myself in front of a building that I had never noticed before. It was the Rubin Museum of Art, a museum featuring art and textiles from Eastern religions. On the building was a sign that read "We do not remember days, we remember moments." Something about that short phrase captured my attention.

When I got home, I googled the quote (the source of which turned out to be the twentieth-century Italian poet Cesare Pavese), which led me to an abundance of literature on the power of the present moment. Intrigued, I dove down a rabbit hole of personal research, one stream of inquiry spilling into the next, which eventually led me to the concept of consciousness.[21] It's a word we all know. As a medical term, its basic meaning is *awake*. For our purposes, however, it means something much more expansive: a state of open awareness that not only allows us to witness ourselves and the life around us but also empowers choice.

Touch your forehead. Right behind your fingers in the most forward part of your skull is the prefrontal cortex, the seat of the conscious mind. This is where we plan for the future and engage in sophisticated reasoning and complex multitasking. Our conscious mind is not constrained by the burdens of the past. It is forward thinking and constructive. It makes us uniquely human—though the rest of the animal kingdom is undoubtedly alive and present, other animals do not seem to share our ability to think about thought, something called metacognition.

Even though consciousness makes us human, most of us are so immersed in our inner world, so unconscious, even asleep, that we aren't aware that there's a script continually running through our minds. We believe that script is the true "us," the Self. But that chatter is just our thoughts. We practice thoughts all day long.

You might have stopped at this paragraph and thought: *You don't "practice" thoughts.* But we do. We practice thoughts from the moment our eyes open in the morning until we close them at night. You've practiced thoughts so consistently and for so long that the act of practicing is beyond your awareness. You practice thoughts in your dream states and in your subconscious. You may label these thoughts as "you," but they are not you. You are the thinker of your thoughts, *not the thoughts themselves.*

Thoughts are electrochemical responses that happen thanks to the firing of neurons in the brain. Thoughts serve a purpose; they allow us to problem solve, create, and form connections. There is, however, such a thing as relying too much on our thoughts. When we're in the "monkey mind," as the Buddha first described it, we never stop thinking; our thoughts jumble together; there is no space to breathe and examine them.

Let's return to Jessica. Her indecisiveness—one day feeling negative, the next feeling positive—was a product of her monkey mind. Some days her thoughts revolved around how lucky she was to have such a great guy in her life, and she fully believed it. And when she fully believed it, it manifested itself in her behavior (moving in with her boyfriend, agreeing to marry him). But on other days, when she wanted him to get the hell away, she believed those thoughts, too, and picked fights, slammed doors, and threw things. The seesawing made her distrust herself, and as a result she began to numb herself with drugs and alcohol as a way to further disconnect from her conscious Self.

Jessica could not move forward because her thinking mind trapped her in a state of reactivity. It was impossible for her to get any clarity about what she wanted because she wasn't tapped into her intuition. We all have an intuition, a psychological and spiritual concept that refers to an innate and unconscious wisdom. It's the evolutionarily driven gut instinct that helped keep us alive throughout human history and still speaks to us; it's that feeling of the hair on the back of our neck standing up when we walk down a dark alley alone, it's the deep belly feeling of distrust we get when we encounter someone we have no logical reason to doubt, it's that spine tingle we get when we meet someone we know is special. This is your intuitive Self speaking from your soul through your physiology. Typically, as children, we are in touch with this spiritual Self-knowledge and have strong instincts. As we grow older and fall under the influence of others, we tend to become disconnected from our intuition. Our sixth sense gets muddied. It's not lost, just buried.

## THE CONSCIOUS SELF AND THE SUBCONSCIOUS SELF

It is only when you are conscious that you are able to *see* yourself, a process of self-awareness that can suddenly reveal so many of the previously hidden forces constantly at work molding you, manipulating you, and holding you back. You can't eat better, stop drinking, love your partner, or improve yourself in any way until you become transparent to yourself. Because if you intuitively know what you need to do to change for the better—why don't you do it? It's not a moral failure; it's because you're stuck repeating these more or less automatic behavioral patterns.

Maybe this situation sounds familiar: You head to work at the same time every day, and the routine to get out the door is more or less memorized. You shower, brush your teeth, make coffee, eat breakfast, get dressed, drive to work, and so on. You barely have to think consciously about doing any of these things because you've done them so frequently that your mind is on autopilot. Have you ever traveled to work and wondered, *How did I get here?*

When we're running on autopilot, a primitive, or subconscious, part of our mind drives our reactions. Astonishingly, our subconscious stores every single experience we ever have. This however isn't just a neutral storehouse for facts and figures; it's emotional, reactive, and irrational. Every moment of every day, this subconscious mind is shaping the way we see the world; it is the primary driver of most of our (often automatic) behaviors. Anytime we are not fully conscious, our subconscious mind is hard at work being "us." How we think, speak, and respond—all of this comes from the subconscious part of ourselves that has been conditioned by thoughts, patterns, and beliefs that became ingrained in our childhoods through a process called conditioning.

Running on autopilot is a function of our conditioning. Most of us are stuck in subconscious programming; in fact, some brain scans reveal that we operate only 5 percent of the day in a conscious state;[22] the rest of the time, we are in subconscious autopilot. This means that we are making active choices during only a small sliver of our days and letting our subconscious run the show the rest of the time.

## HOMEOSTATIC IMPULSE

The overwhelming pull of the subconscious mind makes it hard for us to change. We are not evolutionarily wired for change. When we do try to push ourselves out of our autopilot, we face resistance from our mind and body. This response has a name: the homeostatic impulse. The homeostatic impulse regulates our physiological functions from breathing to body temperature to heartbeat. And it all happens at the subconscious level, meaning that we do not actively initiate any of them; they are automatic. The goal of the homeostatic impulse is to create balance in the mind and body. When there's dysregulation, the imbalances can be problematic and even self-betraying.

The subconscious mind loves existing in a comfort zone. The safest place, it turns out, is one you've been before because you can predict the familiar outcome. Habits, or behaviors that we repeatedly return to, become the subconscious's default mode. Our brain actually prefers to spend most of its time coasting on autopilot—it is best able to conserve its energy by knowing what to expect. This is why our habits and routines feel so comforting and why it's so unsettling and even exhausting when our routines are disrupted. The trouble is, following our conditioned routine keeps us stuck in that routine.

This gravitation toward the familiar kept our ancient ancestors safe from various threats such as wild animals, food shortages, and hostile enemies. Any behavior that kept us alive—fed and housed—would be repeated and favored by the homeostatic impulse, all without our actively making a choice in the matter. Today in our world of relative comfort (speaking from a developed-world perspective), our minds and bodies have not evolved past that reactive state in which everything unfamiliar or slightly uncomfortable is viewed as a threat. There is also the reality that Black, Indigenous, and People of Color (BIPOC) living in even the developed world face daily threats from our oppressive systems. Because of these instinctually driven reactions, when we try to change our habits many of us remain trapped in cycles of disempowerment. Instead of understanding that this comes from an evolutionarily honed body response, we tend to shame ourselves. This shame is a misreading of our physiology.

Every time we make a choice that is outside of our default programming, our subconscious mind will attempt to pull us back to the familiar by creating mental resistance. Mental resistance can manifest as both mental and physical discomfort. It can take the form of cyclical thoughts, such as *I can just do this later* or *I don't need to do this at all*, or physical symptoms, such as agitation, anxiety, or simply not feeling like "yourself." This is your subconscious communicating to you that it is uncomfortable with the new territory of these proposed changes.

## BREAKING FREE

As Jessica's wedding day loomed, her anxiety bloomed and was channeled into planning various details about the wedding. She wasn't anywhere near a bridezilla but would share with me that she felt out of control, making it seem as though her big day was actually a burden. She and I remained consistent with our work together, trying to harness her powers to witness and awaken her consciousness. It was around that time, a few years into our sessions, that I finally learned about a devastating loss she suffered—brought into our session when she reported she had recently become upset over thoughts of the father-daughter dance she would not have.

When she was in her early twenties, Jessica's father, a rock in her life and a beloved member of her larger community, passed away suddenly. This kind of tragedy would devastate anyone, but Jessica's decision to not even mention his death until five years into our relationship showed me how deeply she had repressed the loss. It was worth exploring whether her possibly unresolved feelings were emerging in these daily cycles of reactivity, through her patterns of anger at her partner and overall consistent daily stress. Because Jessica had never faced her grief head-on—the feelings felt too big and scary to handle, so she stuffed them away in order to carry on with her life—she was stuck in a loop. Her body became acclimated to the loop, making her feel more comfortable when avoiding her own deeper feelings rather than facing them. I mentioned to her that it was unusual that her father had not come up sooner in our conversations and asked her why she thought she didn't tell me about such a pivotal and traumatic event. She expressed surprise that she hadn't yet mentioned him and uncertainty about the effects of this loss; that was how far she buried her grief.

As she began to plan her wedding, her father became a more frequent topic. His obvious absence made it impossible for her to continue denying his place in her life. Still, she rarely showed any emotion in relation to his loss. She remained composed, almost numb, when discussing him. As the wedding neared, we began to talk about him more and more, and at the same time we worked on cultivating her awareness of the many ways that her past grief was filtering her view of the present. She was able to witness how she was doubling down on surface stressors as a way to distract herself from the unacknowledged pain of her father's death.

Together we explored the importance of cultivating the power of her conscious awareness to break those automatic reactions. We worked on grounding her attention back in to the present moment before diving into a knee-jerk overreaction about the wedding cake or seating arrangements. We explored how she could best use practices of breathwork and meditation. What was most impactful for Jessica was physical movement, especially yoga. For many people, physical movement is useful in honing the attention muscle that is so key to consciousness. Yoga, which is considered a "top-down" practice (meaning that the brain sets the intentions that the body follows), can be an especially powerful means of helping the mind settle into the present moment by focusing our attention as we practice channeling our breath and challenging our body. The attentional control she developed through her yoga practice helped her to begin to take a second before reacting. This helped her create a space for her to begin to consciously witness more fully what was going on for her. It was from this foundation of consciousness that she would create future change.

Yoga was so transformative for Jessica that she decided to train as an instructor. In doing so, she followed a rigorous program that forced her to confront many of the default states of reactivity she had been living in. Once she allowed space for self-witnessing and was able to sit with the discomfort of the sometimes overwhelming feelings activated in challenging physical poses, our therapy started to click. The more engaged she became with her yoga practice, the more she started to live in the present moment. She began to switch out of autopilot mode and see a glimmer of herself instead of merely jumping from one feeling to the next. As she became more present, she was able to pause and witness her thoughts and behaviors for what they were: transitory states that could be managed. Her attention muscle helped her develop more awareness of her thoughts; then she learned how to sit through the discomfort of witnessing them, building a sense of resilience and empowerment. That became a catalyst for her inner transformation.

The more Jessica trained in her yoga practice, the more conscious she grew. In fact, part of what was happening was that she was literally changing her brain at the physical level. When we develop our attention muscle, a process called neuroplasticity takes place. Neuroplasticity is a concept introduced in the last fifty years, when researchers discovered that our brains remain structurally and physiologically changeable throughout life (despite previous beliefs that the possibilities for change ended in our twenties). The brain is remarkably able to reorganize itself and grow new connections between neurons. Research shows that practices like yoga and meditation that help us to focus our attention on the present moment, are especially powerful in restructuring the brain. When new neural pathways are forged, we are able to break free of our default patterns and live more actively in a conscious state. In fact, functional MRI (fMRI) brain scans confirm this,[23] showing tangible evidence that consistent consciousness practices actually thicken the prefrontal lobes, the area where our conscious awareness actually lives. Other forms of compassion-based meditation (or just closing your eyes and thinking about someone you love) help strengthen an area called the limbic system, which is the emotional center of the brain. All of this work helps to rewire our brain, disrupt our default thought patterns, and wake us up out of our subconscious-driven autopilot. From this foundation of consciousness we can then begin to witness the conditioned patterns in our thoughts, beliefs, and relationships. This honest self awareness shows us our pathway towards change and ultimately healing.

## THE POWER OF BELIEF

In 1979, the Harvard psychologist Ellen Langer recruited two groups of elderly men from nursing homes in the Boston area to live for a week in a monastery in New Hampshire and take part in a groundbreaking study on the power of belief and its effect on aging.[24] The first group of men were told to live as if the clock turned back twenty years overnight. They were asked to try to actually *live* as younger versions of themselves. The second group would remain in the present time period but were urged to reminisce about the past.

Everything in the first group's area of the monastery, which had been decorated for the study, supported the participants' transformations back to their younger selves. The furniture was midcentury modern. Past issues of *Life* magazine and *Saturday Evening Post* were scattered around the living quarters. The men watched Ed Sullivan on a black-and-white television, listened to the vintage radio, and screened

1950s movies such as *Anatomy of a Murder*. They were encouraged to discuss events from that past time: the launch of the first US satellite, Fidel Castro's rise in Cuba, and their fears about escalating Cold War tensions. All mirrors were removed, replaced by photographs of the men twenty years earlier.

The study lasted only one week, and the changes the men experienced were astounding. Both groups showed vast improvements on every measure—from the physical to the cognitive and emotional. All of the men were more flexible; they stooped less, physically; and many of their fingers, riddled with arthritis, were more dexterous and even appeared healthier. Independent onlookers who, unaware of the study, were asked to compare "before" photos to "after" photos taken a week later, estimated that the "after" photos had been taken at least two years prior to the "before" photos.

The changes ran deeper than the physical and were most profound for those who embodied their younger selves. Sixty-three percent of them demonstrated measurably higher intelligence scores after a week, compared to 44 percent in the other group. Across the board, all of the men in the first group reported improvements in all five senses, from an ability to taste more flavors in food to better hearing and vision.

I'm sharing this study to show the incredible power of our thoughts, which can influence us in many ways. That these remarkable changes happened in an older population, who are typically more resistant to change, is evidence of the potential for similar transformation in your own life.

Instead of fixating on related negative thoughts—as studies show we do 70 percent of the time[25]—I want you to try to witness your body's sensations when you're feeling threatened. In other words: I want you to *become conscious*. Do you see yourself growing defensive, with tightened shoulders and jaw muscles, when you FaceTime with your mother? Do you withdraw, disconnecting from or becoming hyperaware of your body's sensations, when you walk into an unfamiliar environment? Witness without judgment. Just observe. The path forward is to learn yourself. Learn how to spend time alone, to sit still, to really hear your intuition and witness your entire Self—even, and especially, the darkest parts you'd most like to keep hidden.

There is tremendous freedom in not believing every thought we have and understanding that we are the thinker of our thoughts, not the thoughts themselves. Our minds are powerful tools, and if we do not become consciously aware of the disconnection between our authentic Selves and our thoughts, we give our thoughts too much control in our daily lives.

To begin this work, we must be in an environment that we consider safe and supportive. We cannot become conscious in a hostile environment, especially not at first. We need to be in a place where it will be okay to let down some of our defenses, take chances, and let ourselves go. For those of us who are living in unsafe physical environments, especially those under our current oppressive systems, our safest places can be found in short, quiet moments within ourselves.

It's time to try a few exercises that will help you access this consciousness. It will be helpful to use these prompts for a few minutes every day. Why? Because to effect change, you will need to create a routine that you stick to, a small daily promise to yourself that you can practice keeping for yourself during your healing journey. You'll notice that as you begin this practice, there may be a lot of discomfort. This is because the mind is screaming "Hey, wait! This is uncomfortable! We want to operate on our familiar programming!" This may manifest as some form of agitation. It may be helpful to try to practice breathing through this, and *try not to judge the experience*. If the discomfort becomes too intense, empower yourself to stop, and most importantly, acknowledge yourself for identifying your limit. Rest, of course, and know you can return to practice the next day.

Remember, this may feel awkward and silly at first. Stick with it. This consciousness building exercise sets the foundation for the work that follows.

## DO THE WORK: BUILD CONSCIOUSNESS

1. Find one to two minutes in your day when you can practice being focused on and truly present in whatever you're doing. This could be while you are doing the dishes, folding laundry, or taking a bath. It could mean stopping on your walk to look up at the clouds or taking a moment to really smell the aromas of your work space throughout the day. Make a conscious choice to witness the entirety of your experience in that moment. Say to yourself, "I am in this present moment." Your mind may respond with a steady stream of mental resistance because it's being jolted out of its conditioning and it's being watched. All sorts of thoughts may come up in your mind. This is okay. Just practice witnessing them.

2. Ground yourself in the moment. Our senses allow us to leave the monkey mind and find a deeper connection to the present moment. Let's say you've chosen to do this exercise while doing dishes. Feel the soap on your hands. See how the soap bubbles over your hands; feel the slickness of the dishes in the sink; smell the scent of the air. This will enable you to stay in this moment without your mind commanding you out of it. Doing this will become more and more comfortable with practice.

3. After practicing this for one to two minutes, acknowledge that you gave yourself this time. This will allow your mind and body to understand how it feels and give you a moment to thank yourself for the time you took to do *the work*.

4. Repeat this exercise at least once a day. As you get more comfortable, you'll begin to notice more moments when you can repeat the practice.

## FSJ: CONSCIOUSNESS BUILDING

I will now join you on this journey, sharing with each of you the same Future Self Journaling prompts I used each day to begin to create new habits in my daily life. Early in my journey, I began to practice keeping a small daily promise of creating one new experience of consciousness in my day. Each day in my notebook, I copied similar versions of the following statements, giving myself a consistent daily reminder of my intention to change. This helped me make new choices consistently throughout my day helping me to create new habits over time. To help you with this process, you may want to use the following example (or create a similar one of your own):

**Today I am practicing** being conscious to myself and my daily patterns.

**I am grateful for** an opportunity to create change in my life.

**Today, I am** conscious and aware whenever I choose.

**Change in this area allows me to feel** more aware of myself and my patterns.

**Today, I am practicing when** I bring my attention back to the present moment.

---

The goal from here is to practice making this new choice throughout each day. To help me remember my consciously set intention, I set reminders for myself on my phone for random times throughout the day. (Yes, technology can sometimes be our friend.) Each time my reminder went off, I checked in with myself noticing where my attention was. I discovered very quickly that it wasn't in the current moment. Not at all. I found I loved to spend time rehashing past stressful experiences in my mind. If I wasn't reliving the past, I was worrying about multiple inevitable calamities that could cause me future stress. My conscious power to create change was nowhere to be found.

# 3

# A New Theory of Trauma

I met Christine during the early days of sharing my healing journey on social media. Like Ally, Christine connected with my posts about the concept of self-betrayal, or the consistent denial of our authentic wants and needs leading to destructive or self-harming behaviors.

Christine readily admitted that she was a "self-help addict." There wasn't a wellness fad she hadn't tried. She would buy the books, go to the seminars, even try the weeklong workshops in around-the-world places—all to the same end: disappointment. No matter what she did, she ended up in the same place she started. She would throw herself fully into a practice or experience in the beginning, and find herself straying after a few weeks. Bored. Uncomfortable. Done with it.

Her number one problem, she told me, seemed superficial, but it plagued her: She hated her belly. Her "tummy chub," as she called it, bothered her since early adolescence. Though she had never been overweight, she constantly felt that her stomach was gross, as though it were an alien part of her body that didn't belong. When she started to explore her nutrition, she discovered that she often could not remember what she consumed in a day. Sometimes she would forget that she was eating even as the food hit her mouth. She described nights of completely zoning out while eating a pan of brownies. It was only after coming back up for air that she realized she was so unconscious of the food she ate that she barely registered flavor or taste.

This type of experience is typical of someone experiencing a state of dissociation—a coping mechanism of physical and mental disconnection from our environment in response to consistent stress or overwhelm. A person is physically there yet mentally gone. It's a protective response to an event or situation that feels too big or threatening for the conscious mind to attend to. Dissociation is a very common stress response for those who are living with childhood trauma. Psychiatrist Pierre Janet, who coined the term, described it as a "splitting off" of the self.[26] I describe it to my clients as the feeling of departing in a "spaceship," a kind of metaphysical detachment of the self from the body. Christine's food dissociation showed me that she was attempting to escape something that had nothing to do with eating.

Over time, Christine began to talk about her past. She came to realize her family had not provided a trusting or supportive environment and that her mom often bullied her and enlisted her siblings to pile on. In the absence of safe, secure relationships, she kept a terrible secret that tortured her: a close friend of the family, a man in his forties, had begun sexually abusing her when she was nine years old.

The man had convinced Christine that what he was doing to her was a secret and that if she told anyone, she would get into trouble—a common strategy used by sexual predators. The abuse went on for several years. Her family even teased her about the man's clear preference for Christine. "You're his favorite," her mother would say. Her siblings would get annoyed when he brought her gifts or took her on special outings. "You're such a suck-up."

Christine knew intuitively that what was happening was wrong but she learned to reject her intuition and believe her perpetrator. She coped by disengaging—mentally leaving as her body endured the abuse. Repeatedly disconnecting from her intuition, she eventually learned that she could not trust herself, instead looking to the thoughts, beliefs, and opinions of others.

Her dissociative behavior became a default coping strategy—and in adulthood that meant leaving the present moment when she was experiencing uncomfortable feelings. Witnessing this pattern in adulthood helped her better understand that this was a learned behavior from childhood where she left the present moment in order to emotionally cope.

## TRAUMA: A MISUNDERSTOOD CONCEPT

Trauma, as the majority of mental health professionals understand it, is the result of a deeply catastrophic event, like severe abuse or neglect. Such events are life altering, splintering a person's world into a "before" and an "after"—as Christine's sexual abuse did. The Centers for Disease Control and Prevention provides a scale called the Adverse Childhood Experiences (ACEs) test,[27] which mental health professionals use to assess the level of trauma in their clients' lives. The ACEs questionnaire includes ten questions that cover various types of childhood trauma, including physical, verbal, and sexual abuse as well as experiences of witnessing such abuse or of having an incarcerated family member. Every "yes" answer to the ten questions results in one point. Research has shown that the higher the score, the greater the chances of negative life outcomes, from higher rates of substance abuse and suicide to increased risk of developing chronic illnesses.

The ACEs framework is important because it clearly maps out how traumas sustained in childhood leave lasting imprints on our bodies and minds. The ACEs shows that what happens in childhood, especially when it was a highly negative experience, stays with us for a lifetime.

When I took the ACEs, I scored a 1 (worldwide, nearly 70 percent of people score at least 1[28]). That result reflected the same message I received during my training—that the word *trauma* applied only to someone like Christine, who experienced extreme abuse. I would never have thought of my own childhood as traumatic in any way. I came from what I viewed as a "normal" family. My dad worked hard and came home every night at the same time. We never went without food. My parents weren't drinkers. They were still married. There was no extreme verbal abuse and no physical abuse at all.

Yet I had almost no memories from childhood. The milestones that typically make up a person's existence—first kiss, prom, holidays—all of those were blank for me. I also struggled with facial recognition. I could barely ever register a familial resemblance. (Babies, to me, were not "spitting images" of their parents at all. To me, they were . . . babies.) When I watched docudramas, I could never tell the difference between the person being interviewed and the actor in a reenactment scene.

I didn't realize any of that was unusual until I shared the blankness with others, who would get annoyed when I couldn't remember a shared memory or make fun of me when I had a hard time recognizing someone from my past whom I should have had no problem identifying. Some people couldn't believe it. "You must be lying! How could you forget?" It became a joke with my friends: "Nicole has the worst memory!"

I should add that I did remember emotions—I still had "feeling memories" or impressions of the past, I just didn't connect those feelings with concrete experiences. I can feel what it was like to lie in bed at age six and cycle through the list of ways that my world could shatter: my parents could die, someone could break into the house, we could all die in a fire, the list went on and on. This anxiety state is a feeling memory and an expression of my family's fear-driven refrain, "It's always something." That "something" could be a pissed-off neighbor, an overdue bill, a snowstorm, or a fight with another family member. If it happened to one of us, it happened to all of us. We were united in a cycle of outrage and anxiety.

Unlike the rest of my family, though, who struggled to cope with living in such a highly fearful state, I never *appeared* overwhelmed. They called me the aloof one, the laid-back, chill child who was easy and go-with-the-flow. It appeared like nothing ever bothered me. That aloofness was a coping strategy, my mind's protection from the stress:

I would detach, distance myself, get into my "spaceship." I was so disengaged from myself, so far away on that spaceship, that ultimately I stored very few memories from my childhood and retained barely any recollections from my twenties. Just because my mind wasn't present to what was unfolding around me doesn't mean that my body doesn't remember.

Dr. Bessel van der Kolk, a trauma expert and the author of the ground-breaking book *The Body Keeps the Score: Brain, Mind, and Body in the Healing of Trauma*, describes dissociation as a process of "simultaneously knowing and not knowing" and says that traumatized people who disengage "simultaneously remember too little and too much."[29] Trauma lodges itself in the body in diffuse ways, which we will discuss in more detail in the next chapter, and its most profound impact may be in the way it affects the nervous system's fight-or-flight stress response.

It was only later in my life, after years of offering therapy to people such as Christine, that I started to find commonalities among people who experienced childhood trauma: many coped by building individual "spaceships" that led to lifelong patterns of disengaging, detaching, and making few memories. This discovery posed the questions: If nothing "traumatic," as I once understood it, had ever happened to me, why couldn't I remember most of my childhood? Why did I have such a hard time connecting with and taking care of myself emotionally? Why did I consistently betray myself? How could Christine and I express the same trauma responses when our childhood experiences were so different?

Little did I know then that what I suffered was a form of *spiritual* trauma and I was living the consequences of that trauma in my everyday life, just as Christine was.

## WIDENING THE DEFINITION OF TRAUMA

I have treated people all over the ACEs spectrum—from those who had "perfect" families with trauma scores of 0 to those who had ACEs scores close to 10, with more traumatic experiences than many of us could imagine, let alone survive.

Though their histories differed drastically, the dynamics followed a similar script. Many were functional perfectionists, overachievers, or addicted to different substances or behaviors. There was a lot of anxiety, depression, lack of confidence, low self-worth, and an obsession with being viewed a certain way. There were problematic relationship patterns. And of course, there was the "stuckness," the inability to move forward from patterns of behavior that seemed ingrained. The patterns were telling a story—one that would shed light onto how pervasive trauma in childhood truly is.

The reality is that there are many people who cannot point to several moments (or even one moment) that broke their life apart. Many might not be able to admit that any part of their childhood was damaging. That doesn't mean that there wasn't trauma present—I've yet to meet a person who has not experienced some level of trauma in their life. I believe that our understanding of trauma should be widened to include a diverse range of overwhelming experiences or, as the neurologist Robert Scaer defined it, any negative life event "that occurs in a state of relative helplessness."[30] trauma is

The ACEs framework, though useful, does not tell the full story of trauma. It does not take into account the range of emotional and spiritual traumas, which are an outgrowth of consistently denying or repressing the needs of the authentic Self that so many of us have experienced. In fact, the ACEs assessment, surprisingly, doesn't even take into account the myriad ways that the outside environment—really, society at large—can traumatize us. There is not one question in the ACEs test about overt racism—such as discrimination and abuse, which are obvious forms of racial trauma—let alone any reference to the subtler, more pervasive and harmful forms of bigotry and bias that exist in the infrastructure of society. When you live in a world that is unsupportive and outright threatening—in the education system, prison system, health care system, and most workplaces—you are existing in an almost constant state of trauma. Marginalized groups, especially BIPOC, are navigating systemic oppression, discriminatory laws, and a prejudicial framework that may place them squarely into "a state of relative helplessness," the essence of Scaer's definition of trauma.

In other words, traumatic experiences aren't always obvious. Our perception of the trauma is just as valid as the trauma itself. This is especially true in childhood, when we are most helpless and dependent. Trauma occurred when we consistently betrayed ourselves for love, were consistently treated in a way that made us feel unworthy or unacceptable resulting in a severed connection to our authentic Self. Trauma creates the fundamental belief that we must betray who we are in order to survive.

## CHILDHOOD CONDITIONING

A parent-figure's role is to be a guide. A loving parental relationship provides a secure base for a child to return to as they venture out into life, with all the ups and downs associated with this great transition. A guide is largely nonjudgmental, allowing the child to exist as they are. A guide is more likely to observe and act from a state of awareness and wisdom. This allows the child to experience the natural consequences of their actions without intervention and laying the foundation for them to build self-trust. Think of the guide as a wise teacher, someone who has faith in the foundation they have provided and trusts that the student will be able to weather what life brings. The child then internalizes this faith. This doesn't mean that the child avoids pain, loss, anger, or grief—the wide array of human feelings—instead, the guide or parent-figure has provided a base of security and resilience for the child to return to when hard times come.

If parent-figures have not healed or even recognized their unresolved traumas, they cannot consciously navigate their own path in life, let alone act as trustworthy guides for someone else. It's very common for parent-figures to project their own unresolved traumas onto their children. When even well-meaning parent-figures react under the influence of their own unconscious wounds they, instead of offering guidance, may attempt to control, micromanage, or coerce a child to follow their will. Some of these attempts may be well intentioned. Parent-figures may consciously or unconsciously want to keep the child safe and protected from the world so that the child will not experience the pain that they, themselves, have. In the process, they may negate the child's wants and needs. Even when this can seem intentional, these reactions often stem from their own deep-rooted pain, which may not be visible on the surface. Many of us were raised by parent-figures who had difficulty navigating their emotions as a result of their own unresolved childhood pain. They may have projected this pain onto us directly, when they urged us not to cry, or indirectly, when they withdrew in response to our displays of emotion. According to Lindsay Gibson, a psychotherapist and the author of *Adult Children of Emotionally Immature Parents: How to Heal from Distant, Rejecting, or Self-Involved Parents*, this lack of emotional connection in childhood leaves "a gaping hole where true security might have been. The loneliness of feeling unseen by others is as fundamental a pain as physical injury."[31] This emotional loneliness continues into adulthood when we repeat these patterns of emotional avoidance, shut down, and shaming.

I imagine it may be becoming easier to see how trauma is intergenerational, passed down from one parent-figure to the next to the next to the next—to us. Central to this process is the concept of conditioning, in which beliefs and behaviors are unconsciously imprinted onto us. Anyone who's ever spent time with a young child knows that children mimic others' behaviors: whether influenced by a friend or classmate or cartoon character, they do as they see. This is how conditioning works. We learn what is modeled to us by others, especially our primary parent-figures. Our attachments in our earliest years set the groundwork for our subconscious beliefs. We learn what a relationship looks like from watching those closest to us in relationships. We learn how to feel about our bodies by observing how our parents feel about their bodies. We learn whether or not to prioritize self care. We learn spending habits, worldviews, and beliefs about ourselves, others, and the world. We stored these beliefs as well as countless other messages in our subconscious.

We are constantly looking to our parent-figures for guidance and as mirrors; the way they engage with their reality is likely how we will engage with ours. We inherit their ways of seeing and interacting; we inherit their beliefs, habits, and even their coping strategies.

Just as you learn how to witness yourself consciously, *the work* is to consciously observe your loved ones and your bonds to them. It took me a long time to come to the conclusion that there was unresolved trauma from my childhood. I was not willing to admit it to myself for a long time. I would have fought you tooth and nail if you suggested that my childhood was less than perfect. This didn't come just from an idealization of my past; it also came from a culturally ingrained protection of the family unit. Admitting publicly that everything was not all rosy would have been deeply disrespectful. We were one big happy Italian family! How dare you suggest otherwise?

For years I remained resistant. I had denied my own reality for so long that it would take a lot of work for me to shift my perspective and start to see the past through the lens of childhood wounding. I had rejected my needs for so long that I wasn't even aware of them. As with most of us, many of the habits I learned in childhood, I repeated and carried with me throughout my life. Many of us never stop to think: Is this really *me*? How many of us find ourselves celebrating holidays the same way we did in childhood without even imagining doing it a different way? How many aspects of your life have you actually chosen—and how many have you inherited?

Identifying your wounding is a fundamental step on the healing journey, and it's rarely an easy one. This reckoning often unearths deep reservoirs of pain, sadness, and even anger that have long been suppressed so that you could, at least on a surface level, function and move on. As you dive deeper into this work, it is important to keep in mind that sometimes old scars will be opened and an outpouring of feelings will come with the process of healing wounds from childhood. Just remember: this, too, can be a moment of witnessing. Begin to practice being kind to yourself and your loved ones, regardless of what comes up. How a parent-figure treated you as a child is not a reflection of who you are. Or even who they are. You do not need to be a reflection of their unprocessed trauma.

What follows is a new framework for understanding childhood trauma, with archetypes I've developed based on the common dynamics I've observed in my extensive clinical practice as well as within the SelfHealer community. These are by no means hard-and-fast categories. You might identify with one dynamic strongly, or several of them may resonate. You don't have to fit into a box; I just want to help you think about your primary relationships and the conditioning you've experienced. The first step to healing is awareness.

## THE ARCHETYPES OF CHILDHOOD TRAUMA

### Having a Parent Who Denies Your Reality

A typical example of reality denial occurs when a child, feeling uncomfortable around a relative, tells his mother and is met with a response like "Oh, she's just trying to be nice. You'd better be polite." (We saw this to an extreme degree with Christine and her family's view of the man abusing her.)

When a parent-figure denies a child's reality, they are unconsciously teaching the child to reject their intuition, their "gut feeling." The more we learn to distrust ourselves, the deeper this intuitive voice withdraws, becoming harder and harder to hear. This results in lost intuition and internal conflict. We learn that our judgment cannot be trusted and look to others to shape our reality.

Denying a child's reality can take on subtle forms. A child might confide in their parent-figure that their friends didn't want to sit with them at the school lunch table. For the child in that moment, it was an extremely distressing situation, resulting in them feeling rejected at a time when the need for peer validation is an important part of development. The well-intentioned parent-figure might respond with some degree of dismissal, "Don't worry, you'll find new friends. It isn't a big deal. It will get better. It's only your first day!" Anyone with their own level of unresolved feelings will generally feel uncomfortable with a child's expression of feelings and may cope by attempting to dismiss them. The child's experiences may activate similarly painful past memories for the parent-figure (these are often unconscious) who tends to push the child to repress or ignore the feelings that are coming up. The problem is that the child was having a legitimate feeling and looking to be comforted and supported; instead they were told that the pain was inconsequential. Through repeated similar experiences, a child is taught that their perception of reality and related emotional experiences are not trustworthy.

Our childhood realities can also be denied when our parent-figures and families dismiss objective issues. I once had a client whose father was a functional alcoholic. Though he had a job and provided financially for the family, the minute he walked through the door, he'd crack open a beer and drink through the night until he either got hostile and started yelling or passed out. When my client was old enough to notice and comment on his father's behavior, his mother dismissed his fear and excused her husband's behavior as a result of a "hard day at work." This denial was a learned behavior modeled by my client's mother who was raised in a household that denied the reality of a family member's substance use. Over time, my client began to inherit his mother's way of viewing his father's behavior, talking to himself about how hard his father worked. It wasn't until he lifted the curtain a bit and acknowledged the rows of empty bottles and the nightly drinking that he began to see his father's behavior for what it was.

## Having a Parent Who Does Not See or Hear You

We've all heard the saying "Children are meant to be seen, not heard." It was a slogan of sorts that summed up our older generations' mindset around raising children. This mindset was born out of an understanding that the only needs children had were basic, such as food and shelter. Resource scarcity was a reality for many members of these generations, many of whom were locked in survival mode. These adults often defined successful parenting as the fulfillment of basic survival needs with little energy or attention left for emotional needs. The effects of this survival-based parenting style have been passed down through inherited trauma and we are living with its long-term consequences.

Not being seen or heard in childhood is an experience of feeling emotionally disconnected from a parent-figure. Sometimes this involves severe neglect, though often it comes in the form of more subtle experiences. It can look like a parent-figure who is overwhelmed by their own feelings and distracted by chronic stress, or by contrast, one who is in a state of complete emotional shutdown and unable to listen to and support their child's emotional expression. Another version of this looks like a parent-figure operating on autopilot, running from task to task, distracted in their own mind, and unable to truly see their child in front of them. This prevents any deeper emotional connection with their child because mentally the parent-figure is simply "not there."

It is painful not to be heard. It is upsetting to be ignored. It is confusing to learn that we must hide our true Selves in order to be loved. Being acknowledged is one of the deepest human needs. If your childhood thoughts or ideas are not "heard," your mind feels dismissed. If your childhood Self-expression is not "seen," your soul feels diminished. This lack of acknowledgment can also take the form of your future being spoken for or predetermined before your passions and life's path can be fully known. Experiences such as these make it hard for us to learn how to trust our inclinations and follow our intuitive needs.

For parent-figures reading this, it's important to remind yourself that children exceed us in their connection to their intuition and their core Self. As adults, we easily get lost in our own steady stream of thoughts. Children are still highly intuitive, their world is in flux, still being formed. In providing a secure and open space for your children to explore, you will also learn about yourself and the possibilities that each of us contains when we are free to express our authentic Selves.

## Having a Parent Who Vicariously Lives Through You or Molds and Shapes You

This type of parent-figure is typically known as a "stage parent"—someone who is overzealous and pushes their child to become an actress or a singer to fulfill the parent-figure's own needs for fame, achievement, or attention. Though this archetype is most often associated with performance (and unfairly with mothers), this kind of behavior isn't limited to the stage.

It's easy to vilify stage parents, as they are often portrayed in popular culture as outright abusive. Often the push to make a child succeed comes from a very natural parental instinct: pride. Unfortunately, pride turns sour when the motivation to push a child to succeed originates from an unprocessed trauma. Parent-figures who live out their lives through their children carry a deep-seated, painful belief that they are a "failure" or in some way inadequate, and often project this core belief onto their children. Let's say a father wanted to be a basketball player and broke his leg before he was able to make his college team, or maybe a mother wanted to be a doctor and that path wasn't open to her, so she became a nurse. The result is that the child may feel an oppressive amount of pressure to succeed—and abandons parts of their authentic Self in order to please the parent-figure. Ultimately, trying to establish one's own validity through the successes of another leads to disappointment on the parent-figure's side. It also leads to resentment on the part of the child who neglected their own needs to fulfill another's unmet needs. Anytime an intrinsic need is denied, resentment soon follows.

This loss of Self can manifest in a number of ways in adulthood, and I've seen it play out most often as either severe indecisiveness and procrastination or as an obsessive need to succeed. To clarify, sometimes the stage parent acts with intention (this is associated with the more maligned Hollywood parent who pushes their kid on stage for financial gain), though many other times the parent truly desires a better life for the child. Molding and shaping takes many forms and occurs when a parent-figure consistently projects their own wants, needs, or desires onto their child—such as telling their child to avoid certain friends or focus on certain classes in school. It can be something as subtle as telling a child, "You're going to be an amazing mother one day." This is often a completely unconscious process. Parent-figures who are doing this likely don't see that they are engaging in possibly problematic behavior. In fact, many see it as an act of love (and for them it often is). On occasion, the outcomes can be devastating for some of those in traditionally desirable professions (lawyers and doctors,[32] for example) who struggle to cope with the misalignment of their careers, use substances, experience mental health issues, and in extreme cases, even commit suicide.[33,34]

## Having a Parent Who Does Not Model Boundaries

Boundaries are clear definitions of our personal limitations. Children instinctively understand boundaries. They respond to them and can clearly state their own boundaries and follow through with maintaining them, regardless of others' reaction to them (just watch how a toddler almost instinctively shakes their head "no" in response to something they don't like). Some adults, however, have fewer boundaries and typically have a difficult time maintaining the ones they do have. Many of us grew up in homes raised by parent-figures who did not fully understand how to use or maintain their own boundaries, making them unable to model appropriate limits for us.

In my therapy practice I heard frequent historical reports of a parent-figure's reading of a childhood diary. This violation of private space often resulted in a shaming confrontation for the child and sometimes even punishment based on what was read (as happened to me). These experiences teach us as children that loved ones can and do cross one's boundaries. In instances of frequent boundary crossings, children may internalize a belief that such boundary crossings are part of "closeness" and maybe even "love," allowing them in future partnerships. A child may do the opposite, becoming highly secretive and protective with their personal details.

Another common boundary crossing occurs when one parent-figure complains to a child about the other parent-figure. Several of my clients told me that personal details about parental relationships (such as infidelity or financial issues) were told to them in childhood. The parent-figure, unable to appreciate that the child is not a peer, may be seeking emotional comfort from their child. In such instances, a child may feel overwhelmed by these personal details and have their own conflicted feelings about hearing the negative comments about another loved parent-figure.

## Having a Parent Who Is Overly Focused on Appearance

As we know, the need for outside validation doesn't just stop once we "grow up." Instead, the impulse to be liked and admired follows us through our lives. Parent-figures may project this need onto their children in a number of ways. Sometimes, it can be obvious: the parent-figure who comments on a child's weight or obsesses about the child looking "presentable" at all times; the parent-figure who is overly concerned with minor details, such as how a child wears her hair. Children learn quickly that some parts of their physical appearances are "acceptable" and some are not. This begins a lifelong practice of believing that receiving love is conditional on one's outward appearance.

This same imprinting happens when our parent-figures are overly fixated on how *they* look, modeling behaviors such as obsessive dieting, paying extreme attention to grooming, or excessive exercising. It can take the form of deeming certain foods "bad" or "fattening." It can also take the form of commenting about the body or appearance of friends, family, or public figures. Direct statements don't necessarily have to be made to the child, because, as we know, a child is a sponge who notices when one's core beliefs are overly image focused.

This can also be observed on a larger scale when parent-figures behave a certain way outside versus inside the home, training the child to see that humans can have "pseudoselves." An example of this is family members who are constantly bickering or yelling inside the home but once in public speak and act lovingly or at least politely, upholding personae that are, in fact, masks. Children learn quickly that they must shift who they are depending on where they are—just as they saw modeled—in order to survive and be loved.

## Having a Parent Who Cannot Regulate Their Emotions

Emotional regulation is the process of experiencing an emotion, allowing the sensations to pass through the body (rather than trying to distract oneself with, say, drugs or alcohol or an iPhone or food), identifying it ("I am angry right now" or "I am sad"), and breathing through it until it eventually passes. The practice of emotional regulation enables us to remain centered and calm through the various stresses that life brings and return to a physiological baseline.

Most of us did not have parent-figures who were able to identify, let alone regulate, their feelings. Instead, when they were emotionally flooded or experiencing many intense feelings at once, they didn't know what to do. Some may have projected the overwhelming emotional energy outward, screaming, slamming doors, and throwing things or storming off. For others, the emotions project inward, resulting in some kind of withdrawal—this looks like parents using the silent treatment or "icing" someone out. Icing behavior takes place when a parent-figure becomes emotionally distant or withdraws love from a child, usually as a result of feeling emotionally overwhelmed. Not being able to control their own feelings about a particular experience, the parent-figure shuts down and shuts out their children. Many SelfHealers resonate with this experience; some of them identify with the phenomenon of a parent who used the "silent treatment" as a punishment. In our healing circles people have spoken about parent-figures who disengaged; those who stopped speaking to them; those who deployed other family members to reject them. When we have loved ones who shut down instead of managing their feelings, we are modeled an overall lack of emotional regulation and often do not develop coping skills that enable us to build emotional resilience of our own.

## Coping with Our Traumas

"You're a pig! You're white trash! You're an embarrassment to the family!" my mother once shockingly yelled at me.

That terrible moment was one of the rare examples of my mother's eruptions after years of suppressing her emotions. It happened after my sister's wedding. I was the maid of honor and allowed to bring three of my closest friends from college to the reception. One of those close friends happened to be my secret girlfriend, Katie.

No one, not even our friends, knew that Katie and I were dating. We weren't ashamed, exactly; it was just my first same-sex relationship, and I didn't feel the need to proclaim it to the world, let alone to a family who never talked deeply about anything. The morning of the reception, my friends and I began to drink heavily. I remember sobbing while watching the father-daughter dance, which on the surface I'm sure appeared odd to my friends and family as I couldn't have cared less about wedding traditions. Below the surface, it stung with a deeper sense of loss, knowing that I would not be able to give my dad this ritual; there was no way that I was ever going to have a traditional wedding! The night went downhill from there, and the sadder I became, the more I withdrew into myself.

Katie was also drunk and was upset by my distanced behavior. Every time she tried to dance with me, I brushed her off. Then she tried to kiss me, and I gave her the look of *Cut it out*. She got angry and stormed off. A scene followed, and it became obvious to everyone in the wedding hall that there was something romantic between us.

I was enough in denial to believe that we got away with it. No one mentioned Katie that night or the next day. It was only a month or so later, after I returned to Cornell University in upstate New York, that my mom appeared unannounced. She drove up with my father from Philadelphia that day, and once I answered the door, she flew through it and yelled those painful words. She continued yelling as I tried to get her out of my apartment. The scene became loud enough that a neighbor came out to see if I needed help. I got her out of my apartment building and back into the car with my father, who sat with his head down, not saying a word. I found myself very caught off-guard, as my mom rarely if ever showed this degree of emotion, making this outburst destabilizing for us all.

When I returned to my childhood home months later for summer break, my mom acted as if I didn't exist, as if she could walk right through me because I was invisible, a ghost. If we passed in the hallway, she would walk by with her head up and her gaze focused past me. My father played along with my mother's silence, though he still spoke to me. This was the trauma of my childhood fully realized. I was so unworthy, so unlovable. I didn't exist. It was almost a relief to become the physical manifestation of what I so feared. It was what I was training for my whole life. It was my "spaceship" in action.

The emotional withdrawal continued for weeks, until one day out of the blue my mom started speaking to me again and acted as though nothing had ever happened between us. We never spoke about my sexual orientation again, and she fully accepted my future girlfriends as if she had no history of behaving any other way. In fact, we never spoke about that interaction again. After years of repression, her body had ejected all her feelings all at once, resulting in an outsized, destructive outpouring of emotion. When the dust eventually settled, it was as if she could hardly believe that she'd had that reaction—that she was capable of such emotional expression.

In and out of romantic relationships as a young adult, I kept finding myself in the push-pull dynamic of emotional reactivity and emotional withdrawal. I often picked relationships where I could remain emotionally distanced, removed, often emotionally unavailable. When I continued to feel my emotional needs and deep desires for connection unmet, I would react, calling or texting too often, throwing tantrums, and picking fights. If I eventually did get an emotional reaction I on some level craved, I would then detach and dissociate, feeling overwhelmed—I'd become the ghost I learned to be as a child. I blamed *them* when the relationship inevitably turned south. Looking back, the reality was that I was stuck in conditioned patterns that were all coping strategies, or ways to manage and control my inner turmoil.

In 1984, two groundbreaking psychologists who studied stress and emotion, the late UC Berkeley professor Richard Lazarus and UC San Francisco professor Susan Folkman, presented a theory of coping, which they defined as "constantly changing cognitive behavior efforts to manage specific external and internal demands that [exceed] the resources of a person."[35] In other words, coping is a learned strategy to manage the profound unease in the body and mind that stress generates.

Lazarus and Folkman outlined adaptive and maladaptive coping strategies. Adaptive coping is an action we take to help us return to feelings of safety, such as facing a problem head-on or redirecting negative thoughts. The key here is being *active*; adaptive coping requires effort and a conscious acknowledgment of the discomfort. It can be harder to use an adaptive coping strategy when we were not modeled them or taught how to use them.

Maladaptive coping strategies, often learned from our parent-figures, give us a brief distraction or reprieve from the discomfort (say, by drinking alcohol at a wedding, as I did) or avoiding any emotional reaction (as I also did when I dissociated). Either of these attempts at relieving our distress, however, ends up in more disconnection from the authentic Self.

How we cope with a particular environment has less to do with the environment and more to do with our conditioned coping strategies around stress. Let's say two people have the same high-stress, performance-based job. Sonia deals with the stress by taking on adaptive coping strategies: going to the gym regularly to help channel her stress or calling a best friend for support. Michelle, who is contending with the same pressures, may use substances to zone out and escape reality. Though she may feel better in the moment, when she wakes up the next morning, she feels foggy, unfocused, and miserable. The stress and shame is now compounded and the cycle of maladaptive coping continues.

I've observed many maladaptive coping strategies in my clinical work. Some of the most common include:

- **People pleasing.** Once you meet the demand, the stress is (temporarily) gone.
- **Anger or rage.** If you can discharge the emotion onto someone else, you've released it.
- **Dissociation.** You "leave your body" during a stressful event so that you don't "experience" the trauma in the first place. Sexually, this form of detachment can involve having sex with people we aren't truly interested in; instead, it might involve dedicating ourselves to our partner's pleasure, without any awareness of or attention to our own.

All of these coping strategies enable us to avoid repeating or reliving our past trauma, delaying immediate pain. They do not help us fully meet our physical, emotional, and spiritual wants and needs. When our needs are consistently unmet, our pain and disconnection are compounded. Self-preservation leads to self-betrayal. It's a loop we can easily get stuck in. The cycle of unresolved trauma, repetition of maladaptive coping behaviors, and consistent denial of Self allows the pain to live on in our mind and body, where it can eventually make us sick.

## THE POTENTIAL FOR CHANGE

We all carry unresolved trauma. As we've seen, it's not necessarily the severity of the event itself but our response to it that determines the imprint it makes. Resilience is learned through conditioning; if we didn't see it modeled by our parent-figures when we were young, we may have never learned it. When we do *the work* of resolving trauma, we can become more resilient. In fact, these experiences can become catalysts for profound transformation.

When I share information about trauma with my online Self-Healers community, I receive a lot of feedback from people asking questions such as "Are you saying everyone is traumatized?" or "How do I not traumatize my children?" Here's the thing: Trauma is part of life. It is unavoidable. Your very first experience on this earth—birth—was a trauma, possibly for both you and your mother. Just because we've experienced trauma does not necessarily mean that we are destined for a life of suffering and illness. We don't have to repeat the patterns that shaped our early lives. When we do *the work*, we can change. We can move forward. We can heal.

Trauma may be universal, and it's also individual, affecting each *whole* person—the nervous system, immune response, every part of their physiology—uniquely. The first step toward healing in mind and body is knowing what you're dealing with—identifying the unresolved trauma. The next step is understanding the long-term effects of this trauma and how your learned coping strategies are keeping you stuck.

---

## DO THE WORK: IDENTIFY YOUR CHILDHOOD WOUNDS

To gain awareness of your personal childhood wounds or suppressed emotions, take some time to reflect and write using the prompts that follow. You need to respond only to the experiences that resonate with you. Many people with unresolved trauma, including myself, don't have many memories, making some of these questions difficult to answer. Explore whatever does come to mind.

### HAVING A PARENT WHO DENIES YOUR REALITY

Remember a time in childhood when you went to your parent-figure(s) with an idea, feeling, or experience and they responded in an invalidating way. For example, their response could have been some version of "It didn't happen that way," "It's not a big deal," "You should just forget about it." Spend some time connecting with your child self, exploring what you may have felt when your parent-figure(s) responded in those ways. To help you reflect, feel free to use this journal prompt:

In childhood, when my parent-figure(s) ____________, I felt ________________.

### HAVING A PARENT WHO DOES NOT SEE OR HEAR YOU

Remember a time in childhood where you wanted to be acknowledged by your parent-figure(s) and they seemed distracted, busy, or otherwise made you feel unacknowledged. Spend some time noting the past circumstances that led to you feeling unseen or unheard. Then reflect upon and write about the ways you may have tried to get their attention. Did you "perform," "act out," or become withdrawn? To help you reflect, feel free to use this journal prompt:

In childhood, when my parent-figure(s) ____________, I felt ________________.

To cope, I ________________.

### HAVING A PARENT WHO VICARIOUSLY LIVES THROUGH YOU OR MOLDS AND SHAPES YOU

Do you remember a time in childhood when you got messages about who you were (or weren't)? Did you have a parent-figure(s) who said, "You're so sensitive like your mother" or "You need to get straight A's to make the family proud"? Were you as impassioned and committed to those goals as they were, or did you feel as though you were going through the motions just to please them?

Spend some time noting the different messages you may have received about yourself in childhood, also noting the different ways you may have been influenced by your parent-figure's directly or indirectly expressed wishes. To help you reflect, feel free to use these journal prompts:

IN MY CHILDHOOD . . .

I received the following messages about myself:

____________________

I was aware that my parent-figure(s) wished the following of me:

____________________________

### HAVING A PARENT WHO DOES NOT MODEL BOUNDARIES

Spend some time thinking back to your experiences with personal limits and their violations in childhood, as well as about the different sorts of limits (or lack thereof) modeled by your parent-figure(s) overall. To help you reflect, feel free to use these journal prompts:

IN YOUR CHILDHOOD . . .

Did you feel free to say "no"? Or did your parent-figure(s) tell you to behave a certain way? ___________________

Did your parent-figure(s) set clear limits on their time, energy, and resources in their relationships? ______________

Did your parent-figure(s) respect your privacy, or did they invade it? Examples of privacy violation include: transgressions such as reading a diary, listening to phone calls, or other snooping behavior.

______________

Did your parent-figure(s) allow you to have conversations, interactions, and experiences with people in your life without inserting themselves into them? ______________

## HAVING A PARENT WHO IS OVERLY FOCUSED ON APPEARANCE

In childhood, many of us received direct and indirect messages about our appearance. A parent-figure(s) may have even commented directly on certain aspects of your appearance with statements such as "You should wear your hair down," "Your thighs are getting bigger," "Do you really think it's a good idea to have seconds?" or "You'd look a lot better if you didn't wear clothes like that." Sometimes such statements may also be directed at others. Your parent-figure(s) may have commented on aspects of other people's appearances, highlighting some qualities positively and others negatively. Your parents' attention to or rituals around their own physical appearance also modeled beliefs and values about what is acceptable and what is not. To help you reflect, feel free to use this journal prompt:

What are the messages you received regarding appearance?

______________

## HAVING A PARENT WHO CANNOT REGULATE THEIR EMOTIONS

One of the most important aspects of your emotional health is how you regulate and process your emotions. In childhood, you learn emotional regulation by watching how your parent-figure(s) express their feelings (or don't) and by the way they respond when you express yours. Spend some time reflecting on how emotions were handled in your childhood. To help you reflect, feel free to use these journal prompts:

When your parent-figure(s) had strong feelings (such as anger or sadness), how did they respond? For example, did they slam doors, vent, scream, or give the "silent treatment"? ____________

Did your parent-figure(s) have a specific coping strategy? For example, did they overspend when shopping, use substances, avoid certain (or all) emotions entirely? __________

When your parent-figure(s) had strong feelings, how did they communicate with you or those around you? For example, did they resort to name-calling, blaming, shaming, or the silent treatment?

______________

After strong feelings, did your parent-figure(s) take time to explain or help you process your own feelings around what happened?

______________

In childhood, I received the following messages about feelings in general or my feelings in particular: ________________

# 4

# Trauma Body

The breaking point for me, at least physically, came the day I fainted—passed out cold.

I'd been experiencing symptoms of dysregulation for years. Like a game of Whac-A-Mole, I tried to fix each problem individually when the symptoms became uncomfortable. The dissociation, I thought, was a function of my personality. *I have a bad memory!* The anxiety was a result of both my genes and my current circumstances, I rationalized to myself—*I'm living in New York City on my own. My mom is sick*—so I went to a psychiatrist for medication to get me through the rough patches. The headaches were also genetically inherited. The brain fog came from working too hard. I had no clue why I was so constipated, again seeing a similar pattern in my mom and sister and not bothering to think too hard about it. Instead I downed bottles of brewer's yeast and prune juice and numerous over-the-counter medications. It was all individual issues with individual treatments. Nothing was connected.

Around that time, I moved from New York City to Philadelphia to pursue postdoctoral psychodynamic work at the Philadelphia School of Psychoanalysis. Since I was physically closer to my family, I saw them more frequently than I had in years. At the same time, I was seeing my own analyst once or at times twice a week to augment my own psychotherapy work and began to pick at the scabs of childhood traumas that I had long forgotten. Therapy gave me insight into how problematic my family dynamics were—how my family "othered" anyone outside the family unit and worked so hard to present a face of harmony and unity to the world and in reality lived in a feedback loop of anxiety and fear. I saw my mother's difficulty showing true affection and love, which came from the scarcity—not just material but also emotional and spiritual—created by her parent-figures, who never expressed love themselves. I saw my own protective mechanisms—the disengagement, the perfectionism, the numbing—as conditioned trauma responses that my mother passed on to me from her own deep-rooted pain.

The realizations were stark and upsetting. I didn't have any place to put them. So I started seeking chaos with Lolly—picking fights, pushing her away, and then freaking out when she left. It was the same pattern I repeated for years with my other romantic partners—cycling between emotional disconnection and the inevitable panic that resulted when the distance became too overwhelming.

Then I started to faint.

The first time was at a housewarming party at my childhood friend Amanda's apartment. (That it happened at the house of a person who was linked to my childhood is not lost on me.) It was a warm summer day. She had a pool at her apartment complex, which she was psyched to show off, and as we walked around it, I started to feel uncomfortable. The sun's heat felt strong against the back of my neck. I began to sweat. I suddenly felt light-headed, and the sky seemed to spin. *All right, Nicole,* I remember thinking. *Get it together.*

I opened my eyes. Lolly and my friend stared down at me with concern.

"Are you okay?" Lolly asked as Amanda, a trained EMT, assessed my cognitive state. She saw me hit my head quite hard on the concrete and was concerned that I suffered a concussion. I insisted that I was fine, even though I did feel dizzy and slightly nauseous.

The fall wasn't the *aha!* moment it should have been. I chalked it up to a freak accident. I returned to work as unsettled and detached as ever. Increasingly, I began to notice other issues with my cognition. I often struggled to find the right words. During one therapy session, I lost my train of thought so completely that I let the silence hang in the air for several minutes, apologizing profusely to my client for the lapse.

Then I fainted again. During the Christmas holidays that year, Lolly and I spent significant time with my family. We went out to pick up oyster-shucking knives. I remember walking into the hardware store, feeling dizzy and thinking about how hot it was under the harsh store lighting.

Once again, I looked up to a group of concerned faces.

Obviously, something was seriously wrong with my nervous system. It was only once my body actually screamed out for me to pay attention that I finally did.

## TRAUMA BODY

It's no exaggeration to say that every client who arrives at my office experiencing psychological symptoms also suffers from underlying physical health issues. Unresolved trauma weaves itself into the very fabric of our being.

As we know from ACEs, traumas make us more likely to develop a host of physical and psychological conditions, from depression and anxiety to heart attacks, cancer, obesity, and stroke. The research is unequivocal: people with unresolved trauma get sicker and die younger.

The ways in which trauma affects the body are varied and complex, and physical dysfunction boils down to one common denominator: stress. Stress is more than just a mental state; it is an internal condition that challenges homeostasis, which is a state of physical, emotional, and mental balance. We experience a physiological stress response when our brain perceives that we don't have adequate resources to survive an obstacle or threat (which is the general state of affairs when it comes to unresolved trauma). Addiction and stress expert Dr. Gabor Maté, who is the author of many books including *When the Body Says No: The Cost of Hidden Stress*, calls this the "stress-disease connection."[36]

When we are stressed, the body shifts its resources from maintaining homeostasis, that happy place of well-being and balance, to protecting itself. Stress is unavoidable (just trying to avoid it would stress you out!). Normative stress, for example, is a natural part of life: birth, death, marriage, breakups, job loss—these are all part of the human experience. As an adaptive response, we can develop coping strategies to help return us to our psychological and physiological baseline: seeking supportive resources, learning how to self-soothe, and assisting our often stuck nervous systems to return to homeostasis. This process of leaving and then returning to our baseline of balance is called allostasis. It allows us to develop the biological capacity for resilience.

The body's stress response, often referred to as our fight-or-flight mechanism, is probably familiar to you. Fighting and fleeing are two of the body's instinctual, automatic reactions to stress (the third is freezing—more on that soon). When we encounter a threat, either real or perceived, the brain's fear center, the amygdala, lights up. Once activated, this area of the brain then sends messages to the rest of our body that we are under attack, prompting the various systems of our body to mobilize the necessary resources to help us survive.

Whereas normative stress helps us grow and adapt, chronic stress—stress that is constant and persistent—wears us down and harms every system in our body. When we are chronically stressed and unable to return to homeostasis—because we never learned or developed adaptive coping strategies or because the stress feels too overwhelming to cope with at all—our bodies overactivate certain systems and suppress others. In cases of chronic stress, our adrenal glands release cortisol and other stress hormones, such as adrenaline, continuously.

Stress also activates the body's immune system, prompting it to become hypervigilant and primed to react at the mere suspicion of trouble. Our immune system learns from our behavior and habits beginning from when we are in utero and continuing throughout our lives. Once our immune system gets the signal that we're living in a near-constant threat state, it repeatedly sends out chemicals that cause inflammation throughout the body. These chemicals act as a kind of fire starter for a wide array of symptoms of imbalance and dysfunction, increasing our risk of developing autoimmune diseases, chronic pain, and other diseases ranging from heart disease to cancer.[37]

Cytokines—molecules that work to coordinate cell-to-cell communication—are one of these inflammatory chemicals. Cytokines incite the immune system to act when faced with injury or toxic invaders. They are responsible for the inflammatory symptoms we've all experienced when we've been ill—fevers, swelling, redness, pain—and when they overreact or "storm" our body, the results can be deadly.

If the immune system is constantly misdirecting its inflammatory chemicals, like the cytokines, the body's ability to respond to real illness is diminished. At the same time, inflammation occurs all over the body and may even affect the brain. The impact of stress and trauma on our immune system and brain is so significant that scientists have launched a new field of inquiry into the mind-body connection called psychoneuroimmunology. Inflammation in the brain has been identified in various forms of psychological dysfunction and mental illness—from depression and anxiety to outright psychosis.

Given these possibly devastating consequences, it is critical to address an overactive fight-or-flight response. If left immobilized, or stuck in this response, our immune system will continue to activate a full-body inflammatory reaction. "As long as the trauma is not resolved," wrote Dr. Bessel van der Kolk in *The Body Keeps the Score: Brain, Mind, and Body in the Healing of Trauma*, "the stress hormones that the body secretes to protect itself keep circulating."[38,39,40,41] The body must also devote excessive energy to "suppressing the inner chaos" of trauma, or the activated fight-or-flight response, which further pushes us into a state of dysregulation. It's a vicious cycle, a physiological loop repeated over and over again.

Stress affects every system of the body, including the gut—it's no coincidence that gastrointestinal (GI) problems are one of the issues most commonly cited by people dealing with anxiety. When we're stressed or frightened or anxious, our body has trouble digesting food and can either hold on to it for too long—resulting in constipation—or release it too quickly—resulting in irritable bowel syndrome (IBS) or diarrhea. Stress affects our food choices and the makeup of the microbiome in our gut, which is constantly communicating with our brain (something we will discuss in detail in chapter 5). In these cases, your body is denied essential nutrients—either because it isn't breaking down the food you eat fast enough or it's discharging it before it begins to process it. Without a well-functioning digestive system, we become sicker in all areas of our body.

The stress-disease connection is especially damaging for oppressed populations.[42] Oppressive environments enforce a near-perpetual trauma state in individuals, inducing stress responses that are chronic and unending. It's no wonder that there has been a documented connection between oppression and higher rates of physical illness and psychological distress. Research shows that BIPOC experience higher rates of depression and anxiety and are more likely to develop hypertension, artery calcifications, lower back pain, and cancer. In one sobering study,[43] a group of Black women was followed for six years after completing a survey about the level of discrimination they faced in their daily lives. Those who reported more incidents were at greater risk of developing breast cancer than those who reported fewer. We are at the very beginning of our understanding of the broad effects of systemic oppression. Thankfully, there is a growing body of literature devoted to investigating its fallout. There are several books that I feel are essential reading, which I have included in the Suggested Further Readings section at the end of the book. In the end, all studies confirm this fact: racism, bias, and bigotry make their way into the body's cells, changing the body in fundamental and destructive ways that are passed down through generations. The effects of racism exist in blood and bones.

## INTRODUCTION TO POLYVAGAL THEORY

As we've seen, unresolved trauma, coupled with poor coping strategies, affects the body physiologically. Stress alters your reality. There is no part of your universe that stress does not mold. The smell of freshly cut grass might transport you to a childhood trauma. A stranger's face might make you feel defensive or afraid without any cause. Hearing a sitcom jingle from your childhood could suddenly make you feel sick to your stomach. If you are a BIPOC in America, simply walking down the street or watching the news of daily violence against people who look like you can activate your trauma response. Some of you never feel safe; you may always feel like the sky is about to fall.

During the time I started having fainting episodes a few years after my move to Philadelphia, I understood that I was stressed out though still felt confused about why I was passing out. There was no stress that I could identify that seemed threatening enough to warrant such a strong response in my body. Why was my body in a state of heightened activation without there being any immediate threat?

Later, when I started researching psychiatrist Dr. Stephen Porges's polyvagal theory, which offers revolutionary insights into trauma and the body's stress response, I discovered why, seemingly out of nowhere, I began to faint. Polyvagal theory helped me understand just how it is that trauma lives in the body and continues to shape our world.

The term *polyvagal* refers to the vagus nerve, which connects the brain and the gut. The vagus nerve has many branches of sensory fibers that run throughout the rest of the body—from the brain stem to the heart, lungs, genitals, you name it—connecting every major organ to the brain. The location and function of these nerves help us understand why the body reacts so swiftly when we're stressed: why our hearts race when we run into an ex; why feelings of panic make us feel short of breath; and why I started fainting (or losing consciousness) out of the blue.

When we are in a state of homeostasis, the vagus nerve acts as a "neutral break," keeping us calm and open, helping us be our most social selves. When the vagus nerve is activated and it enters its defensive system, fight-or-flight responses can manifest themselves almost immediately.

## SOCIAL ENGAGEMENT

Most of the people I treat live in a near-constant fight-or-flight mode. This stress response is an automatic function of something called the autonomic nervous system, the part of the nervous system that regulates involuntary functions, including heartbeat, breathing, and digestion.

The autonomic nervous system is all about properly allocating our body's resources. It constantly scans our environment for cues: Should I be careful here? Is this a dangerous situation? Is this person a friend or foe? Am I properly hydrated and fed to deal with any threats? The autonomic system uses something called neuroception—a "sixth sense" that operates outside our conscious awareness—to assess our environment and put people, places, and things into one of two boxes: safe or unsafe.

When the autonomic nervous system deems a situation safe, our vagus nerve tells our body to relax. This is when our parasympathetic nervous system, something called the "rest and digest" system, kicks in. The vagus nerve sends signals to the heart to slow down. Our digestion hums away happily, properly dispensing nutrients to our body. Our lungs inflate and take in more oxygen. In this calm state, we enter what is called social engagement mode, where we are primed to feel safe, secure, and able to connect easily with others.

When we are in social engagement mode, we even look more engaging and friendly. Our smiles seem more authentic (the vagus nerve connects to the muscles of the face), and our voices sound melodic and friendly (the vagus nerve also connects to our larynx, or voice box). Our hearing improves, as the vagus nerve connects to muscles in the middle ear, which open up so that we're better able to hear calm human voices. Even our saliva glands are activated, greasing the wheels of our most potent instrument for connecting with the world around us: our mouth.

When we are in this receptive, parasympathetic state, our resources are allocated to higher executive functions in the brain, such as planning for the future, self-motivation, problem solving, and emotional regulation. Now that we're not consumed with survival, we are free to be our authentic selves. This is a state of play, joy, compassion, and love. I call this the "learning brain"—it is flexible, open, calm, peaceful, and curious, all key states for achieving milestones in neurological and behavioral development in childhood. We are more likely to make mistakes and learn from them. We are more likely to get up when we fall.

## FIGHT OR FLIGHT

When we feel threatened, our body enters activation mode, the home of the fight-or-flight response, activated by the sympathetic system, the yin to the parasympathetic yang.

In activation mode, the vagus nerve sends SOS signals to the sympathetic nervous system, making our hearts pump harder and faster, activating stress responses in our adrenal glands that increase our cortisol levels, and raising our body temperature, making us sweat.

In this heightened state, we literally experience the world differently. Pain doesn't register. We focus on louder, more distressing sounds. We lose nuances in our sense of smell. And in activation mode, we look different. We grow dead-eyed. Our brows furrow. Our shoulders hunch, and we take on a defensive stance. Our voices take on an unnatural, stressed-out tone. The muscles of the middle ear close, and suddenly we register only high and low frequencies (what are known as predator sounds). Everything filters through a lens of possible threat: A neutral face becomes hostile. A fearful face grows angry. A friendly face is suspicious. Our body has primed itself for battle, an evolutionary necessity that we inherited from our ancestors. It's an innate adaptive response that we learned when we had to face constant threats—in the form of wild animals, famine, and war. All of this is helpful and protective if we are in fact facing this level of threat. The same supercharged response occurs during the mundane, everyday trials in life, for example, when you receive a text from your boss or watch your computer crash when an assignment is due.

In addition to all the health issues associated with this chronic stress state, people who struggle with an overactive sympathetic response system (what is known as poor vagal tone) report hosts of troubling issues. Some of the most common emotional and relational patterns include:

- Lack of emotional resilience
- Inability to form meaningful connections
- Issues with concentration
- Difficulty performing higher-functioning cognitive tasks, such as planning for the future
- Trouble delaying gratification

It's important to note that we enter fight-or-flight mode entirely subconsciously. Our body's reaction to threat is instinctual and involuntary; it is not a choice we make. We cannot blame someone who believes they are being attacked for lashing out any more than we can blame someone for sweating too much when they exercise.

## IMMOBILIZATION

The two most commonly known stress responses—fighting and fleeing—don't tell the full story of the body under attack. As Dr. Porges pointed out in his legendary paper on the polyvagal theory back in the 1990s, there is also a third mode: immobilization, or "freezing."

Our vagus nerve has two pathways. Social activation and engagement mode are on one pathway. This pathway is myelinated, meaning that it's sheathed with a layer of fat to make it engage quicker and shut off faster. The second pathway is unmyelinated and therefore less reactive and slower to shut off and more primitive. In fact, we share this pathway not with our ape ancestors but with reptiles.

When the second pathway is activated, we become immobilized. Our whole body shuts down. Our heart rate and metabolism slow to a crawl. Our bowels either release completely or clench up and hold. Our breathing may stop. We may pass out. This happens when our body feels that there is no hope for survival. Justin Sunseri, a polyvagal-informed therapist, describes immobilization mode beautifully: "If you see a bear, your mobilization mode may be activated, as your body primes you to either run or flee. But if the bear is already on top of you, your body might just give up and play dead."

This is dissociation mode. People who enter this mode leave their bodies psychologically. Many, like me, may appear present, interacting with others, though mentally be far off on their own "spaceship." Some detach so completely that they view the event as a dream. Others develop amnesia. Whatever the degree of dissociation, this evolutionarily programmed trauma response explains why many of us have so little memory of past experiences—if we were never truly present when events occurred, we have no event memory to return to. It also explains how hard it is to disengage from this detached state and return to the present moment. The unmyelinated nerve makes it almost impossible to recover quickly once you've entered this mode.

## THE SOCIAL WORLD

So many of my clients, friends, and members of my online SelfHealers community have come to me with interpersonal issues that reflect disconnection: *I just can't seem to connect with anyone. I want friends, but I can't seem to cultivate any emotional depth. No one knows the real me. I can't find love.*

Once I dove into the polyvagal literature, I realized that the inability to form true intimacy with others is usually not about some defect in personality but a product of our vagal tone, a measure of our nervous system's response to our environment. When we have poor vagal tone, we have higher sensitivity to perceived threats in our environment, which overactivates the body's stress response and leads to reduced emotional and attentional regulation overall.

Those of you who experience the discomfort of social anxiety might recognize this disconnect. Imagine walking into a party filled with strangers. You might have obsessed over what to wear to the party, planning every detail, every possible conversation topic, or you may have felt totally neutral about the party—no warning signs that you might feel uncomfortable and act accordingly. Either way, none of it matters once you actually walk into the room.

Suddenly, all eyes are on you. Your face grows hot and red when you hear laughter, which you're certain is about your outfit or your hair. Someone brushes past you, and you feel claustrophobic. All the strangers seem to be leering. Even if you know rationally that this is not a hostile place, that no one is looking at or judging you (and if they are, who cares?), it's nearly impossible to shake the feeling once you're trapped in it.

That's because your subconscious perceives a threat (using your nervous system's sixth sense of neuroception) in a nonthreatening environment (the party) and has activated your body, putting you into a state of fight (argue with anyone and everyone), flight (leave the party), or freeze (don't say a word). The social world has become a space filled with threat.

Unfortunately, this kind of nervous system dysregulation is self-confirming. While it is activated, anything that doesn't confirm your suspicions (a friendly face) will be ignored by your neuroception in favor of things that do (the stray laugh you felt was directed at you). Social cues that would be seen as friendly when you were in social engagement mode—such as a pause in the conversation for you to enter, eye contact, a smile—will be either misinterpreted or ignored.

We are interpersonal creatures. We require connection to survive. Yet nervous systems that are dysregulated due to unresolved trauma keep us unfulfilled, outside our emotions, trapped in our inability to connect with others.

## CO-REGULATION

When we're stuck in a trauma response, our neuroception can become inaccurate. It misreads the environment, sees threats where there are none, and returns us to the overactive fight-or-flight state. Then the cycle of activation starts all over again. Understanding *why* this occurs alone won't fix our social issues. The trouble is that our nervous system states are feedback loops. As Dr. Porges put it, "We mirror the autonomic state of those around us."[44]

When we feel safe, it is reflected in our eyes, our voice, and our body language. We are fully present, and there is a lightness and ease in our manner. This sense of safety is passed on to others in a process called co-regulation. When others are reassured that you are not a threat, they, too, will feel safe and enter the same social activation mode that sets them at ease. Our energies and states are transferable. We feel better and calmer around certain people because our nervous systems are responding to theirs. Oxytocin, the bonding hormone, flows, helping us to bond emotionally and, in the case of romantic relationships, physically. The sense of security creates a cospace of comfort. It's a mutual exchange of connection.

The ability to co-regulate is established in childhood. As we've seen, we are conditioned by our parent-figures in ways that are both subtle and profound. One of the most important behaviors we learn from our loved ones is the ability to apply internal coping strategies that help return us to the safe and creative space of social mobilization or social engagement during times of stress. If you lived in a house surrounded by calm and healing energy, your system not only internalized that environment but mirrored it. Our vagal nerve will return us to our parasympathetic state of balance or homeostasis when it feels there is a safe space to return to.

If you lived in a chaotic house where overreaction, rage spirals, disengagement, or fear were the norm, your internal resources were likely tied up in the management of stress (survival, really) and could not freely return to the safe social engagement mode. As we've learned, children are dependent creatures. If a parent-figure provides a chaotic, stressful environment, the child will internalize that state and generalize: *My parents feel threatened. I am threatened because they are not attuned to my needs. The world is a threatening place.* This "survival brain" (as opposed to the social engagement's "learning brain") is hyperfocused on perceived threats, thinks about things in hard-and-fast black and white, and is often circular, obsessive, and panic driven. We are very fearful about making mistakes. We thrash around, break down, or shut down when we fail.

At the party, for example, we likely couldn't escape our vagal response, because we were passing that state along to people whose paths we crossed. The others at the party then reflected our activated state back to us, keeping us stuck and leading us along a path of emotional addiction.

## EMOTIONAL ADDICTION

When trauma is not properly addressed it is left to drive our narratives and shape our autonomic responses. Our mind and body become reliant on the strong physical response that comes from the release of neurotransmitters associated with that experience and solidify it in the neural pathways of our brain. In other words, the brain learns to crave the feelings associated with the trauma response. This is the loop of emotional addiction.

A typical day of emotional addiction might look like this:

You wake up in the morning, and dread washes over you. The alarm is buzzing, and it's time to get up and get ready for work. Immediately you have the same thoughts you have every morning: *I need coffee. My commute is forty-five freaking minutes. I have to shower. I wish it was Friday.* Your mind is doing what it always does, providing you with the endless narratives of the many things you need to do (though you desperately wish you didn't have to) before you have done them. Your body responds to your stressful thoughts: your heart rate increases, your breath shortens, your nervous system upregulates, your stress hormones are released—all before you've left your bed. On the way to work, there is traffic. You expect the traffic because it happens almost every day, but your mind still races with critiques about how you should have left earlier and how much you hate your commute. You experience a buildup of frustration and anger, which you discharge onto your coworkers once you get into the office. You complain to them, and it feels good to be heard, but when you open your email, your heart starts racing again and your stomach tightens. You spend some more time venting, which again feels good, and the cycle of emotional activation continues.

When you arrive home, you're exhausted, which is a normal response to a day of living on an emotional roller coaster. To relax, you reach for a glass of wine. Because you're so exhausted, you're unable to be present and connect with your partner. You turn on Netflix and begin binge-watching. The stressful crime show allows you to feel the same emotional spikes you've felt all day. You love the uncertainty and the way it leaves you on the edge of your seat. You feel somewhat content (and more relaxed because of the wine) and eventually fall asleep on the couch, wake up at 2:00 a.m., and then throw yourself into bed just to repeat the same pattern when you wake up.

Our body learns to engage in patterns like these to feel like our familiar self. Ideally, when we experience a powerful emotion, either our activation or our immobilization mode is triggered and we return to our baseline social engagement zone quickly. Those activation states are supposed to feel unpleasant and dangerous, and for those of us stuck in the loop of emotional addiction, the rush feels good. It might be the only time we feel anything at all. Our body responds to those feelings by releasing hormones such as cortisol and neurochemicals such as dopamine that fundamentally change our cellular chemistry. We now need to seek out the same kind of emotional hit again and again. Even if an emotion makes us stressed or sad, it often feels familiar and safe because it provides the same type of release that we experienced as children.

In my childhood home, for example, stress and fear ruled. Those feelings bound us together and provided a stand-in for emotional intimacy, which was largely absent. Instead of connecting authentically, we connected over drama and pain, frantically coming together over each new crisis (Mom's health! A rude neighbor!). The "downtimes," when we didn't experience these feelings, felt dull in comparison to the jolts of outrage, fear, and anger.

When I wasn't in the emotional addiction cycle, I didn't feel like "me." My body became so accustomed to adrenaline, cortisol, and other powerful hormonal responses that I continued to unconsciously seek them in adulthood to repeat the emotional baseline established in childhood. Without them, I felt bored and agitated.

That was why I would nitpick when things were calm in my romantic relationships, throw myself into a panic about upcoming work I was tasked to complete, or push myself into a state of anxiety while trying to unwind and relax. My body was feeling uncomfortable and pulling me back into the familiar stress of my childhood.

Some of my clients have described how the outrage they experience from watching the news actually makes them feel pleasurably "charged." They want that rush of anger or disgust. It's the one thing that makes them truly *feel* because their body has become so accustomed to operating from a highly charged baseline. Our relationships are another common place where we act out our emotional addictions. Many of my clients found themselves in relationships with people who are unpredictable or unreliable. They were unsure of and unclear about their emotions, which leaves them feeling anxious. Most of their thoughts revolved around their love interest and how they felt about them. Any action or behavior the other person engaged in became something my clients overanalyzed. Intellectually, they were seeking a completely different kind of partner. They wanted someone who would commit and who would be clear about their feelings. Yet they kept returning to the same relationship dynamics because it felt exciting. Addicted to the cycle of unpredictability and the powerful biochemical response they get from it, they couldn't pull away.

Over time (as with other addictions, such as to sugar or sex, or drug or alcohol dependency), our body needs more and more intense experiences to receive the same chemical "hit." Our subconscious leads us into situations where we can get that hit in increasingly powerful doses: unpredictable relationships, news media that leave us feeling scared and angry, social media that allow us to pick fights online. This is why we are drawn to vent to friends and chronically complain; these behaviors help us remain in a heightened state. Nonactivated peace is dull and unfamiliar. Our body and mind seek the familiar, even if it is painful, and many of us are left ultimately feeling ashamed about and confused by our behavior.

## COMING FULL CIRCLE

Consistent cycles of emotional addiction exacerbate other dysfunctions of the trauma body, including the chronic inflammation and gut issues that are key physical symptoms expressed by every single one of my clients.

Because the vagus nerve is connected to the gut, if we have a dysregulated vagal nerve or poor vagal tone, our digestion suffers. When we enter the fight-or-flight mode, the cascade of stress hormones activates our body to pump out inflammatory chemicals, such as cytokines, which create even more inflammation. Our nervous system—and our unconscious addiction to keeping it in a highly activated state—is at the heart of many of our psychological and physical symptoms.

Understanding why the nervous system becomes dysregulated—and realizing that stress reactions take place outside our conscious control—can help normalize these behaviors and explain why so many of us feel alone when we're in a crowded room, why we put substances into our body to numb our natural physiological responses, why we lash out, run away, or disengage. As we have seen, these are all automatic responses that are conditioned by experiences with co-regulation in childhood or a lack thereof.

*However*, this is not the end of the story.

As we will see in the next chapter, there are ways to improve our vagal tone and help manage our nervous system responses. Learning how to harness the power of the vagus nerve was the most impactful and empowering discovery of my early healing journey, and I hope the tools that follow help you to do the same.

---

## DO THE WORK: ASSESS YOUR NERVOUS SYSTEM DYSREGULATION

**Step 1. Witness yourself.** Nervous system dysregulation is a term used to describe symptoms that come from repeated activation or extended periods of stress. Ideally, when you face a stressful situation head-on, your nervous system becomes activated and then returns to a baseline state of balance, which allows your body to "rest and digest." If your nervous system cannot regulate itself, however, you cannot recover from stress and you may have the following symptoms:

- **Possible psychological plus emotional symptoms:**
  - *Activation symptoms:* Shame, guilt, mood swings, fear, panic, aggression, anxiety, rage, terror, confusion, self-blame, overwhelm

  - *Shutdown symptoms:* Inability to connect to people or experiences, feeling "spacey" and numb, inability to think clearly, fear of speaking up or being seen

- **Possible physical symptoms:**
  - *Hypervigilance symptoms:* Insomnia, nightmares, jumpiness (easy to startle), fear of loud sounds, trembling, shaking, racing heart, migraines, digestion issues, autoimmune disorders
  - *Tension symptoms:* Teeth grinding, migraines, muscle tension or aches, exhaustion, chronic fatigue

- **Possible social symptoms:**
  - *Attachment symptoms:* Push-pull or avoidant relationship patterns, consistent fear of abandonment (often resulting in "clinginess" or the inability to be alone)
  - *Emotional symptoms:* Boundarylessness or overly rigid "absolute" boundaries without flexibility, social anxiety, irritability, social withdrawal

For a week, spend some time tuning in to your body each day (you can use the Consciousness Building exercise on page 37 to help you do this). Witness and note when you are experiencing any of the above symptoms of nervous system activation.

**Step 2. Restore balance to your nervous system.** Achieving an awareness of your state of nervous system activation will be an important part of your healing journey. Incorporating the following practices daily will help you regulate your nervous system. Over time this practice will help give you the ability to engage with yourself, others, and the world in new ways.

Choose one of these practices to focus on each day, and practice only to the degree of intensity or effort that feels comfortable. Those of you who are already keeping a journal or notepad for this work may want to note how your body feels and responds to each practice.

- **Find your ground in the present moment.** Find a smell, a taste, or a visual in your current environment. Practice actively focusing your full attention on those sensory experiences.
- **Do a visualization meditation.** Close your eyes and take a deep breath. Picture a white light coming from your heart. Repeat the words "I am safe, and I am at peace" as you place your hands on your heart. Do this three times throughout the day. First thing in the morning or right before bed is a great time for this.
- **Be conscious about your consumption of information.** When you consume information, your nervous system consumes it, too. Be mindful of how you feel in your body as you consume various kinds of information. Do you feel replenished and restored or depleted and fearful? Disconnecting from media that activates anxious feelings can be helpful.
- **Find nature and witness it.** Go outside and just experience any small aspect of the natural environment that is accessible to you. Notice the colors of flowers. Sit under trees. Place your bare feet onto grass or into water. Let the wind blow on your skin. Nature is a natural balancer of our nervous system and gives us a "reset."

As you begin to use these new tools to help restore balance to your nervous system, remember that small, consistent practice is key. Many of you have been living a lifetime in a dysregulated body, so healing, which will happen, will take time.

## FSJ: RESTORING BALANCE

Here is an example of the Future Self Journaling prompts I used each day to begin to create a new experience of nervous system balance in my daily life. To help you with this process, you may want to use the following example (or create a similar one of your own):

**Today I am practicing** restoring balance to my nervous system.

**I am grateful for** an opportunity to create calm in my life.

**Today, I am** bringing one moment of much-needed calm to my body.

**Change in this area allows** me to feel more peace.

**Today, I am practicing when** I find safety in the present moment/do one visualization meditation/am conscious about my information consumption/spend one minute witnessing nature.

# 5
# Mind-Body Healing Practices

The insights I gained into the nervous system and polyvagal theory allowed me to shed something that had long been holding me back: shame. I now understood that so many of the aspects of myself I was struggling with—my behavior, my cyclical thoughts, my emotional explosions, my detached relationships—had a physiological basis. They were the reactive impulses of a dysregulated body. *I* wasn't bad. *I* wasn't damaged. In fact, those habits and behaviors were learned responses that my body used to *keep me alive*. They were survival mechanisms. Applying qualifiers like "good" or "bad," I now realized, grossly oversimplified the wildly intricate interplay between mind and body.

Though there were aspects of my being that were outside my conscious control, that didn't necessarily mean that I was at the whim of my body. It did not mean that because I lived with unresolved trauma and struggled with inflammation and poor vagal tone, I could never change. In fact, just the opposite was true: if my body could learn dysregulated ways of coping, it could also learn healthy routes to recovering. Thanks to epigenetics, we know that our genes are not fixed; thanks to neuroplasticity, we know that the brain can form new pathways; thanks to the conscious mind, we know the power of our thoughts to effect change; thanks to polyvagal theory, we know that the nervous system affects all other systems of the body. As I started to shed layer after layer of ignorance about the connections among my mind, body, and soul, for the first time really witnessing myself, I began to comprehend the potential within to *heal*. We can unlearn and relearn as adults, even if we've endured significant trauma in our past. We can harness the power of our bodies to heal our minds and the power of our minds to heal our bodies.

Do you remember Ally, the remarkable woman whose SelfHealing journey we encountered in chapter 1? Her story taught me so much about the incredible power of all of us to change. Ally's transformation started with the "dark night of the soul" she experienced after being diagnosed with multiple sclerosis and having an adverse reaction to new medication. She was left with the shock and uncertainty of a chronic diagnosis and an aching desire for a better life.

Ally first started to keep small daily promises to herself, and over time she started trusting herself enough to begin witnessing her own trauma responses. She allowed herself to experience the "big feelings," as she called them, recalling moments from her childhood when she was severely bullied. She started to note her body's responses to that fear and sadness and held space for those emotions without judgment or reproach.

Ally began to listen to her body, and it pushed her to harness the power of her nervous system response in the most empowering and joyous ways possible. She listened to her intuition, and it told her to sing. She signed up for vocal lessons, fighting against her tyrannical inner critic (her subconscious push to remain comfortable) and battling the fear that coursed through her body before each session, spiking her adrenaline and ultimately filling her with excitement and pride. With practice, she released the need for perfection and threw herself into the play and joy of creating. Now she sings, plays guitar and violin, and is beginning to take the small steps to write her own music. She was even cast in a musical, which made her inner child (something we will learn more about in chapter 7) beam with pride.

Along the way, she began a yoga practice, which strengthened her body that for months was confined to her bed and couch. This expanded her capacity to endure discomfort and helped her develop resilience in the face of stress. In addition, she made impactful changes to her diet as she followed the anti-inflammatory Wahls Protocol, a food program that has helped many people struggling with autoimmune disorders.

Ally knew none of this at the time, and with each of the practices she was honing and strengthening the connection between her mind and her body, specifically her nervous system, helping her return her body to balance and heal itself. The results were dramatic: she lost eighty pounds, her cognition improved, and she was no longer impacted by mental cloudiness and memory loss. She felt motivated, clearheaded, and filled with purpose. Most astoundingly, she no longer takes any medications for MS. As of this writing, she is in full remission.

"I left behind what was familiar for something very unfamiliar and where I am now is somewhere I never thought I'd be," she said in a podcast interview. "It's better than I ever could've imagined would be possible. Life is crazy and beautiful and challenging and sometimes dark and stormy and also light filled, and I'm thankful for mine."

Ally's dramatic transformation provides a beautiful testament to the power of the mind-body connection. Her dedication to her well-being shows us that investing in our mental and physical health requires daily, committed effort. Her story also serves as an inspiring reminder that no matter how broken, out of control, tired, or hopeless we may feel, change is possible.

## TOP DOWN, BOTTOM UP

Healing starts with learning how to tap into the needs of our body and reconnecting with our intuitive Self. It begins with the act of witnessing: *How is my body reacting? What does my body need?* Asking these questions and listening to her body's responses led Ally to discover her passion for singing, which activates the vagus nerve and helps to rebalance the nervous system. She didn't know anything about how her nervous system worked, and through listening to her body, she gained an intuitive sense of how to activate it in healing ways. We can all learn from Ally and use the helpful feedback our bodies offer us.

Even though our nervous system reactions are automatic, there are ways to improve your vagal tone, manage your trauma-conditioned responses to stress, and return more quickly to the open, loving, safe space of social engagement mode. This is such a fruitful area of research right now that many researchers are studying the use of vagal tone stimulators (essentially implants that deliver electrical impulses directly to the vagus nerve) to treat an amazing array of illnesses, from epilepsy to depression to obesity to recovery after heart and lung failures. The way to do this without intervention is to activate the parts of our autonomic system that are within our control, such as our breath and voice.

As you may remember, the vagus nerve is a bidirectional communication pathway that carries information from your body to your brain and from your brain to your body. The brain-to-body conversation is called a top-down process. "Top-down processes" recruit your brain to guide your body on a path toward healing. An example of a top-down practice is meditation, which in the act of training your attention helps regulate your autonomic nervous system responses. A similar though opposite reaction happens with bottom-up processes, wherein you use the power of your body to affect your mind. Most exercises that engage the polyvagal nerve that we discuss here employ bottom-up processes, such as breathwork, cold therapy, and the physical aspects of yoga.

Though many bottom-up and top-down processes are out of our control, we can consciously choose specific interventions that actively decrease our psychological stress, slow the sympathetic responses in our nervous system, and even strengthen our musculoskeletal and cardiovascular systems. In addition, when we activate, challenge, and tone our vagus nerve in a safe and controlled environment, we build tolerance and learn how to live with discomfort, which is key to building resilience, the ability to recover quickly from hardship.

As you begin to work on toning your vagus nerve, it may be helpful to know that you will undoubtedly experience uncomfortable internal pushback. It's never beneficial to flood ourselves with discomfort; easing our way into it can bring us closer to healing. It's important that this work be done in a safe, stable place, where the stress and challenge to our bodies and minds are under our control. That way we can push ourselves within safe confines, which prepares us to deal with stresses outside our control.

What follows are some of the most effective, practical ways we can harness the healing power of our bodies to regain balance and build resilience. All of these practices are important tools for strengthening the mind-body connection and promoting healthy vagal tone. These are foundational steps on the path to holistic healing.

## HEALING THE GUT

Most of the clients I've worked with express complicated feelings surrounding food and often live with chronic gut and digestive issues. For these clients, it is helpful to gain an awareness of the effects of their nutrition on their body and thus their mental state.

Very few of us meet the nutritional demands of our body. Instead, we tend to eat based on how we feel—sad, bored, happy, lonely, excited—or, on the flip side, we make food choices out of necessity, habit, or obligation. All of this input around food disconnects us from the actual *needs* of our body. This isn't hardwired but learned. When we're babies, we're driven by our essential needs. When we're hungry, we cry; when we're full, we turn away. Babies are very clear about their likes and dislikes (much to the distress of worried parents around the world); they are driven by their bodies. As we grow older and are modeled other reasons to eat and drink, we stop listening to these innate needs. Chronic and overwhelming stress we experience in childhood can make it harder for our bodies to rest and digest properly. This is confirmed by repeated studies on the role of trauma and the development of GI issues in adulthood.[45] If we listen to our body closely enough, we can relearn what was lost, because our body speaks loudly through messages sent between our gut and our brain. We just have to pay attention.

We have around 500 million neurons in our gut, which can "talk" directly with the brain via a pathway known as the gut-brain axis, one of the most studied examples of the mind-body connection. The gut-brain axis is the highway that enables the exchange of a range of information, including how hungry we are, what kind of nutrients we need, how quickly food is passing through our stomach, and even when the muscles in our esophagus contract. Our friend the vagus nerve is one of the key messengers that facilitate the sending of these signals back and forth between our gut and brain.

The gut is also home to an extensive network of nerve cells along the gut wall that make up what is known as the enteric nervous system (ENS). This is a meshlike system of nerve cells that is so complex that researchers often refer to it as our "second brain." Like the neurons found in our actual brain, these cells are constantly in communication with various regions of the body, signaling the release of hormones and sending chemical messages all throughout our body.

The ENS gathers information from the microbiome, the diverse array of bacteria, fungi, and other microbes that live inside our gut. Gut microbes make neurotransmitters as they break down the food we eat, sending these microbial messages to our brain. Those microbes influence our reality. Just think about when we have to speak in front of a group of people and we say "I feel sick to my stomach." This is not a metaphor. Our emotional state actually does make our stomach feel sick. In fact, 90 percent of the neurotransmitter serotonin, commonly referred to as "the happy hormone" (though it is also involved in sleep, memory, and learning), is made in our gut. This finding has led to the theory that a group of antidepressants called selective serotonin reuptake inhibitors (SSRIs), such as Prozac, actually act on the serotonin produced "below the neck" in the ENS. This profound insight overturned an older belief that these neurochemicals were made only in the brain. When we were sick psychologically, we thought, the root cause must be identified and treated "above the neck." We now know that the brain is only one small part of a larger interconnected network.

In a trauma state, physical dysregulation in both the nervous system and the gut impairs our digestion, working against our ability to properly absorb nutrients from our food. When our body is stressed, we cannot enter the parasympathetic state that sends messages of calmness and security to our body. Without these necessary messages, we either expel our food or hold on to it, resulting in symptoms such as diarrhea and constipation. Our body's dysregulation is likely mirrored in the gut, where an imbalanced microbiome also hinders the extraction of nutrients from our food. Over time, our bodies become chronically deprived of the nutrients they need and no matter how "healthy" or plentiful our diet is, we can often end up undernourished and hungry.

If our diet isn't so healthy, things get worse. Our intestinal lining becomes inflamed when we consume foods that cause damage to that lining, including sugar, processed carbohydrates, and inflammatory fats (such as trans fats and many vegetable oils). These foods provide sustenance for the less desirable occupants of your gut microbiome (some microbes are good for you, while others can make you sick). This collection of microbes lays the groundwork for a condition called gut dysbiosis, in which the balance of your inner ecosystem favors the "bad" bugs.

When dysbiosis occurs, a condition called leaky gut typically follows. Leaky gut is just what it sounds like—a gut lining that instead of acting as a barrier has become permeable, allowing bacteria to leak out of it and into our body's circulatory systems. When bad bacteria leaks into the bloodstream, our immune system responds, recognizing those bacteria as a foreign invader and ratcheting up our immune response.This, as we learned, spreads inflammatory chemicals all over our body, including the cytokines we learned about in the last chapter. A chronically inflamed gut often leads to larger, systemic inflammation,[46] in which inflammation runs rampant throughout the body. This can make us feel sick, lethargic, and even, in some cases, psychologically ill.

Gut dysbiosis, studies suggest, may be a possible root cause for some conditions that we label "mental illness," including depression, autism, anxiety, ADHD, and even schizophrenia.[47] Several animal studies have shown a direct link between a decline in the health of our microbiome (as a result of poor diet and environmental influences such as stress and toxic chemicals) and a sharp rise in the symptoms associated with anxiety and depression[48] in humans. In fact, in some studies, people who suffered from depression had lower levels of specific beneficial bacterial strains—*Coprococcus* and *Dialister*—than did controls.[49] Other studies have offered evidence that people diagnosed with more severe forms of schizophrenia tend to have higher levels of the bacterial strains Veillonellaceae and Lachnospiraceae.[50] This research has been so promising that there is now an emerging field of medicine called neuroimmunology, which is devoted to exploring the gut–immune system–brain connection. Early research in this field indicates that inflammation in the body can cross the blood-brain barrier and enter the brain, and an inflamed brain can lead to a host of neurological, psychological, and psychiatric conditions. There is promising evidence that when the gut wall is healed via dietary interventions along with supplemental probiotics, some mental health symptoms may be alleviated. Several recent studies have found that the use of probiotics has reduced distressing social and behavioral issues in children with more severe forms of autism spectrum disorder.[51]

The quickest way to improve your gut health—to support your microbes and maintain the integrity of your gut wall—is to eat *whole, nutrient-dense food*. The direct line between the gut and the brain makes each meal an opportunity for healing and nourishment. It is helpful not to think of deprivation when we cut processed and unhealthy foods out of our diets and instead view doing so as an exciting opportunity to improve our physical and mental well-being one bite at a time. It's rare to find a psychologist who will ask you what you're eating, though food plays an incredibly important role in mental wellness. In addition to consuming nutrient-dense foods that make you feel your best, adding fermented foods, such as sauerkraut, yogurt, kefir, and kimchi, to your diet can also be helpful, as they are rich in naturally occurring probiotics.

Another popular nutritional approach that has gained widespread appeal and is supported by various academic studies is intermittent fasting.[52] Planned fasts, or intervals of not eating, give our digestive system a break within healthy bounds, which challenge our body in beneficial ways and improves our vagal tone. This could involve full-day fasts, ten-hour windows of eating, or just snacking less frequently during the day. Fasting gives our digestive system a rest, freeing up the energy that would be devoted to digestion for use elsewhere. It can also help to increase our insulin sensitivity and regulate our blood sugar, keeping us from becoming a "sugar burner" who is always hungry and looking for the next sugar fix. Until I changed my nutrition, I was a notorious sugar burner; my girlfriends always knew to pack snacks for any outing or else the day would end poorly for both of us. I ran on hit after hit of sugar and was constantly ravenous. Studies have shown that intermittent fasting increases mental acuity, learning, and alertness[53] (but I will warn you, other studies have also shown increases in irritability,[54] especially in the beginning, before your body gets used to it).

When we fast and change our nutrition, our body learns how to get energy from alternate forms of fuel, such as fat and protein. This allows it to live on other fuel sources and go longer between meals without discomfort because it is *getting what it needs*. When we eat processed, sugar-laden foods, we're hungry all the time because our body is starved for the nutrients it requires. This nutrient depletion continues to send hunger signals to our brain, causing us to feel the need to snack often and, for some of us, to engage in overeating or bingelike behaviors. We eat and eat yet never feel satisfied, because nutritionally our body is not getting what it needs.

Of course, intermittent fasting may not be appropriate for everyone, especially those with a past history of eating disorders. Anyone with a history of restricted eating patterns should not engage with this practice.

## HEALING SLEEP

When we start paying attention to how our nutrition influences our body and mind, other opportunities emerge to learn how our daily choices may not be serving our body's essential needs. After food, the most common way we let ourselves down happens every night: most of us don't get enough sleep.

This starts young. For me, having anxious thoughts at night began in childhood. I would lie awake in bed at age five, frightened, certain that every thud or thump in the night was a burglar or a kidnapper ready to hurt my family. My body was stuck in a state of anxiety thanks to my heightened sympathetic system (and none of this was helped by my diet at the time, which consisted of a steady stream of ice cream, cookies, and soda). My mind was constantly scanning my body, noting the gut imbalances, the adrenaline rushes, the nervous system hypervigilance. When my heart and breath raced, my mind made up a story about a break-in. My stomachaches, bloating, and constipation translated into nervousness and fear. I tossed and turned and got poor-quality sleep many nights.

We now know that inadequate sleep is incredibly damaging—especially to a growing body. When we sleep, our body repairs itself. This is when our gut gets a chance to take a break from digestion, our brain "washes itself" and clears away debris, and our cells regenerate. Sleep is a time of ultimate healing. All of the organs and systems of our body, including our nervous system, benefit from sleep. We know this because of the work done on sleep deprivation, which is linked to depression, cardiovascular illness, and even cancer, obesity, and neurological conditions, such as Alzheimer's disease. People over the age of forty-five who sleep for less than six hours a night are 200 percent more likely to suffer a heart attack or stroke than those who sleep longer.[55]

Sleep is key to mental and physical health, yet few of us prioritize it in any meaningful way. There are so many simple ways we can prepare our sleep spaces and our bodies to give us the best chance of getting a night of restful, healing sleep. The first step is to assess how much we actually sleep. So many of us are unsure or even outright delusional about our sleep habits. We may get into bed around 11:00 p.m., and we'll often spend an hour being activated while scrolling through our phones before we actually shut off the lights. Keep tabs on your sleep behaviors. Try to honestly notice your personal sleep patterns.

The most important way to improve your sleep is to help ease your parasympathetic system into its happy place of relaxation. Substances such as coffee and alcohol, which directly work against the most important stage in our sleep cycle, rapid eye movement (REM), are the biggest physiological barriers to getting into this restful place. Try to limit your alcohol and caffeine consumption to certain hours (preferably stop drinking alcohol three hours before bed and limit coffee to before noon). Maintaining a consistent bedtime routine is also important, as it primes your body to enter the parasympathetic state in the lead-up to actually getting into bed. These days, I get a prompt from a sleep app around 5:00 p.m., even before I start dinner, to start the winding down process (my bedtime is around 9:00 p.m.). A few hours before bed, I turn off my screens. I spend some time reading or listening to music and make sure to limit the hours I spend in front of the TV in the lead-up to bedtime. Taking a bath, getting a massage from your partner, snuggling with a pet—all of these things can promote a sense of calm that will make it easier for you to fall and stay asleep.

## HEALING WITH BREATH

We know that our autonomic nervous system is automatic (it functions outside of our awareness), though there is one part of our body's systems that is under our conscious control. We can't tell our heart to beat more slowly or our liver to detox our body faster, but we can slow and deepen our breath, thereby decreasing our heart rate and calming our mind. We can draw in more air, helping us move air from our lungs to the rest of our body and oxygenating all of our cells. We can also do the reverse, awakening our sympathetic response by taking rapid, shallow breaths. We can escalate and deescalate all with the power of our breath.

Doing breathwork engages the autonomic nervous system; it's like doing planks for the vagus nerve. As we know, the vagus nerve is a two-way information highway that not only connects the brain and the gut but also connects various parts of the body, including the lungs, heart, and liver. When we use our breath to subdue our arousal system, we communicate to the brain that we are in a nonthreatening environment, a message that is shared with the other systems in our bodies. This is a bottom-up approach to polyvagal toning.

Studies have shown a link between daily breathwork practices and increased longevity.[56] The theory is that by managing our stress response, we decrease our inflammatory response and stimulate hormones that maintain the parts of chromosomes (called telomeres) that are associated with longer life. According to James Nestor, the author of *Breath: The New Science of a Lost Art*, a two-decade-long research study of 5,200 people showed that "the greatest indicator of life span wasn't genetics, diet, or the amount of daily exercise, as many had suspected. It was lung capacity. . . . [L]arger lungs equaled longer lives. Because big lungs allow us to get more air in with fewer breaths."[57] Shallow breathing (mouth breathing in particular) can create or worsen a variety of illnesses, from hypertension to attention deficit hyperactivity disorder (ADHD). It strips our body of essential nutrients and weakens our skeletal structure.

One of the most extraordinary utilizers of the power of breath is Wim Hof, popularly known as "The Iceman." Wim set a Guinness

World Record for swimming under ice, took a two-hour ice bath, and ran a marathon barefoot and without a shirt above the Arctic Circle (!). "Your mind makes you strong from within. It is your wise companion," he wrote in his book *Becoming the Iceman*. "If you can grab the wheel of your mind, you can steer the direction of where your mind will go."[58]

To put it simply, Hof's breathing technique involves inhaling through the nose and exhaling through the mouth, then holding the breath, which challenges and expands the lungs. He often couples this with exposure to cold, another kind of bottom-up approach that tests our body limits and stresses the vagus nerve in beneficial ways.

I'm a little less hard-core. I like to ease my body into challenges. There are many breathwork practices to explore and my personal favorite place to start, if you have the space and time to engage in a slightly longer practice, is this:

1. Try to start this on an empty stomach (morning or night is best).
2. Sit or lie down in a comfortable place with few distractions.
3. Take in a deep breath from the lowest part of your stomach.
4. When you can't take in any more air, stop and hold your breath for two to three seconds.
5. Exhale nice and slowly without any force. Take one cycle of regular breathing (in and out).
6. Repeat ten times.

I do this every morning a few moments after waking to start the day. Most days I practice for five minutes, which sounds short but is deceptively challenging when you're new to the practice. As a beginner, this exercise should take no more than one minute, max. Over time you can add more reps.

It took me years of daily practice to get to this point. Initially, I had a hard time breathing from my belly and found it nearly excruciating to sit still for even a few minutes. Over time and with consistent practice,

I cultivated my ability to consistently use deep belly breathing throughout the day, instead of my regular shallow chest breaths. Over time, as my nervous system reset, I found that I was generally calmer and more at peace, which in turn enabled me to breathe more deeply. Today, with consistent practice, I am able to intentionally use deep breathing as a tool to calm my body when I'm emotionally activated and need it most.

## HEALING WITH MOVEMENT

Any activity—running, swimming, hiking—where mind and body are linked in a safe place helps us "widen the window," as Dr. Porges wrote, of stress tolerance. Exercises that challenge your mind and body reduce your risk of developing cardiovascular disease and dementia and may even slow the aging process.[59,60] Physical exercise deepens sleep and improves mood by releasing neurochemicals in the brain, including dopamine, serotonin, and norepinephrine, which all make you feel happier and less stressed. In general, cardiovascular exercise, which increases oxygen and blood circulation all over the body, creates measurable changes in the brain, increasing the size and health of the organ while stimulating new neuronal pathways and strengthening existing ones.

An ultimate "window-widening" exercise, given its direct activation of the vagus nerve, is yoga. Dr. Porges is also a huge advocate of yoga (he's written extensively about its benefits on vagal tone in academic journals). Yoga engages both the mind and body by combining the regulatory power of our breath with movement. As we advance in the practice, increasingly challenging poses begin to test our body's physical limits, further stressing our system, and offering an opportunity to reconnect with the calming power of our breath. Regular yoga practice has been shown to have more diffuse effects on the body (likely because of the strengthening of the vagal response over time), including reducing inflammation levels and regulating blood pressure. It does not seem to matter what kind of practice we engage in—Kundalini, Hatha, Ashtanga, even a hot-yoga hybrid.

Dr. Porges started studying yoga in the 1990s in India and found that many yogic practices are designed to activate the body's stress responses of fight, flight, or freeze. The whole idea behind yoga, he said in an interview, "is that through training, you can begin going into these immobilizing states normally linked with faint and freeze, but more aware and less frightened." He described it as "the ability to go deep inside oneself and feel secure" in response to a perceived threat.[61] This is key to healing: learning the power of your body and your mind by testing their outer limits. As we take on deeper and more taxing postures, our vagus nerve learns how to control our stress response and return more readily to the state of calmness and safety where healing happens. We learn how to "bounce back" faster or become more resilient in the face of controlled physical and mental adversity. In one study, people who were practicing yoga for six years or longer could keep their hands in ice water for twice the time of controls who never practiced it.[62] The yoga practitioners did not distract themselves from the pain, as the nonyogis did, but actually leaned into the sensation and found ways to focus on and channel the pain as a way to get through the sensation—the essence of a resilience exercise.

## HEALING WITH PLAY

Joy, the expression of pure happiness, is a mere memory for most of us. We've forgotten the happy freedom of doing something for the mere delight of doing it—not for any secondary gain, requirement, or external motivation. When we were children, we did things just because we wanted to. Many of you can remember a time in your childhood when you felt this way; maybe it was while taking a dance class, running around freely on the beach, or expressing yourself artistically through drawing and painting.

As adults, we can still experience a similar joyous freedom when we allow ourselves to play. This might involve dancing without ego's interference, playing music on toy instruments, or dressing up and entering an imaginary world. When we lose ourselves in this way, we are sometimes able to enter what is referred to as a "flow state" of pure enjoyment of the *doing*. This state functions very similarly to the feeling we get when we're lost in conversation with someone we love, caught up in a moment, living almost outside the boundaries of time. This joy is healing in and of itself.

When our play is social, we can challenge our neuroception (the part of our nervous system that scans the environment for signs of danger). When we horse around with someone, play a pickup game of soccer, or even compete against a friend in a video game, we shift into and out of fight/flight/freeze modes and our safe social engagement mode of calmness and security. This helps teach our body how to recover quickly, in a similar way as we learn to during a yoga practice. Creating artificial alternation between danger and safety in a fun and open space ultimately "improves the efficiency of the neural circuit that can instantaneously down regulate fight/flight behaviors," wrote Dr. Porges in an article on play and the vagus nerve.[63] We learn how to switch off those fight/flight responses and return to our safe baseline instead of remaining chronically activated helping decrease chronic sickness.

A common favorite playtime activity that engages the vagus nerve is singing. Singing feels pleasurable for many of us. We may have been conditioned to keep our voices to ourselves when others said we couldn't carry a tune. Try to remember back to when you were a child and the various ways singing was used to develop self-awareness, confidence, and joy. The benefits of singing do not stop in adulthood. Belting out your favorite song will help tone your vagus nerve in many of the similar ways that breathwork, yoga, and play do. If you can sing with others, the benefits are even greater; the co-regulatory force of a room full of singers is incredibly uplifting. Even singing to yourself in the shower can be healing.

As you may remember, the vagus nerve connects to many muscles in the face and throat, including the larynx and vocal cords. When we are in a place of safety and security, our voices sound different and we hear a wider range of tones, especially in human voices. We can help create that sense of calmness via the muscles in our mouth and neck when we sing. The science journalist Seth Porges (a son of *that* Dr. Porges) also suggests that we listen to midfrequency music to open up our middle ear muscles (the same muscles that are activated when we are in the happy place of social engagement mode).[64] One of the most effective places to look for midfrequency music? Disney movie soundtracks. So yes, put on that *Lion King* opening and belt it out to your heart's content.

## CONTROLLING EMOTIONAL ACTIVATION IN REAL TIME

Over time, through each small daily promise I made to myself, I built a new foundation for healing. This foundation helped my body and all of its systems return to the balance it so desperately longed for. I started choosing foods that allowed my body to feel energized and nourished. I prioritized sleep. At the same time, I worked on different exercises to activate my consciousness. I started a daily meditation and breathwork ritual, deepened my yoga practice, and incorporated play, finding time to sing and dance and hike in nature.

It took years to incorporate all of these elements. Without a formal guide, I was bringing in different techniques to heal my gut and immune system allowing my long-lost intuitive voice to guide my healing journey. The first time in a long time that I made contact with that inner voice was when my cat George went missing. Lolly and I came home from a weekend trip and couldn't find him. We looked around the house, and as I searched room after room, I could feel myself getting agitated. My agitation escalated. I started screaming "Open the oven! Open the oven!" and flung open the oven door, expecting to find his dead, burnt body. I stormed about all in front of my nephew, who at the time was five or six and came home with us. My face flamed red, and my heart beat into my ears. I had lost control.

Five minutes later, I calmed down enough to develop a plan to find George, calling neighbors and the vet until we eventually tracked him down. I apologized to Lolly after it was all over, saying, effectively, "I'm sorry I lost my shit."

She responded, "I understand. I really don't think you even *meant* it."

The idea that I hadn't *meant* to behave the way I had touched something inside me. There was a part of me, the authentic part of me, that knew she was right. While I had been going through the freak-out, I could sense on some level that I wasn't truly frantic. It was as though I had been playing a role, acting out the family dynamics of my conditioning, freaking out just as I had been trained to. The authentic part of myself though knew it wasn't real. My heart rate really had risen, of course, and my adrenal glands produced cortisol, as those systems were activated by my sympathetic response, and yet a small part of me agreed with Lolly, knowing deep down that I *didn't* really mean it.

That signaled to me that there was something deeper going on, and I started to pay more attention to what was setting me off and how my body reacted when it lost control. Fast-forward several years into doing *the work*. This time our cat Clark went missing. (I really do have adventurous cats!)

Clark, a very "doglike" cat, must have gone out and gotten lost. I was concerned, though this time, as we searched for him, my nervous system didn't become hyperactivated; I remained calm and focused. While it took almost three weeks, we eventually found him, too, and that time I didn't kick and scream and hurt the ones I loved in the process.

Today I am embodied. I know how it feels to be in my physical self, how sensations pass through me: the butterflies in my stomach when I'm nervous or excited (it turns out that although they feel the same, they are actually two different feelings), the pangs of hunger when I truly need to eat, the feeling of satiety when I've had enough food. Previously, I was so disconnected that I never truly connected to those sensory messages.

I'm also less hunched over, less tense overall. I have more energy. I wake at 5:00 a.m. and feel productive and clearheaded throughout the day. I was the person who couldn't remember words. The person who fainted. The person who was so clenched up and repressed that she couldn't evacuate her bowels properly.

This doesn't mean I don't ever experience a trauma reaction anymore. I'm not always shiny and clearheaded, and I still lose my shit sometimes. When I do, I offer myself grace and compassion. I see the reactions for what they are: the results of an overtaxed autonomic system that feels threatened.

Our bodies truly are incredible. We now know that we are not "destined" to be sick just because our family members are. Nothing is set in stone. Our cells respond to our surroundings from the moment of conception. We've seen how our environments—from our childhood traumas to the food we choose to put into our bodies—mold us, especially our nervous system, immune system, and microbiome, systems that are particularly responsive to stress and trauma. We've learned about the power of the autonomic system to shape the way we see and inhabit the world and the incredible role of the vagus nerve, which travels from our brain to every system in our body. I've devoted so much time to this because understanding these processes provides a window into the resilience of the body and the possibility of transformation.

The next step is applying this empowered state of consciousness and belief in transformation to the mind—understanding our past selves, meeting our inner child, befriending our ego, and learning about the traumatic bonds that continue to shape our world. This wisdom helps free our minds in the same way we've freed our bodies.

Let's go.

## FSJ: BREATHWORK

Here is an example of the Future Self Journaling prompts I used each day to begin to create a new practice of breathwork in my daily life. Each day in my notebook, I copied similar versions of the following statements to provide myself with a consistent reminder of my intention to change, to make new choices, and over time to create a new habit.

**Today I am practicing** using a deep belly breath to help calm my body and bring me a sense of safety and peace.

**I am grateful for** the opportunity to learn a new way to regulate my body.

**Today, I am** calm and grounded in my body.

**Change in this area allows me to feel** better able to tolerate stress.

**Today I am practicing when** I remember to use my deep belly breath when I begin to feel stressed.

# 6

# The Power of Belief

It's been said that we tell ourselves stories in order to live. These stories are often based in our actual experiences—believing we're desirable because we were pursued romantically from a young age. Sometimes these stories, often created in childhood, are never updated and don't reflect our current reality. Those of us like myself, who might have been shy as a child, may continue to consider ourselves a "shy person" even though we no longer feel or act that way.

We often tell ourselves stories as an act of self-protection. In childhood, we are not mentally or emotionally capable of understanding that our parent-figures had a whole life outside of the one we know. As children, we are limited by what we can cognitively and emotionally understand based on our developmental age. Given these limitations, we may believe that we are bad when a parent-figure raises a hand to us, instead of knowing that this person, on whom we are dependent for our survival, has difficulty managing their anger. Sometimes our reality is too painful to understand or process, so we make up an alternative story that guides us through the darkness. A child who feels neglected might make up a narrative about how the parent has an "important job," making an excuse for their absence without having to dig into the harder truth.

Like all of us, I am made up of many such narratives (which are also called core beliefs): *I'm the Christ child. I'm unemotional. I'm anxious.* Core beliefs are the many stories about ourselves, our relationships, our past, our future, and the innumerable other topics we construct based on our lived experiences. One of my deepest narratives, one that ran the show for years without my knowledge, became clear to me once I started doing *the work* of becoming conscious and witnessing my internal world. That story is: *I am not considered.*

This has been an issue in almost all of my romantic partnerships. It has kept me reserved and pathologically self-sufficient in my friendships and professional life; it can even rear its head when someone cuts me off in line, when the narrative in my head tells me: *You don't matter.* Why? In that instant, I truly believe that a complete stranger doesn't consider me, just as my mother couldn't. I'm a ghost that they can walk right through.

This flash of insight came during a meditation practice when a memory popped into my mind's eye of my mother in the kitchen at our home in Philadelphia. I must have been four years old.

My dad came home from work at the same time every night. An hour before he arrived, my mom would start getting dinner ready, setting the table, making sure the food would be hot for his arrival. As she prepped, she would stand by the window that looked out onto the street where my dad walked home from the bus station. You could spot him coming—exactly the same every night—at least five minutes before he arrived home. The predictability and routine of her days kept her safe from her own childhood trauma of unpredictability and scarcity—from the overall emotional unavailability of both parents to the sudden death of her father. I'm sure that the stability my father provided with his rigid scheduling and insistence on "togetherness," or the infrequency of the time they spent separately, soothed my mother considerably.

That night, my father did not show up as expected. Ten minutes passed, and he still wasn't there. Fifteen, twenty, thirty minutes—he was late. From my favored position under the kitchen table, I watched my mother grow increasingly tense. I spent hours under that table, pushing the pedals of my little scooter, using my legs to propel me around and around and around. I considered it to be a place of safety and refuge from the chaos (despite the superficial dressings of domestic harmony) that surrounded me, with the added energy expenditure helping to relieve my near-constant inner turmoil.

Time ticked by. Now my mom didn't even pretend that she wasn't upset. She stared out the window, wringing her hands. She didn't need to say anything; I could *feel* her worry. My little legs pushed faster and faster, a physical representation of my mother's anxiety. As her unspoken anxiety increased, she was entirely unaware of the small creature unraveling under her feet. She was not emotionally attuned to me in that moment and not present in any way to my needs or fears. She simply could not be. I became a nonentity, unacknowledged, as she was consumed by her own anxiety and the trauma response that narrowed her focus to the threat at hand. Without the developmental maturity and wisdom to understand this evolutionary human experience, I was left with a painful reality. It was during these small moments that I began to create this core belief: *I am not considered.*

Then, suddenly, there he was, walking down the hill. Almost immediately, the energy of the room shifted, and my mom returned to preparing dinner.

I learned a second lesson in these moments as well. I began to learn that the only relief from internal agitation would come from outside of me. Like my mother, I always seemed to be waiting for some representation of my father to make me feel safe. I saw it in the frantic uneasiness that washed over me if a text message to a partner went unanswered or the (highly electrifying) fear that coursed through my system if someone was out of my reach emotionally. When I felt desperate, irrational, or unloved, I felt at home. It was my mother at the window all over again: *This person doesn't consider me, yet I need this person to live.*

## THE ORIGIN OF BELIEF

I shared this story with you as an example of how something seemingly mundane—my father coming home late from work, no big deal—can contain messages that get installed in the beliefs that shape us.

Let's take a step back. What is a belief, exactly?

A belief is a practiced thought grounded in lived experience. Beliefs are built up over years of thought patterns and require both interior and exterior validation to thrive. Beliefs about ourselves (our personality, our weaknesses, our past, our future) are filters that are placed over the lens of how we view our world. The more we practice certain thoughts, the more our brain wires itself to default to these thought patterns. This is especially true if the thoughts activate our stress response and vagus nerve. This creates an internal turmoil that can easily become compulsive over time, which is the definition of the conditioned trauma reaction we know as emotional addiction. The habit of thinking a particular thought over and over again changes our brain, our nervous system, and the cellular chemistry of our entire body, making it easier to default to such thought patterns in the future. In other words: the more we think something, the more we are likely to believe it. Our practiced thoughts become our truth. Remember, for most of us who have these conditioned patterns of physiological dysregulation, doing *the work* to rebalance our nervous system is necessary before we can truly change our deep-rooted beliefs.

When a belief is repeatedly validated, it can become what is called a core belief. Core beliefs are our deepest perceptions about our identity; they were installed in our subconscious often before the age of seven. These are the stories of who I am—*I'm smart, I'm personable, I'm outgoing, I'm introverted, I'm not good at math, I'm a night owl, I'm a loner*—that provide the framework of our "personality." Though it may seem as though our core beliefs are our own because we've practiced them without question, they came to us mostly from our parent-figures, home and community environments, and earliest experiences. Many of our core beliefs, unfortunately, are shaped by traumas.

Once a core belief is formed, you engage in what's called a confirmation of bias; information that does not conform to your beliefs is discarded or ignored in favor of information that does. If you believe you're unworthy, you'll see a job promotion as something that happened by mistake knowing it's only a matter of time before you're discovered to be the impostor you really are. When you make a mistake at work, either by happenstance or self-sabotage, it will be filtered through the lens of inevitability: *Of course, I slipped up. I'm not worthy.* We universally lean into something called negativity bias, in which we tend to prioritize (and therefore value) negative information over positive. This is why you can see a glowing performance review and forget it shortly afterward, though you'll never forget the sting of a colleague's criticism.

This bias is evolutionarily hardwired. In the early days of our species, we were much more likely to survive if we focused on the things that could kill us rather than the things that made us happy. Just like the autonomic nervous system's fight-or-flight response, this bias is built into our operating system at the physiological level and is largely out of our conscious control. If we weren't able to filter and prioritize sensory input, we would be constantly overwhelmed by the onslaught of information coming at us. There is *a lot* going on in our world at all times. Just try to acknowledge the totality of the world around you right now. If your brain took in all of those stimuli at the same time, it couldn't function.

This subconscious filtering is the work of the reticular activating system (RAS), a bundle of nerves located on the brain stem that helps us sort out our environment, allowing us to concentrate on the things around us that we feel are essential. The RAS acts as the brain's gatekeeper, using beliefs formed in our early life to sift through incoming information and prioritize evidence that supports these beliefs. In this way, the RAS actively recruits information that reinforces what we already believe to be true.

Here's a common and familiar example of the RAS at work: Let's say you're shopping for a new car. You go to the dealership and find one model you're pretty sure you want, and you spend time online researching everything about that car. Suddenly you notice that everyone and their mother seems to be driving that model, though you could swear you hardly ever saw one on the road before. The RAS can make it feel as though the universe is sending you a message. Maybe it is—it's your own universe, devised by your own incredible brain.

The RAS does more than create confirmation bias when we're car shopping. One theory of depression, though overly simplified, believes that people who are depressed filter the world through a negative lens. Think of your last truly bad day, when one negative thing happened after another and nothing seemed to go your way. It probably felt as though you were truly unlucky—though the RAS was also at work, deprioritizing the positive or even neutral parts of your day. This is why it can sometimes feel impossible to lift yourself out of a fog of dread; your RAS won't let you.

The brain can sometimes use the RAS filter as a defense mechanism. I have met many people who claim that their childhoods were rosy and perfect and refuse to acknowledge any negativity or hardship, despite evidence to the contrary. An idealized view of our childhood becomes a core belief that may come from self-preservation. In real life, no childhood is perfect. Allowing ourselves to honestly witness the entirety of our past and current experiences is fundamental to our healing.

Just as we learned in chapter 2 that we are not our thoughts, we are also not our core beliefs. This is often harder to accept, as our core beliefs are so ingrained, such a part of our identities, that they are hard to part with. The more you learn about the childhood brain and how these core beliefs are formed, the better able you will be, over time, to witness and become aware of them—and ultimately actively choose which ones you want to retain and which to leave behind.

## WIRED FOR SURVIVAL

It may be hard to remember this when you're sitting next to a crying baby on an airplane or pleading with a tantrum-throwing toddler, though early childhood is a moment of pure spiritual essence. The childlike wonder, the play, the truth telling—these are expressions of the authentic Self, or what I consider to be *the soul*. We haven't yet accumulated the lived experience that disconnects us from this authentic Self. We haven't yet formed our core beliefs.

You can think of a baby's brain like the operating system of a smartphone—it's up to the child to "download" everything from how to walk to what to believe to how long to cry to get food. It's no wonder that babies look at the world with literal wide-eyed wonder, almost as if they're in a blissed-out, hypnotic state. They are living in a constant state of receptivity and learning.

Infancy is a time of endless invention. We learn language, movement, social interaction, and cause and effect—all in service to our survival. Neurons, the building blocks of our brains, are communicating with one another through synchronized electrical impulses called brain waves. These brain waves give rise to everything that makes us our human self—our behaviors, our emotions, our thoughts, even the mechanics of our bodies. It's a beautiful symphony, a unique song never before played, all going on in a newborn's mind.

We now know it's also a time when our core beliefs about ourselves and our place in the world are formed. This starts the moment we exit our mother's womb. Once we emerge into the world, the neural pathways in our brains are hyperstimulated, forming, and honing as we try to make sense of the strange new world and our place in it. This can be a frightening time because we are in a state of complete dependency and the unknown is terrifying. This fact is no different for children. Though our brains are not yet mature enough to fully grasp the implications of this dependency, we can still feel the fear that is inherent in our vulnerability. This is impacted by our environment—in both the immediate sense (what is or isn't available in terms of basic necessities, such as food, shelter, and love) and the macro sense (such as living in a developing country or under systemic oppression or during a pandemic). During this time of intense need, all of these factors shape our sense of security and comfort—or lack thereof—and leave lasting imprints on our body, mind, and soul.

The most significant imprinting comes from the people we are most bonded to: our parent-figures. Emerging neuroscience supports the overwhelming effect parent-figures have on their babies' brains. One study found that when adults and babies look into each other's eyes, their brain waves actually sync, creating a "joint networked state"[65] that connects the two people in a silent language of communication.

Without our parent-figures, we will starve—not just physically but emotionally, too. Our main objective is to receive love. If we are loved, it's likely we will be safe, fed, and generally cared for. This state is the most beneficial mode for brain development in childhood; it's the social engagement mode, which we learned about in chapter 4. It's a state of peace where we feel safe and secure to play, take chances, and learn. This safe state is essential for achieving milestones in neurological and behavioral development. This "learning brain" allows us to feel secure enough to take chances; to be more likely to get back up when we fall.

We look to our parent-figures for clues about how to connect, how to navigate the world, and how to cope with stress, which is called co-regulation (you saw this in action in my kitchen window story). Co-regulation is not only a learning experience for the mind, it's also a learning experience for the body. This is when our parent-figures teach us how to moderate our emotional reactions and return to the social engagement mode baseline. When we don't learn this regulation or don't feel safe enough to attempt to learn it, we enter a state of fight/flight/freeze activation in which our neuroception scans the environment and sees threats everywhere.

When we are stuck in fight/flight/freeze mode, we devote our resources to managing stress, and, to put it simply, our child brain suffers. Childhood is a time of great vulnerability. Unable to survive on our own, a parent-figure's withholding of anything perceived to hinder our survival sends stress signals flooding through our bodies. The resulting "survival brain," as I call it, is hyperfocused on perceived threats, sees the world in black and white, and is often obsessive, panic driven, and prone to circular reasoning. We can break down or shut down when faced with stress.

This is especially true between conception and age two, when an infant brain functions on the slowest brain wave cycle with the highest amplitudes, called the delta state. As adults, by contrast, we enter delta state only when we're in deep sleep. The delta state is a learning and encoding mode. There is no capacity for critical thinking, as the spongy newborn brain is fully devoted to absorption.

The brain develops further from around ages two to four, as the brain waves shift to the theta state, the same state that is documented when adults enter hypnosis. In the theta state, children focus inward. They are connected to their imaginations at the deepest levels and often have trouble distinguishing dreams from reality. Though toddlers do develop critical thinking skills around this time, they are still absorbed in an egocentric state, a stage of development when they cannot see any perspective but their own.

This is not the definition of "egocentric" that we see associated with self-centered people in adulthood. Egocentrism in childhood is a developmental stage in which there's an inability to understand the difference between the self and others. In egocentrism, the belief is that everything is happening *to* us *because of* us. As a result of our brain's development, we are literally unable to view the world from another's perspective, even when the "other" is our parent-figure, sibling, or other close relative. As children, when any of our physical, emotional, or spiritual needs are consistently unmet, we inaccurately assume responsibility for this neglect, often internalizing false beliefs (*No one is helping me because I'm bad*) and then generalizing them more broadly (*The world is a bad place*). This egocentric thinking can be seen as we try to make sense of emotionally painful experiences with our parent-figures. A child, after being yelled at by dad after a stressful day at his office, is unable to understand that they are not the cause of his anger.

It is not until the next stage of cognitive and emotional development, around age five, that our analytical mind takes over. Though there may still be trouble discerning what is real and what is imaginary, this is when children begin to use rational thought and to understand the consequences of cause and effect (*When I don't listen, I have to take a time-out*). This stage is followed by the beta state, the lowest-amplitude and fastest waves, which we begin to enter at age seven. This is when a critical, logical, engaged thinker is becoming more present. This is the adult mind in progress. By then, however, we have already amassed the core beliefs and subconscious programming that will continue running our daily lives as adults.

## CHILDHOOD INTERRUPTED

As our brains develop, our needs expand from the basics of shelter, food, and love to broader, more complicated and nuanced requirements for physical, emotional, and spiritual wholeness. Spiritually, our individual souls have three basic needs:

1. To be seen
2. To be heard
3. To uniquely express our most authentic Selves

Few people, let alone stressed parents, have the tools to meet all of these needs all of the time. Even the most fully realized families have limitations. When children's emotional needs are not adequately or consistently met, they often develop a subconscious core belief that they are *not worthy* of having these needs met. When they are emotionally denied, they overcompensate—exaggerating some parts of themselves and denying others based on what they perceive to be validated, or considered *worthy*, by their parent-figures.

A parent-figure who is feeling overwhelmed by and uncomfortable with their own emotions, when seeing their child distressed, might say "You're too sensitive." The child, whose main objective is to receive love, will suppress or hide their perceived sensitivities in an attempt to continue to do so. If this pattern continues, the child might "toughen up" or detach, ignoring their authentic Self and presenting a false self, which emerges from a core belief that parts of their identity are unacceptable. I see this a lot with my male clients and friends. For some who grew up with the model of toxic hypermasculinity, where men are discouraged or shamed for expressing emotion, even acknowledging that they have an emotional world may be challenging. In cases like these, we're fighting not just the conditioning of our parent-figures and family unit but society at large.

Often, these small consistent messages become internalized as core beliefs. Some of you, when helping your mom take care of your siblings, might have been told "You're so helpful. You're going to be such a great mother yourself someday." Heard consistently enough, your core belief may then become "I need to care for others in order to be loved." Over time you may find yourself feeling selfish for caring for yourself or even acknowledging your own needs. Alternatively, you may have been consistently told "I wish you could be more like your brother." That core belief—that you are not as good as a sibling—might translate to a low sense of self. It might make you more likely to compare yourself with others, never believing that you are good enough as you are. Or you may, as I did, receive awards and recognition without doing too much active work, which made you internalize a belief that *I enjoy only things that I'm naturally good at and will quit anything that challenges me or is not immediately easy*. This used to be a central part of my core belief: I wanted to play only if I was going to win.

It's important to point out that though parent-figures do create the bulk of our core belief system, our beliefs are also influenced by the wider environment. Our educational system, which lacks the ability to tailor its approach to individual children, engages in a "one-way model" of teaching that forces them to adapt to the larger institution in order to achieve and be validated. The pressure is compounded by our peers, who validate certain behaviors, styles, or parts of our appearance. We are often placed into categories such as "nerd," "slut," or "jock" that create narratives around identity that we unconsciously internalize. A young girl who finds herself struggling with math in a culture that believes women underperform compared to men at hard sciences may internalize an inaccurate truth about herself. Once we've internalized the belief that we aren't pretty, thin, or smart enough, our RAS will continue to look to find a source of information in our society to confirm this.

Even in adulthood, we tend to see the world through the filters applied by the core beliefs—often negative—that we developed during these "sponge" years of childhood. Continuing to strengthen these core beliefs at the expense of a more accurate, complete, and updated narrative results in increasing disconnection from our authentic Selves. This is one reason why nearly every adult is desperate to be seen, heard, and externally validated. Our need for validation may manifest itself as codependency, chronic people pleasing, and martyrdom; or, on the other side of the spectrum, it may manifest itself as anxiety, rage, and hostility. The more disconnected we are, the more depressed, lost, confused, stuck, and hopeless we feel. The more stuck and hopeless we feel, the more we project our emotions onto the people around us.

Our beliefs are incredibly powerful and continue to shape our daily experiences through our subconscious minds. These beliefs, especially the core ones, weren't formed overnight. They won't change overnight. With dedication and persistence, they can be changed. To truly change, you have to learn who you really are—and a part of this includes meeting your inner child.

## DO THE WORK: DO A CORE BELIEFS INVENTORY

Spend some time reflecting on and journaling about your core beliefs. If you feel intimidated by the word *belief* or are unsure of what yours are, it's okay. Remember, a belief is simply a practiced thought. You hold core beliefs about yourself, others, the world around you, the future, and many other topics. Begin to pay attention to and notice the themes and narratives that run through your mind all day. Notice and write down any and all themes that arise. To help you reflect, feel free to use the following journal prompts, adding any other areas or themes that you notice.

While witnessing my thoughts throughout the day, I am noticing themes:

About myself: ______________________________

About others or my relationships: ______________________

About my past: ______________________________

About my present: ____________________________

About my future: _____________________________

## FSJ: CREATING A NEW BELIEF

Now that you understand that beliefs are just practiced thoughts, it shouldn't come as too much of a surprise to learn that in order to create a new belief, you will have to begin to practice a new thought. From the themes and narratives you just noted in the Beliefs Inventory, pick one to begin to change. Not sure which one to pick? Go with your first instinct. If you're still unsure, think about the one that would have the most impact on your life if you believed differently.

Once you identify the belief you'd like to change, think about what you'd prefer to think. This could be as simple as noting the opposite of your currently held belief. For example, if you find an "I'm not good enough" theme in your thoughts, as many of us do, you will want to believe that "I'm enough."

**Old belief:** ______________________________________________

**New belief:** ______________________________________________

______________________________________________________________

This will be your new daily affirmation or mantra. Now you will want to practice this new thought. A *lot*. Some of you may want to write this new affirmation or mantra somewhere, anywhere, or everywhere. Each time it catches your eye, recite this new thought to yourself. Others may resonate more with a particular time of the day when they will practice this new thought, such as during a morning or evening routine.

Don't worry if you find it difficult to accept this new thought as true. In fact, don't even think for one second that you will think this new thought is true. You won't, not for a long time, at least. Practice anyway. Over time you will retrain your brain to begin to consider the very small possibility that this new thought may someday hold even the tiniest bit of truth. Try not to obsess over when that day will come and one day you just may find that glimmer. I know I did.

# 7

# Meet Your Inner Child

The first thing anyone would notice about Anthony was his thick New York accent, one that reminded me of my time spent riding the subway around Brooklyn.

Anthony was the "black sheep" of his big, Catholic, Italian family—even though he tried his best to follow along with the crowd. He was taught a general sense of right and wrong, with some wrong-doings warranting you a trip straight to Hell.

Even as a young boy, Anthony felt he was different or *bad* in a way his brothers were not. His *"badness"* started before he was even school age, when he was molested by a neighbor, another child himself, who was practicing the abuse he suffered in his own home. Anthony saw the sexual abuse as a likely message from God telling him that he was an evil person, especially because it happened with another boy. He became convinced of his inherent *badness* when his father started acting physically, verbally, and emotionally abusive when drinking. These instances of abuse often came as a reaction to Anthony's somewhat more mild-mannered and emotional nature—qualities that separated him from his brothers. To escape the increasing discomfort of his home life, as a young teenager he began spending more time with older neighborhood boys. Eventually, one of these older boys began another round of sexual abuse, with Anthony believing that it was he who "asked for it" and enjoyed the encounters he had with that predator.

Anthony knew intuitively that the abuse was wrong, that it was not something he wanted, and that he was suffering. When he got up the courage to tell a close family member, he was dismissed as a troublemaker. Meanwhile, his father's physical abuse and drinking escalated to the point that Anthony was removed from his home and sent to live with a relative. Following his removal from his father's home, Anthony fell into a dark depression and began secretly drinking himself.

Soon after, he began acting out sexually, obsessively collecting pornography VHS tapes and stacks and stacks of pornography magazines. He eventually began isolating himself from others and living within his own sexual fantasies. He continued to attend weekly church services with his relative's family, where continuous messages that sex and sexuality were sinful and against God's will were blast from the pulpit. This made him feel even more ashamed about his frequent and ever-insatiable sexual thoughts, urges, and behaviors. Not feeling safe enough to share his growing compulsions and fetishes with anyone else, he continued to view his secrecy as further indication of his sinfulness. Healing, he had learned, could come only through prayer, repentance, and self-inflicted punishment, though by that time he had already deemed himself "unfixable." He decided that going away to college, away from the judging eyes of his church and family, would provide the only possible relief from his endless pain. He used the move as an opportunity to flee the existence and experiences he had come from, entirely unaware that he was only relocating the abused and shamed child within.

Based on appearances alone, Anthony seemed perfect. He was an attractive, physically fit man working as a hypersuccessful stockbroker on Wall Street. This allowed him to live in luxury, surrounding himself with the finest things. In addition to those things, he lived a shadow existence that kept him cut off from his close friends. To relieve the stress of his high-pressure, demanding job, he began drinking more heavily in private, not wanting others to see yet another one of his *bad* habits. During those times of secret and isolated drinking, he began to look outside of his pornography collection in the hope of finding the sexual experiences that would finally fulfill his deeply felt insatiability. He would cruise online platforms that catered to unique sexual fantasies, picking up women with whom he'd have meaningless and sometimes physically aggressive consensual sex. Immediately after the release, he would be filled with an overwhelming self-loathing. He felt that the shame of these encounters would swallow him up, and he'd stare up at the ceiling and beg for forgiveness and peace. One of Anthony's core beliefs was *I'm a highly sexual bad person*, and he continued to strengthen that narrative.

After years of living a hidden life, he suffered a breakdown, which culminated in his cutting his remaining ties with friends and family members. He confined himself to his house for months, drew the blinds, and shut himself off from a world he was never equipped to handle. He entered into a deep fog of unrelenting depression, losing hope that he would ever be "normal." Eventually, he emerged from the womb of his home, ready to start addressing his deep inner conflicts.

Anthony had never before uttered the truths about his sexual compulsions and concerns of sexual addiction to anyone. Prior to his breakdown and isolation, the thought of doing so had been nothing short of debilitating. With the help of a supportive trauma therapist, he began to speak of his hidden sexual compulsions and concerns about being sexually addicted for the first time. It was as if a dam broke inside him. He now understood that he had been groomed and victimized by his abusers and that he did not bring the abuse on himself. He had unveiled his secret, yet he was still living with so much pain.

That was when he decided it was time to meet his inner child.

## ATTACHMENT THEORY

Before we introduce the concept of the inner child, it's important to provide some context about the importance of our earliest childhood bonds. To put it simply, our relationship with our primary parent-figures is the foundation of the dynamics of all the relationships we have in adulthood. We call these relationships attachments. In 1952, psychoanalyst John Bowlby presented a theory of attachment[66] after studying children and their relationship with their mothers at a London clinic.[67] The children would display a variety of "social releasers," such as crying or smiling, to get parent-figures' attention. He came to the conclusion that their intense reactions emerged from a survival instinct. The attachment between mother and child, which he defined as "lasting psychological connectedness between human beings," was "evolutionarily beneficial" for both parties but especially for the child, who is utterly dependent on others to live. Attachment, he concluded, is essential to social, emotional, and cognitive development in babies. The developmental psychologist Mary Ainsworth continued Bowlby's work, creating the Strange Situation Classifications. This technique assessed different attachment styles by observing a child's response when the mother briefly left the child in a room (sometimes with a stranger present) and returned. Ideally, when present, a parent-figure serves as a safe base for the child, who, once settled, will feel free to roam, play, and explore. This isn't always the case. Ainsworth and her colleagues observed and outlined four different attachment styles that emerge during the first eighteen months of life:

1. **Secure.** A securely attached infant may get upset for a brief period of time after the mother leaves the room but will recover quickly. When the mother returns, the child is open and receptive to the reunion. The mother appears to have provided a positive, stable environment that acts as a secure home base in which the child can explore and interact. (To put it into the physical terms

we learned earlier, secure attachments allow for children to freely enter the nervous system's social engagement mode.)

2. **Anxious-resistant.** The anxious-resistant infant may be so stressed and distressed by the mother's absence that they remain upset the whole time the mother is gone. When she returns, the child isn't comforted easily, remains clingy, and may even punish the mother for leaving. This is typically an outcome of a misattunement between the child's needs and the parent-figure's attention, illustrated by the child's inability to be soothed or return to safety upon the mother's return.
3. **Avoidant.** Children in this category show almost no stress response when the mother leaves and almost no reaction when the mother returns. These children do not seek out their mothers for comfort. Some actively avoid the mothers. This is typically a product of a disconnected parent-figure (a disconnection that runs along a spectrum) who leaves the child to navigate feelings on their own. These children don't go to their parent-figure for help with their emotional state, because their parent-figure doesn't really ever provide that support.
4. **Disorganized-disoriented.** These children show no predictable pattern of response. Sometimes they are extremely distressed and stressed; other times they show no reaction at all. This is the rarest attachment style of the four and is typically associated with the childhood traumas found on the ACEs, such as severe abuse and neglect. The child's world is so unpredictable that their body doesn't know how to react or find safety.

The safer and more secure the bond between a child and their immediate parent-figures, the safer and more secure the child feels in the world at large. Research has shown time and again that people who had secure attachments in infancy tend to have secure attachments in adulthood, showing the remarkable, lifelong effects of our parental bonds. Brain scans have supported this conclusion, showing that children who had secure attachments at fifteen months had a larger volume of gray matter (the part of the brain that contains cells and nerve fibers) than those who did not,[68] suggesting that they had healthier brain function. The inability to form secure attachments in childhood, moreover, has been linked to social anxiety, conduct disorders, and other psychological diagnoses.

In recent years, some researchers and clinicians have expanded the idea of attachment theory beyond the immediate parent-figure to the larger family unit. One example of this is family systems theory, developed by Dr. Murray Bowen, which extends attachment theory to the entire family unit, including siblings and close relatives. This is an important addition, in my opinion, because it extends our networks of existence from us as individuals, outward from our immediate environments to our greater communities and worlds at large.

Even though I'm not one to rely on labels, I do think it's helpful to understand which attachment style most resonates with you. What you will hear from marriage and couples counselors around the world is that our attachments live on within us, especially in our romantic bonds. This is also the empirical basis of the work to follow, as the wounds of our inner child that are carried into adulthood are often attachment based.

## INTRODUCING THE INNER CHILD

When I was a child, I never looked overwhelmed. I appeared as if nothing ever bothered me. I'd get a faraway look on my face, and it was as if Nicole had left the room, yet I remained physically present. In fact, I had such big emotions that they nearly erupted out of my pores. I didn't know how to deal with those powerful feelings, so I learned how to distance myself from them as a survival mechanism.

The more I practiced disengagement, the better I got at negating my interior world. I distanced myself from my self—my body, my sensations, my feelings. I got into my "spaceship" to protect myself from the consistently overwhelming experiences. Others described me as laissez-faire and aloof. I internalized those descriptors. I truly believed that I was an unemotional person, that being unaffected was a part of my core being. There was a fire hidden deep down, and I couldn't access it or even identify it. Instead, I felt detached, removed, and unable to find pleasure or joy in anything. In my early teens, after I took my first puff from a plastic water pipe filled with marijuana and drank my first shot of whiskey, I would go on to use substances to externally engineer my disengagement from reality.

No matter how emotionally receptive I believed I was being, I didn't feel connected to people. Though I could have fiery blowups with partners (I was terrified that they would leave me, just as my mother at the window had been terrified that my father might never come home), most of the time, I was detached, avoidant, and unresponsive. It was as if I learned not to love anything too much, because if I truly loved something, it could be taken away from me. It wasn't just a feeling of loss and abandonment; it was a fear that without a certain person *I would not survive.* So I made myself a shell that no one could get into. I made myself into a person who not only didn't know her own needs but didn't have any.

I became aware of this disconnection once I started to notice my thoughts as I practiced self-witnessing. Along the way, I kept running into recurrent narratives, over and over, the familiar theme that *no one considers me*, the same thing I felt when hiding under the kitchen table throughout my childhood. The belief was consistent; I could see it in the way I experienced almost everything, in my emotional reactions, in what filled me with anger and what made me disengage. There was a story being told there; I just wasn't ready to receive the message.

Then I came across the work of the therapist John Bradshaw,[69] who has dedicated his career to speaking about the inner child in people with substance abuse issues. Bradshaw drew from his own childhood, raised by a father who struggled with alcohol addiction. Like many children whose parent-figures struggle with using substances, Bradshaw began to use alcohol himself. The more he studied his family's history as well as the family histories of those under his care, the more he realized that every single one of them was dealing with a deeply wounded inner child. In his book *Homecoming: Reclaiming and Championing Your Inner Child*, he put forward the compelling idea that so many of us end up in "toxic" (his word) relationships because we never addressed the traumas that happened in childhood. "I believe that this neglected, wounded inner child of the past is the major source of human misery," he wrote.[70]

In my own extensive training and practice, I've observed patterns similar to those Bradshaw notes and came to understand we all have a childlike part of ourselves. This childlike part is free, filled with wonder and awe, and connected to the inner wisdom of our authentic Self. It can be accessed only when we are safely in the social connection zone of our nervous system, able to feel spontaneous and open. It is playful and uninhibited or so fully present in the moment that time doesn't seem to exist. This same inner childlike part of each of us, when not acknowledged, can run rampant in our adult life, often reacting impulsively and selfishly.

These reactions emerge from a core wound that the inner child must live with as a response to childhood trauma. Inner child wounds are the consistently unmet emotional, physical, and spiritual needs from our childhood expressed through our subconscious that continue to impact our present self. It's nearly impossible to fulfill all the needs of another human, especially when both people are dealing with their own unresolved traumas. The majority of us feel unseen, unheard, and unloved and we carry this pain with us throughout our lives. Even those we call narcissists aren't truly living in a state of extreme self-love, not at all. In fact, they are big children who are reacting to an inner child wound that is deeply painful.

Our romantic partners tend to activate our wounds at the most intense levels, though we can be emotionally activated by anyone in our lives who touches our wounds. We may argue loudly with partners or friends, slamming doors or stomping around (essentially throwing a tantrum). We may literally grab our "toys" and leave the "sandbox" (refusing to share in success at work, feeling resentful about splitting a restaurant bill when you had less to eat). The inner child is a petrified part of our psyche that formed when we were limited in our emotional coping abilities. This is why many of us act like children when we are threatened or upset. The reality is that many of us are stuck in this childlike state. We are emotionally illiterate because we are little children in adult bodies.

There are common personality archetypes that typically describe our inner child states; many of us will resonate with more than one, but they are helpful in identifying the variations in our inner child reactions. The seven types I've seen most commonly run the gamut from the caretaker, whose self-worth comes from taking care of others, to the life of the party, who appears to be confident and happy but needs constant external validation to feel whole. What these archetypes have in common is that they all emerge from the inner child's need to be seen, heard, and loved. These archetypal narratives were created by those unmet needs.

## THE 7 INNER CHILD ARCHETYPES

**The caretaker.** Typically comes from codependent dynamics. Gains a sense of identity and self-worth through neglecting their own needs. Believes that the only way to receive love is to cater to others and ignore their own needs.

**The overachiever.** Feels seen, heard, and valued through success and achievement. Uses external validation as a way to cope with low self-worth. Believes that the only way to receive love is through achievement.

**The underachiever.** Keeps themselves small, unseen, and beneath their potential due to fear of criticism or shame about failure. Takes themselves out of the emotional game before it's even played. Believes that the only way to receive love is to stay invisible.

**The rescuer/protector.** Ferociously attempts to rescue those around them in an attempt to heal from their own vulnerability, especially in childhood. Views others as helpless, incapable, and dependent and derives their love and self-worth from being in a position of power. Believes that the only way to receive love is to help others by focusing on their wants and needs and helping them solve their problems.

**The life of the party.** This is the always happy and cheerful comedic person who never shows pain, weakness, or vulnerability. It's likely that this inner child was shamed for their emotional state. Believes that the only way to feel okay and receive love is to make sure that everyone around them is happy.

**The yes-person.** Drops everything and neglects all needs in the service of others. Was likely modeled self-sacrifice in childhood and engaged in deep codependency patterns, much as the caretaker did. Believes that the only way to receive love is to be both good and selfless.

**The hero worshipper.** Needs to have a person or guru to follow. Likely emerges from an inner child wound made by a caretaker who was perceived as superhuman, without faults. Believes that the only way to receive love is to reject their own needs and desires and view others as a model to learn how to live.

---

## CHILDHOOD FANTASIES

One common defense against the pain of unmet childhood needs is idealization. Sometimes that manifests itself as a rosy RAS filter, where we look around and block out anything negative, arriving at impossibly optimistic conclusions: *I have the perfect family! My childhood was only happy!* When we cannot reasonably conclude that our family is perfect, we start to engage in alternative, imaginative ways of coping. One such way is engaging in hero-based fantasies or the dream that life could change if only someone or something would swoop in and save us.

One member of my online SelfHealers community, Nancy, shared that as a child, she used to have daydreams involving the band Duran Duran, who arrived in a limousine to take her out of her unhappy home. She spent long hours thinking about how it would happen, how good she would feel, and how the escape would change her life and make her into the person she longed to be: a loved human.

Nancy later dropped Duran Duran from the fantasy, though she didn't stop her escapist longing for a hero. As she grew up, she put that responsibility on her crushes and later her boyfriends, who always failed to live up to the pressure of the unattainable pedestal she placed them on. When they inevitably failed her, she would find another person to fantasize about. That often led to her seeking emotional and physical affairs, each of which would last until she found herself in exactly the same place again: unhappy, unfulfilled, desiring yet another escape hatch.

There is nothing inherently wrong with daydreaming. I think that imagining a different life is actually a productive thought exercise. Nancy's fantasies were not necessarily productive; they enabled her to displace all of her hope for change onto an external figure. Her romantic liaisons provided an escape, and the same principle applies to other fixations: people think they will be "saved" or fulfilled once they get a great job, buy a house, or have children. They check all the boxes, yet once they've achieved their goals, they find themselves just as unhappy if not more so—hence the ubiquitous midlife crisis.

The wounded inner child carries all of these compulsions into adulthood. We carry this powerlessness, hoping that others will change our circumstances and make us happy, externalizing quick fixes and daydreaming of alternate realities. We seek approval from others so that we will feel good about ourselves. We choose the quick fix—drugs, alcohol, sex—to feel pleasure in the moment that will dull our pain. Our real long-term goal is to find that security *inside ourselves*. Our work is to internalize the feeling of being good enough—a state of okayness that is not reliant on others. How can we begin to get to that place? This is the question at the heart of our inner child work.

## MEET YOUR INNER CHILD

As you begin your inner child work, your first step is to accept that you have an inner child that remains present in your adult life. It's important to note that even if (like me) you can't remember most of your childhood, it doesn't mean that you can't access your inner child. It is very likely that what you're doing, feeling, and thinking every day is a living replica of those past experiences in one way or another. It's through these daily experiences that we can *all* access our inner child.

The next step is to acknowledge that our inner child is wounded. This appears simple though can actually be quite challenging. As we learned in chapter 3, just because you can't point to a "before-and-after" moment, it doesn't mean you didn't experience traumas and that those traumas didn't create wounds that live on within you. You might even say, "My childhood wasn't that bad. I shouldn't complain." I hear that a lot. I have to remind you: you are looking backward in time from the perspective of your adult brain with the awareness and maturity that can put things into proper perspective and alignment. Our child brains did not have these capabilities. Everything was bigger, more intense, more extreme than we can imagine now. Give your inner child the gift of acknowledging its wounds.

Accepting that you have an inner child with wounds will help you remove your shame about and disappointment in your inability to change, the "stuckness" that we've discussed. Your inability to move forward or make changes isn't about *you*, it's an extension of the conditioned patterns and core beliefs you developed in your childhood. Your hurt inner child is still hurting. This is just a fact, like a heartbeat. It is not something to be ashamed of.

It's important to acknowledge that even though your inner child is there, it is only a part of you. It is not your essential, intuitive Self. When you react from that wounded place, begin to witness from a place of curiosity. Your goal is to gather information. When you shut down when your mom criticizes your new haircut, what narrative is your inner child telling you? When you erupt in a storm of expletives when someone cuts you off on your way to work, what is your inner child trying to communicate? Honor what your inner child is trying to tell you. Honor its experience.

You don't need to have the answers; just start to listen to the questions. The more you cultivate this listening, the more you will become present and aware. The greater your presence and awareness grow, the greater your ability to distinguish between your inner child reactions and your authentic Self will be. And the better you're able to distinguish between them, the better you'll be able to make choices about how you will behave. This distance will give you the opportunity to choose the way you want to react.

## ANTHONY'S INNER CHILD

Doing inner child work will not rid you of your inner child. Nor will it fully heal the wounds of the past. By the time Anthony came to the community, he had done some research into the inner child healing work of John Bradshaw and found some of my discussions about the inner child helpful. He had begun piecing together the ways his inner child had filtered the core beliefs he held about himself. As a result, he started to unravel the shame-based narratives that surrounded his sexual behaviors and more recent drinking. He disentangled his beliefs about his supposed participation in his childhood sexual abuse, which for so long he accepted as a fact, seeing them only from his child brain. Once he applied the logic of the wise inner parent-figure, he saw from an adult perspective the reality of that experience: he had been groomed by a child predator.

When Anthony began to accept that his inner child (including all of the different painful experiences he lived) was inside and incredibly hurt, he was able to understand how the hurt was pushing him to act out narratives that no longer served him.

At the same time, he identified his overachiever inner child archetype and realized how much he paired achievement with love. Eventually, he quit his high-powered job in business. He recognized how his obsession with success helped him dissociate from his emotional world—how it allowed him to disconnect, just as he did in childhood.

The story doesn't end there. Things are never that simple, are they? Anthony didn't just wrap a bow around his inner child and put it away. There is a temptation to close the book on this work and tell yourself, "I've met my inner child. Now I'm all better. Time to move on." In truth, *the work* is never done.

The true shift for Anthony happened when he settled into accepting that his inner child will always be there cultivating an ongoing dialogue between his present self and his inner child. Speaking more openly about his sexual compulsions and substance use, he came to identify the vicious cycle of shame and coping behaviors (numbing himself with substances or acting out sexually) his inner child had been repeating for years.

When he was very young, Anthony remembered, one day he came home and shared an instance of schoolyard bullying with his dad who had asked why he appeared upset. Not only had his father suggested that he "was making a big deal out of nothing," he seemed to wince when Anthony described how he had reacted earlier that day by crying in front of his peers. It was through this interaction that Anthony realized that his father was ashamed of him and his emotions. It was a gut punch—his first painful experience with shame.

That memory kept coming up in his own therapy, though he couldn't figure out how to get past it. It was only once he started to acknowledge his inner child that he realized that the interaction created an inner wound, which had only been deepened by the abuse he later suffered. In that father-son moment after a particularly difficult day at school, he learned that he should never be open or honest or show weakness, or he would be shamed by those he loved the most. After having even his sexual abuse denied and minimized by those closest to him, he began to hide more and more parts of himself away from the eyes of those around him. To cope with his deep-rooted shame, he began to numb his accumulating pain in secret, looking for whatever could relieve his discomfort for the moment.

At his core, Anthony felt unworthy—a *bad* person—and he began to cope the only ways he knew how, which only added more and more acts to feel ashamed about. Over time, he decided that the only way to move past it was to access and engage the core wounds of his inner child. He has learned that when his shame is activated, his best strategy is to give whatever part of him needs a voice a safe place to express itself, thus helping to break the continued expression of shame and problematic coping.

Like Anthony and myself, I'd love for you to begin to rebuild your connection to your inner child. I've included several writing prompts here that you can use to start a dialogue with the archetype that resonates most with you.

## DO THE WORK: WRITE AN INNER CHILD LETTER TO YOURSELF

**Step 1. Spend some time reflecting and witnessing your inner child** throughout your day, and note which of your inner child archetypes are most frequently activated. Remember, several may resonate, but try to pick one to begin with. Follow your instinct as to which is the best fit, or go with the one that is most frequently or presently active. There is no wrong answer here, I promise. Over time, you can visit each of these archetypes, taking time to acknowledge each of the wounded parts of your child self.

- **The caretaker.** Typically comes from codependent dynamics. Gains a sense of identity and self-worth through neglecting their own needs. Believes that the only way to receive love is to cater to others and ignore their own needs.

*Dear Little Caretaker Nicole,*

I know you have felt you needed to take care of everyone around you, to make them feel better, and to make sure everyone is happy with you. I know this makes you feel really tired and you don't always end up being able to make people feel better. You don't have to do this anymore. You are allowed to take care of yourself now. I promise you others will still love you.

I see you, I hear you, and I love you always,
*Wise Adult Nicole*

- **The overachiever.** Feels seen, heard, and valued through success and achievement. Uses external validation as a way to cope with low self-worth. Believes that the only way to receive love is through achievement.

*Dear Little Overachiever Nicole,*

I know you have felt you needed to do some things perfectly to make others or yourself feel happy, proud, or loved. I know this makes you feel not good enough as you are. You don't have to do this anymore. You are allowed to stop pushing yourself so hard to do things perfectly. I promise you are more than enough exactly as you are.

I see you, I hear you, and I love you always,
*Wise Adult Nicole*

- **The underachiever.** Keeps themselves small, unseen, and beneath their potential due to fear of criticism or shame about failure. Takes themselves out of the emotional game before it's even played. Believes that the only way to receive love is to stay invisible.

*Dear Little Underachiever Nicole,*

I know you have felt you needed to hide some of the things you are good at, the achievements you made, and other good parts of yourself so you wouldn't hurt other people's feelings. I know this does not allow the good things about you to be celebrated and may even make you feel bad about them. You don't have to do this anymore. You are allowed to let others see how good you really are. I promise you can let your goodness show and still be loved.

I see you, I hear you, and I love you always,
*Wise Adult Nicole*

- **The rescuer/protector.** Ferociously attempts to rescue those around them in an attempt to heal from their own vulnerability, especially in childhood. Views others as helpless, incapable, and dependent and derives their love and self-worth from being in a position of power. Believes that the only way to receive love is to help others by focusing on their wants and needs and helping them solve their problems.

*Dear Little Rescuer/Protector Nicole,*

I know you have felt you have to jump in and save everyone around you every time they have a problem, need help, or are feeling sad. I know this makes you feel tired and disappointed in others and you don't always end up being able to make them feel better. You don't have to do this anymore. You are allowed to take a break in solving other people's problems. I promise you can begin to focus on yourself and still be loved.

I see you, I hear you, and I love you always,
*Wise Adult Nicole*

- **The life of the party.** This is the always happy and cheerful comedic person who never shows pain, weakness, or vulnerability. It's likely that this inner child was shamed for their emotional state. They believe that the only way to feel okay and receive love is to make sure everyone around them is happy.

*Dear Little Life of the Party Nicole,*

I know you have felt you have to always be happy, cheer others up, or be "strong." I know this makes you scared to let others see you feeling sad, angry, or afraid, and you feel "bad" when you feel these ways. You don't have to do this anymore. You are allowed to feel any way you feel. I promise you are safe to feel all of your emotions and still be loved.

I see you, I hear you, and I love you always,
*Wise Adult Nicole*

- **The yes-person.** Drops everything and neglects all needs in the service of others. Was likely modeled self-sacrifice in childhood and engaged in deep codependency patterns, much as the caretaker did. Believes that the only way to receive love is to be both good and selfless.

*Dear Little Yes-Person Nicole,*

I know you have felt that you have to say "yes" whenever someone asks you to do something for them, such as hang out, loan your favorite shirt, or do a favor. I know this makes you feel like a bad person if you really want to say "no." You don't have to do this anymore. You are allowed to say "yes" or "no" based on how you feel and what you want to do. I promise you can say "no" and still be loved.

I see you, I hear you, and I love you always,
*Wise Adult Nicole*

- **The hero worshipper.** Needs to have a person or guru to follow. Likely emerges from an inner child wound made by a caretaker who was perceived as superhuman, without faults. Believes that the only way to receive love is to reject their own needs and desires and view others as a model to learn how to live.

*Dear Little Hero Worshipper Nicole,*

I know you have felt that other people know more than you do and have always looked to others to help you make decisions. I know this makes you feel that you are not smart enough, and you don't trust yourself to make your own choices. You don't have to do this anymore. You are able to think about things and make decisions without looking to others for answers. I promise you can trust yourself and still be loved.

I see you, I hear you, and I love you always,
*Wise Adult Nicole*

## INNER CHILD GUIDED MEDITATION

Those of you who are interested in a guided inner child meditation can visit my website, https://yourholisticpsychologist.com.

# 8
# Ego Stories

I've always wanted to be laid back and stress free, someone whom others would describe as "a hippie at heart." In some ways, I am that person.

Then there were always the damn dishes.

At the mere sight of a pile of used silverware or dirty pots and pans in the sink, I'd basically lose it. I'm talking blind rage. In the past, I sometimes became so reactive that I'd have a tantrum—slamming my hands on the countertop, yelling, stomping my foot. A full-body stress reaction would follow: my vagus nerve would activate my nervous system stress response, sending fight/flight/freeze messages to my body. Physiologically, I'd react as though a bear had just jumped on me in the woods, thrashing around to "save" myself from the attack of the dirty dishes.

Sometimes it would go a different way. I wouldn't throw things or get angry. Instead, I'd become as quiet as a stone and stew, immersing myself in a state of internal agitation that would linger for hours. I'd become avoidant and distant, prompting my partner to crowd me with questions.

"Are you okay?"

"Yeah," I'd respond deadpan.

"Are you sure?"

"Yeah, I'm fine."

Either way (fight or freeze), the end result would be the same: a fight with my partner.

I'm sure many of you are thinking *Gosh, that seems like an overreaction to dirty dishes*. (Though some of you may have the same one I'm sure!) The reality is that I could not regulate my emotional state because the dishes touched something deep inside me that I was not yet aware of. It was my subconscious mind communicating with me—whether or not I wanted to listen.

## MEET THE EGO

It's only now, looking back, that I know that those dishes in the sink communicated a narrative: *My partner doesn't consider me.* Remember, this is one of my core beliefs about myself (*I'm not considered*) that came from my childhood. This, my friends, is an ego story.

Despite its pronounced impact on our lives, most of us have no awareness of the ego and how it drives our behavior. The ego, the great protector of the inner child, is the "I" identity. Anything that follows the word "I" is an extension of the ego: *I'm smart. I'm boring. I'm sexy. I'm frumpy. I'm good. I'm bad.* The ego is our sense of self, our personal identity, our self-worth. The ego is a master storyteller (*When my partner leaves dirty dishes in the sink, it means I'm not considered*), creating and maintaining narratives about who we believe we are. The ego itself is not good or bad; it just is.

The ego, developed in childhood, is formed through the beliefs and ideas imparted on us by our parent-figures, friends, immediate community, and greater environment—what we call our personality or self-identity—that live in our subconscious. Ego beliefs don't come out of nowhere; they are grounded in lived experiences.

Throughout our lives we create a story about who we are based on our experiences. This narrative includes aspects of our identity, opinions, and beliefs. The ego works to keep us living within familiar narratives because, though often painful, they are predictable. The predictable, as we now know, feels safer than the uncertainty of the unknown.

The ego, attached to its ideas, opinions, and beliefs, runs as an endless stream of thoughts keeping us locked in our identity. The ego's core objective is to protect our identity at all times and at whatever cost. This rigidity is part of the ego's defensive stance. The ego needs to be an inflexible protector in order to make sure that the softer, more defenseless part of us (namely our inner child) remains safe. That's why the ego is so defensive and fear based. It views everything within the context of a rigid dichotomy: good versus bad or right versus wrong. It is staunchly attached to its opinions and believes that we *are* our opinions. The ego interprets any disagreement or criticism as a direct threat to our very existence. That's because when we are in an egoic state, our beliefs and thoughts are *who we are*; anything that even questions those narratives is adversarial. When our opinions are questioned, the ego believes that our core self is being threatened.

If we do not practice witnessing the ego, it will fight to assert itself and dominate, leading to feelings of insecurity and low self-worth as the ego works overtime to defend "us." Feel that sting? That little undermining comment from a coworker that made your blood boil? The desire to defend, condemn, and win? The need to be right or have the last word no matter the cost? The quick turn to judgment and disparagement? The need to compare and contrast? The feeling that you aren't [fill in the blank] enough? This is the ego in its reactive state. When our ego is activated, everything is personal (as in the egocentric state in childhood, when everything was about us). Everything that happens *to* you, it assumes, happens *because of* you. It's why so many people are obsessed with pleasing or impressing others—and it's a significant part of the reason we feel "stuck."

It can go something like this:

1. I feel anger when I am emotionally activated.
2. I feel emotionally activated when my partner doesn't respond to my texts fast enough.
3. My partner's not answering my texts fast enough means that I am not worthy of consideration, which makes me angry.
4. When I am angry, I yell or scream at or ice out those I love. My ego feels the core wound of unworthiness and projects it outward, preferring to dump the emotion onto others rather than experience the painful emotion of unworthiness.
5. Conclusion: I am a worthless and angry person.

While this of course isn't the truth, the more we listen to our ego, the more these narratives become our reality. Let's say you want to start journaling, and your ego says, "This is a waste of time. You have so many other more important things to do," as a way to save you from the fear of failure or the fear of what you might uncover. Or you take yourself out of the running for a job promotion even though you're overqualified in order to protect yourself from the possible sting of rejection. The more shame we carry, the more the ego wants to avoid future situations where we could experience more shame or any deeper pain. The ego, in an attempt to make sure you're never hurt again, puts up barriers—because in every opportunity for positive change, there is also the chance of the pain of failure.

## EGO ACTIVATION

The ego is hypervigilant, always acting as a bodyguard. It's rigid, often hostile to counterviews, and refuses to compromise or even offer compassion. The ego is in a near-constant defensive stance, ready to spring into action if it experiences any opposition at all. The threats against our ego self can manifest in the following ways:

- "All hands on deck," or strong emotional reactivity (acting out of a protective wound)

- False confidence (some might call it narcissism), which is more often than not a bravado that emerges from feelings of insecurity due to lack of connection to the authentic Self
- Lack of nuance in thinking—everything is right or wrong; there are no gray areas
- Extreme competition (a belief that other people's success undermines or conflicts with your own)

These reactions occur when there is a fusion among your opinions, thoughts, beliefs, and selfhood. This is why ego stories take on a life-or-death quality; when someone disagrees with or criticizes you, that person's opinions don't feel limited to a specific topic and end up being about *who you are* fundamentally. When a belief is threatened, as when someone hates a movie you like (it's a silly example but one that can get us riled up if we're reacting egoically), your whole being is threatened.

Often when disagreement does occur, the goal is not to try to get closer to a shared truth and is instead to invalidate each other's realities, to destroy the other person to establish your own worth and power. That's how disagreements get ugly so quickly. That's why no one ever listens to others. Because if what you believe is who you are, there is no space for conversation or contemplation. There is no space for expansion or adaptability. Sometimes when I watch debates, all I can see is egoic protective stances; all of the wounding and activation from childhood is present right there onstage.

## EGO PROJECTIONS

Our ego works overtime to defend its perception of who we are. To do this, it denies or represses emotions that we feel are *bad* or *wrong* in order to be *good* or *desirable* and receive as much love as possible. These *bad* or *wrong* parts of us are sometimes referred to as "the shadow self."

Adults enable this repression by telling children that some things should be hidden and others should be praised. Out of our vast dependency as children, we learn that to maintain our connections, our lifelines, we must appear acceptable. This is a survival mechanism, an evolutionarily advantageous part of maturing and understanding how to interact with the world. When we consistently repress any part of our authentic Self in order to receive love and the act of repression becomes an ego story, we become who we believe we should be.

This process, as we know, is unconscious. The more we deny parts of our shadow self, the more shame we feel and the more disconnected we become from our intuition. This shame and disconnect are projected onto others. Suddenly, we throw the faults and criticisms we feel about ourselves onto other people. The more disconnected from and ashamed of ourselves we become, the more we see the same in others.

In order to continue to feel valued, safe, and as though we're a good person, we tell ourselves, *We aren't like them.* In reality, at our core we have exactly the same "faults." Let's say you're standing in line to get coffee. A woman cuts in front of you. You're outraged! *This woman is an entitled, arrogant jerk! She's self-obsessed and rude! She's a bad person! She is nothing like me!*

This is an ego story. None of us has the gift to see inside other people's minds. We cannot know what the woman who cut in front of us is thinking. Yet we easily conjure up a tale—painted almost entirely by our past experiences. Our ego projection is unconsciously recreating patterns without ever directly interacting with another person. Maybe a parent-figure told *us* that we were arrogant when we asserted ourselves so we began repressing our own needs and policing the needs of others around us.

Ego stories come naturally to us because uncertainty is frightening. When we don't know why a person is behaving in a way that makes us upset, angry, or uncomfortable, our ego goes into hyperdrive to try to figure out why and keep us safe by insisting that *we* would never do something so terrible. If that *bad* person did that *bad* thing, then, since I'm a *good* person, I would never do it. This is why judging others is so addictive; it relieves us from the ego's internal struggle with shame. When we identify the faults of others, we can ignore our own and even convince ourselves that we are superior. None of this is actually wrong or bad (this is egoic speak!); it's just part of being human.

## HOW TO DO THE WORK WITH YOUR EGO

Now that we've learned about the role of the ego, it's time to start the process of doing *ego work*. The goal of this work is to become aware and conscious, instead of deferring to our ego's reaction of our world. *The work* begins with simply witnessing. When we exist on autopilot, our ego holds the reins, so actively engaging the conscious mind helps loosen our ego's hold on our daily existence. Once we become aware and conscious, we can view our ego's thought patterns and fears and try to view its tantrums and defenses without judgment. Our ego's defensiveness and vulnerability are similar to those of our inner child: Both need to be seen and heard without judgment. Our ego needs space to settle. It needs room to relax and soften.

### Step One: Allow Your Ego to Introduce Itself

The goal here is to see your ego as separate from you and practice being a neutral witness. You can start the act of separation with this short prompt. It takes about one or two minutes.

1. Find a quiet place with no distraction, perhaps where you have previously worked on consciousness exercises.
2. Close your eyes and take one deep, exaggerated breath.
3. Repeat the following affirmation: *I am safe, and I choose a new way to experience myself as separate from my ego.*

I will warn you: this first step, though fast and seemingly simple, is often the hardest. The ego does not like to be witnessed, so engaging with it on the initial observation level can be very uncomfortable. You might feel sensations in your body that are like irritability or even nausea. Your ego might tell you stories about how you shouldn't practice this work because it's too silly. This is all a normal part of the process. Keep going. Getting through this discomfort takes work, so be patient with yourself.

### Step Two: Have a Friendly Encounter with Your Ego

Now I want you to start paying attention to what you say after you use the phrase "I am." When you hear these words spoken or witness yourself thinking them, use them as a cue to start noticing the patterns that follow. For example, *I'm always late, I'm horrible at remembering things, I'm always attracting losers.* No judgment, no exasperation, no disappointment. Just take mental notes or, even better, jot your thoughts down on a notepad or write them in your phone. Notice how often you speak about yourself. How many conversations do you steer away to talking about you? Do you avoid discussing your emotions? How negative are the words that follow the phrase "I am"?

This is your ego speaking. You've been repeating these narratives for so long that you may not even notice them, realize their repetitiveness, or question their truths. This step will pull you out of the comfort of those familiar patterns. Before you became aware of your ego reactions, you unconsciously lived out your patterns, conditioning, and childhood wounds. Ego work gives you an opportunity to choose a new narrative. The more you can repeat these practices, the better (I still do them anytime I feel activated). Repetition will prime new pathways in the brain and allow witnessing to come more easily with time.

### Step Three: Name Your Ego

This may sound silly, but naming your ego is a powerful act of separating from it. Once we can view it and name it, we can disentangle our intuitive Self from the ego reaction—or at least get one step closer to accomplishing this.

I call my ego "Jessica." I watch Jessica come and go. Sometimes she'll disappear for a few hours and then come roaring back with reckless abandon. I notice that certain things make Jessica extra touchy—and that's *fine*.

Sometimes when I feel activated and I can tell that my ego is starting to take over the reins of my mind and I want to throw a tantrum or say something snarky, I'll own it. "Jessica is acting up again," I'll say. It's unbelievably helpful to say those words out loud and helps give me a moment to take a breath and make a choice about whether I want to indulge Jessica or keep her in check.

I've received messages from people with the most hilarious names for their egos. What is yours?

## Step Four: Meet the Activated Ego

As we expand our level of conscious awareness, we can see that we are not our ego stories. Thoughts happen to us. They don't mean anything about who we are. They're simply our ego attempting to defend our identity and protect us from pain.

In this self-witnessing ego state, we can accept and even tolerate attacks on our ego's sense of safety. The next time you're out in the world and you feel emotionally activated, take note of the experience. This is an extension of the first step. Next, keep track of all the times you feel uncomfortable or angry. What was said on the surface? What part activated an ego story?

Here's an example.

> Your sister says, "You look tired." You respond sarcastically, "Of course I look tired. I've been working sixty hours a week and raising a child. Must be nice to have tons of free time. Don't worry, next time I see you, I'll look perfect!"
>
> *What your sister said objectively:* "You look tired."
>
> *What your ego heard:* "She's always so rude and condescending. She never acknowledges the hardships I go through and how much I work to just stay afloat."

Here, the ego felt a core emotion (unworthiness). That was painful, and since you've never learned to process your feelings, the ego came to project it onto your sister. As we know, the ego prefers to dump painful emotions onto others, rather than sit with them.

One example of a way to handle the sister's comment in the above example is to acknowledge your hurt, not bury it. You could respond, "Ouch. That stung. I think I took that way more personally than you intended it."

As we navigate the ego in a more empowered way, we can actually have difficult conversations without feeling under threat when we are questioned or challenged. The more we practice this awareness, the more our ego softens, the greater our confidence grows, and the more the ego can settle and integrate. Though these stages are laid out neatly in this chapter, they are far from linear. You will shift into and out of these stages, first progressing and then backsliding. Your ego is always there.

## The Concept of Self-truth

As you build up attentional controls and practice self-witnessing, you will be forced to start looking more objectively at your behaviors. Self-witnessing is not enough on its own; you also need to be honest about what you are observing. You will benefit from being open and honest about the shadow self that exists within you—within all of us—and come face-to-face with self-truth.

Our shadow self consists of all the unsavory parts of ourselves, about our relationships, our past, and our parent-figures that we are ashamed of and try to deny. Our ego spends a lot of time fighting battles to obscure our ability to see this shadow. As you learn how to question your ego, some of these parts of yourself will become apparent—often through your judgments of and projections onto others. The more you become separate from your ego, the greater your ability to see things from a distance will be.

Our projections, or our internal emotions that we externalize onto others, are messages from our shadow self. Take notice of the voice of criticism or judgment the next time it crops up, as it inevitably will. What is it telling you about yourself? One of my early introductions to seeing my ego stories came when I started questioning my knee-jerk annoyance with people who posted videos of themselves dancing on Instagram. It made me angry. My mind made up so many stories about their self-obsession, their need for the spotlight, on and on. The reality was that I have trouble letting myself go in front of other people and have refused to dance in public since I was a little girl. I was jealous of the freedom and joy I saw in those posts.

When our ego is in the driver's seat, our mind does some pretty remarkable gymnastics to repress or avoid or dismiss or put down. Once you allow what exists, you can view yourself more objectively, more honestly, and ultimately more compassionately.

## The Concept of Ego Consciousness

Living unconsciously and unaware of our thoughts, patterns, and behaviors, we are completely identified with our egoic concept of who we are. Our automatic response is to externalize uncomfortable feelings, blaming everyone else and discharging energy outward. This state of consciousness, also called ego consciousness, leaves us powerless to make our own choices. Without accountability and inner knowing, we are very much at the whim of our environment.

I'll use my dishwashing experience as an example.

When I see a sink full of dirty dishes and start to feel my rage spiral, I begin the process of witnessing. I notice my bodily reactions: heart racing, blood rushing to my face, feeling hot, antsy, ready to burst. As I witness my reactions and give them the space to breathe, not discounting them as "overreactions," I learn from them. I begin to listen to the narrative that they are telling me. I allow myself to think a bit more objectively. My heart is pounding. The blood is rushing to my head. I feel agitated. I'm seeing this from more of a distance, as a kind of insight into my internal world, without immediately entering the rage or disconnection spiral.

I take a second and look even further. There is a feeling of dread in the pit of my stomach. I recognize that feeling from my childhood, and I acknowledge the pull toward the familiar trauma reaction. My subconscious craves the stress cycle of my childhood. The rage and anger, I realize, were not only about the dirty dishes or even about my partner but also about my mother. They were about her emotional distance. They were about her distraction. They were about *not being seen*. The dirty dishes were a kind of time machine taking me back to sitting under the table in Philadelphia, playing with my toy cars while my mom stared out of the window, waiting for my father to come home. They took me back to all of the times and places when I was not seen or heard, when I felt forgotten or ignored, when my mother was so fearful herself she was unable to offer me comfort or safety. My ego created a story to help protect me from feeling that pain again, so acting egoically meant pushing the other person farther and farther away from me as dramatically and even aggressively as possible.

I had never seen myself clearly or honestly enough before to be able to come to that conclusion. Now I could make an active effort to change my relationship with dirty dishes.

It took years, and now I enjoy doing the dishes. I no longer see them as a testament to my worthlessness. The change didn't happen overnight, and it started with this: I practiced new thoughts about the dishes. Even though my subconscious was rolling its eyes, I would tell myself, *You are considered. You do matter* as I ran the hot water and felt soapy water cover the smooth dishes in my hands. Even if I didn't believe it, I said it anyway.

Then I made a ritual out of doing the dishes that made me happy. After I finished, I'd do something only for me. Maybe I'd take a half hour and read alone in my room. Or I'd take a walk with my dog. Over time and with more practicing of these thoughts, my subconscious quieted and the thoughts became beliefs. I still deal with emotional activation—as we will likely always—and over time (lots and lots of time) I channeled my emotional activation into considered, intentional action.

I am no longer the victim of circumstances. I have no control over whether or not others will wash their own dishes, and I can intervene and change the narrative. I don't have to rely on anything external to adjust the way I feel. I feel empowered by those dirty dishes because they give me the choice to take the time and honor myself when I wash them.

After years of doing ego work, I am still activated, especially when I've gone long periods when my ego has appeared to be in hibernation. Or when my physical and emotional resources are low from life's stress and the lack of sleep that so often accompanies these times. Like all aspects of *the work*, this process is continual. You're never done. The mere practice is transformative. The more ego awareness we have, the more we find grace, humor, and empathy in ourselves—and ultimately in the people around us.

The ultimate goal, really the final step in your ego work, is to cultivate empowerment consciousness, or an understanding and acceptance of your ego. Through practice, this state of consciousness will create a space of awareness that will allow you to make choices beyond knee-jerk ego reactivity. These consistent new choices will pave the path toward your future transformations. Contrary to popular belief, your goal is not "ego death." Your ego will always be with you, even when you feel you've mastered it (which is in and of itself an ego statement!). In fact, it will often show up and surprise you when you least expect it to.

To be clear, even with the cultivation of empowerment consciousness, there are many of us who do not have the privilege to effect structural or objective change in our oppressive living environments. Many of us continue to live in poverty or under constant daily threats of racism, where escape is not an option. We cannot *ego work* our way out of systemically oppressed environments. We can, however, empower ourselves with the tools to survive despite and amid our surroundings. My hope is that while we continue to work toward long overdue structural systemic change, we can all empower ourselves with choice, however small, whenever possible.

## DO THE WORK: MEET YOUR SHADOW

To meet your shadow self, take some time reflecting and writing using these prompts.

When you have feelings of jealousy, ask yourself: What do I feel the other person "has" that I feel I am lacking? ____________________

How often do you give others advice, and why do you give it? (There will be clear patterns.) ____________________

How do you speak about yourself to others? (This will help you understand your self-narratives and limiting beliefs.) ____________________

How do you speak about others when they are not around? (This will help you understand your relationship narratives and attachment or spiritual trauma.) ____________________

Anytime our ego, or story about the self, is threatened, we can become emotionally reactive—arguing our points, criticizing others, and throwing tantrums or detaching (usually whatever you typically do when you're upset). As you begin to explore and identify the deeper beliefs driving these reactions, you must realize that they will not go away overnight. As you have been learning throughout this book, our ego stories, as well as our shadow self, are stored deep in our subconscious, directing our reactions daily, and cannot be changed immediately. As you begin this work, you will continue to be aware of your ego, its related reactions, and even your compulsion to react in those old ways. And many times you still will. That's okay.

## FSJ: CHANGING EGO CONSCIOUSNESS TO EMPOWERMENT CONSCIOUSNESS

In order for you to empower yourself to break out of your ego's conditioned habits and patterns, you will want to begin to create a space before you instinctively return to those older ego reactions. To help you with this process, you may want to use the following example (or create a similar one of your own):

**Today I am practicing** breaking old habits of emotional reactivity.

**I am grateful for** the opportunity to choose new responses to my daily life.

**Today I am** calm and grounded in presence.

**Change in this area allows me to feel** more in control of my choices.

**Today I am practicing when** I use my breath to ground my reactions and make space for new, conscious choices.

# 9

# Trauma Bonds

My most frequently uttered phrase while I was growing up was "I'm bored." I was always chasing the intoxicating high of the cortisol roller coaster. Even outside the home or on my own, I could recreate that stress cycle. Sometimes when I couldn't sleep, I'd soothe myself (by throwing myself right back into the stress cycle with which I was familiar) by listing all the ways that my family could die—in a fire, in a flood, during a home robbery.

Later, with romantic partners, I sought the same stress cycles. I'd remain emotionally distant and largely unavailable, a pattern I learned with my mother in childhood. I'd only end up growing resentful over time as I held them solely responsible for the disconnection and distance I helped to co-create. Whenever they tried to move close, I'd push them away, unfamiliar with the intimacy. When they left, I'd panic, running back to the familiar cycle of stress ("*always something*") from my childhood. My mind would race, thinking of all the ways a girlfriend failed me (an unanswered text message, an inconsiderate gift, a stray comment of disapproval). No matter what, I could always find *something* to stress about. Even in the most peaceful moments, my mind would nag: *Something is wrong. Maybe I'm not really attracted to this person. Maybe I'm over this relationship.* I needed that stress response to *feel*. Without it, I felt numb—bored!—and eventually I'd end up pushing the other person away or leaving, confirming my belief that *I will always be alone*.

Looking back, I first became attracted to my girlfriend Sara exactly because she gave me that roller-coaster feeling of uncertainty. I could never really know where I stood with her, and that discomfort felt exciting (and familiar to my dysregulated nervous system). Several years into our relationship, when I started to suspect that Sara was cheating on me with a mutual friend (the *ping* of my intuition felt that something was off), I confronted her. After she denied my allegations, I allowed her to wave me off and call me paranoid because I didn't have enough faith in my intuitive voice to follow it as a guide. When I later found out that it was true that she was cheating on me with that friend, it was as though a boulder crashed down onto my inner child. It wasn't the infidelity that hurt the most; it was her denial of my reality, one of the wounds from my childhood when everything was swept under the rug, including my sexuality. Having never developed a trust in my own reality, I found myself believing hers.

Retrospectively, I can see how I participated in the disconnection that led to our relationship's ending. I know now how dissociated I was then. I know that I was playing the part of the aggrieved party, and the truth is that I wasn't at all present. The whole time I was pointing my finger at her, I kept myself at an emotional distance that left a crater-sized hole in our relationship. One can be only as connected to others as they are to themselves.

When that relationship inevitably erupted, I moved out to a three-bedroom apartment, which I shared with a woman several years older than me. We quickly developed an intense friendship that grew into attraction. It was like the relationship equivalent of drawing yourself a warm bath, soothing and inviting. It's only now, looking back, that I see that that feeling of safety emerged from the recognizable patterns of my childhood.

We connected immediately as we spent more and more time together bonding emotionally around a shared experience of anxiety.

Outside of that very familiar bond, emotionally I remained at a distance. As I had always done, I ran around seeking to please all those around me, though never able to provide what they all desired most—authentic connection.

A few years in, the topic of marriage came up. Marrying seemed like the logical next step. So off we went, flying out of state because it was not yet legal for us to marry in New York.

Shortly after marrying, we moved from New York City to Philadelphia, leaving our routine and particularly active social life behind. In our new home, with fewer distractions, it felt as though a flashlight was shone on the depth of our developed disconnection. I was in a near-constant state of dissociation, unable to give my wife what she felt she needed and also feeling unfulfilled myself. Years of unmet needs were projected on to her, with increasing resentment being soothed by my continued pattern of dissociation. My checking out further activated her anxiety, increasing her safety-seeking through connection, and sending me further in to my own dysregulation and distance. It's a cycle I've observed often in couples I've worked with that spins many into bouts of despair and eventually to divorce.

After one particularly emotional day of work, I came home and started to feel really sick—my heart was racing, and I felt sweaty one second and freezing the next. I put on my sneakers and a heavy winter jacket, because I thought I would need to take myself to the hospital; I believed I was having a heart attack. In reality, I was having an anxiety attack, which even the clinician in me couldn't identify at the time. Surrounded by puffy down, I curled up into a ball and rocked back and forth, telling myself to breathe through the pain. Thankfully it wasn't a heart attack; it was an acute message of the soul. My mind avoided the truth for so long that my body had taken over. I realized that the people I was choosing to love were not random. It was all part of a pattern, a deeper story that started in my attachment bonds in infancy. My current relationship was a part of that pattern, and our marriage was not founded on a solid base of authentic connection.

After a few more grueling months of harkening with my emerging truth I came to one of the most difficult decisions of my life thus far. I listened to my true Self for one of the first times and acted accordingly: I asked my wife for a divorce.

## ATTACHMENT THEORY IN ADULTHOOD

Our dependency on other people to survive and thrive doesn't end in childhood; as adults, we continue to seek out attachments, primarily through romantic relationships. In the 1980s, researchers Dr. Cindy Hazan and Dr. Phillip Shaver applied attachment theory to romantic partners, employing a "love quiz" to assess how secure the study participants' relationships were in adulthood compared to those they experienced in infancy.[71] The results of their research confirmed what many in the psychological community had long suspected: early-infant/childhood attachment provides the basis for romantic relationships in adulthood. It's not a hard-and-fast rule, and typically, if you had affectionate, supportive, and loving bonds in infancy, you are more likely to report having affectionate, supportive, and loving bonds in adulthood; if you had distant, erratic, or abusive relationships in childhood, there's a good chance you will seek out the same kind of bonds in adulthood.

Dr. Patrick Carnes, the author of *The Betrayal Bond: Breaking Free of Exploitive Relationships*,[72] continued this research by coining the term *traumatic bonding* to describe the relationship between two people with insecure attachment. This is a problematic bond that is reinforced by neurochemical expressions of reward (love) and punishment (removal of love). Dr. Carnes focused on the more extreme cases of traumatic bonding—those seen in domestic violence, incest, child abuse, and even "Stockholm syndrome" cases of kidnappings, cults, and hostage takings. In his definition, we enter into a traumatic bond when we seek comfort from the source of our trauma—in this case, the person who is abusing or hurting us. When the source of our trauma is the person we are dependent on, we learn how to cope (in this case receive love) by enmeshing ourselves in that bond. Dr. Carnes described this phenomenon as the "misuse of fear, excitement, sexual feelings, and sexual physiology to entangle another person."[73]

In my more expanded definition, a trauma bond is a relationship pattern that keeps you stuck in dynamics that do not support the expression of your authentic Self. Trauma bonds are often learned and conditioned in childhood, and then repeated in adult relationships (peer, familial, romantic, professional). They are relationship patterns that are based on our earliest, often unmet, needs.

Trauma bonds are not exclusive to romantic relationships, though that is often where they are most obvious. Almost all of us participate in trauma bonds, and it is highly likely your very unique needs —physical, emotional, spiritual—were not always consistently met.

While not exhaustive, common signs you'll witness in a trauma bond include:

1. *You have an obsessive, compulsive pull toward particular relationships even though you know the relationship will likely have problematic long-term consequences.* Often we confuse the intense emotions associated with a trauma bond for love. This plays out in a push-pull dynamic, in which the emotions of fear and abandonment appear to be exciting "chemistry." The flip side of this dynamic can result in boredom, when a "safe" relationship loses the thrill of the threat of loss. Excitement is a powerful motivator that keeps many people coming back.
2. *Your needs are rarely met in particular relationships, or you are unaware of what your needs are in any relationship.* All children have physical and emotional needs. Through our primary parent-figures, we learn how to get those needs met. Your parent-figures may have been unable to meet your needs because they were unable to meet their own. This will leave you similarly unable to meet your own needs in adulthood. This can look like not being able to ask for things or say "no" out of fear or shame. As a result of a lifetime of unmet needs, you may consistently feel resentful, unfulfilled, or needy.

3. *You continue to betray yourself in particular relationships to get your needs met and have a related lack of Self-trust.* When you don't trust yourself, you outsource your worth to others. When you outsource your worth, you become chronically dependent on other people's perceptions of who you are. Rather than making decisions or choices based on your own inner knowing, you make them through someone else's perspective, allowing another person to validate or invalidate your reality. This becomes a vicious cycle that leaves you feeling constantly destabilized—some people describe it as feeling "crazy"—and continues your disconnection from the inner guidance of your authentic Self.

Trauma bonds are the results of relationship dynamics that are rooted in stories about our self, created in childhood and manifested in our adult relationships. They are extensions of how we adapted (or coped) in the absence of having an intrinsic need met. Ego protection stories (such as mine of *not being considered*) were early-life adaptive measures to soothe difficult emotions and cope with trauma. Those coping strategies helped us survive issues with our primary attachment figures, so we held on to them tightly as we entered adulthood and faced perceived "threats" in other bonds. We use them to maintain an armor of self-protection so that our inner child wounds can never be opened again.

The unconscious pull toward these patterns is so strong that we will do almost anything to preserve a relationship founded on a trauma bond—often engaging in acts of self-betrayal in order to receive love. It is the same betrayal we learned in childhood when we were told that certain parts of us were "bad" or unworthy of love, so we repressed or ignored those aspects of our authentic Self. The goal is always to receive love, because bonds equal survival. Love equals life.

## SHAME, ADDICTION, AND TRAUMA BONDS

For people who have experienced trauma, it's easy to confuse the feeling of mental and physical activation for authentic connection. When stress responses are identified as our homeostatic "home" by the subconscious, we may confuse signals of threat and stress for sexual attraction and chemistry. Eventually, we develop an emotional addiction to this heightened state that keeps us stuck in cycles in which we end up in the same relationship dynamics as always—with the same or different partners. This traumatic bonding is an addiction, as real and consuming as any other addiction, that takes us on a similar biochemical roller coaster.

For many of us, our particular cycle of closeness and rejection began in infancy as part of our earliest relationships, so we are compelled to find adult relationships that mirror that conditioned cycle. In childhood, this can look like a parent-figure who was inconsistent in expressing love, showing attention at one moment and complete lack of interest at another. We crave love, so our child brains learn how to adapt. If our parent-figures gave us attention when we misbehaved (even negative attention) we may have purposefully acted out in order to receive more attention. This may not seem as though we're getting our needs met, though we're receiving attention and being seen, core needs in childhood. Our childhood attempts to have our physical, emotional, and spiritual needs met by our parent-figures (however incomplete, impersonal, or even selfbetraying they may be) form the basis of how we meet those same needs in our adult relationships. We gravitate toward familiar dynamics regardless of the outcome.

It's no wonder, then, that children born into environments filled with stress and chaos will seek similar environments as adults. When we exist in a state of fear (of physical harm, sexual abuse, or abandonment) our body is altered on molecular, neurochemical, and physiological levels. The feeling we get from the release of stress hormones and our nervous system response can become addictive if we were conditioned to associate them with the experience of "love." This becomes homeostasis right down to the firing and wiring of our neural pathways in our brain. We are always subconsciously seeking to relive our past because we are creatures of comfort, who love to be able to predict the future, even if that future is certain to be painful, miserable, or even terrifying. It's safer than the unknown.

Sexual chemistry has powerful physiological effects, too. When a romantic relationship is built on extreme highs and lows, it often has corresponding sexual highs and lows that can make us feel extremely *alive*. The hormones released during sex are potent: oxytocin increases the feeling of bonding and acts as a pain reliever, momentarily numbing whatever emotional and physical hurt exists, dopamine improves our mood, and estrogens give women an overall boost. It's no wonder we want more of that rush—especially when it's intertwined with the conditioned dynamics of our childhood. It can be incredibly hard to keep your head above water when the waves are so powerful .

This is why issues often emerge after the sex-infused honeymoon period in the early phases of our romantic relationships. Once we progress past that stage, we often complain of boredom or begin to create our own stress by hyperfocusing on what we perceive to be our partner's faults. When we are conditioned to associate love with a trauma response, we feel dull and numb without it. I've lived this cycle. If there was peace in my relationships, if there wasn't some impending crisis, I'd feel irritated and restless, and I'd make sure to initiate some stress. Addicted to my past, I made it my future. Then I'd feel ashamed for making the same mistakes over and over again.

The shame emerges from the feeling that we should know better—and yet our illogical and ever powerful subconscious keeps us from taking the "better," more rational path. I've worked with so many clients who've found themselves stuck in the attraction/shame cycle that is inherent in trauma bonds. We are often aware that we have this history and are engaging in these patterns; this is typically not lost on us. The red flags are almost always apparent. Even when they're not, many of us have friends and family members who see them and kindly (and sometimes not so kindly) well intentionally try to warn us about them.

When we are engaged in trauma bonding, we are not reacting from our rational mind; we are pulled in by the subconscious wounds of our past, living in autopilot patterns that are rooted in the familiar. As long as you are unaware of these conditioned patterns, even if you do find the "perfect" (whatever that means for you) partner with zero red flags, you'll still feel as though the relationship is missing something essential. There will be no *connection* because you're still trapped in the trauma bond state and no amount of good sense can knock you out of it.

I share all of this to help you understand that trauma bonds are not something to feel ashamed of. There is a cascade of physiological responses running through your body, working to keep you in the exact place you are in. The advice "Just leave" or "You should know better" is not helpful and does not come from a space of understanding the dynamics of trauma. Trauma bonding is a process that has to be unlearned. It takes time and dedication; it takes work.

## TRAUMA BOND ARCHETYPES

As with every other possibility for growth in this book, the first step in breaking trauma bond patterns is witnessing them. We're now going to revisit the childhood traumas I introduced in chapter 3 from the perspective of their effects on our adult relationships. Keep in mind that this is not a neat checklist. Many people identify with several of these archetypes; a few don't see themselves in them at all. Our trauma reactions might not match up neatly with this list; nothing in life ever does. The goal here is to give yourself the permission to go back and ask yourself: *What happened way back when, how did it hurt me, and how do I now cope in my relationships?*

**Having a parent who denies your reality.** Anytime a child was told that what they were thinking, feeling, or experiencing was not valid, a void is created in the Self. Those of us with this wound often continue to deny our own reality to maintain harmony. Such a person doesn't acknowledge their own needs or may be pathologically easygoing. These people can be martyrs, the ones who act selflessly to their own detriment. They are typically conflict avoidant and follow the mantra "If you're okay, I'm okay." Those with reality-denying wounds can even be confused about their own reality, having been disconnected from and distrustful of their intuition for so long. They continue to outsource their decisions and needs to everyone around them. As their needs persist and resentment grows, those of us with these wounds end up holding everyone around us responsible for our choices.

**Having a parent who does not see or hear you.** Those who felt that their parent-figures ignored or neglected their core need of being seen and heard learn early that they must quiet their true nature in order to receive love. We see a similar reaction in those who lived in a family whose members were emotionally immature (i.e., often employing "icing" or the "silent treatment" as punishment). Love is often either scarce or unconditional in such an environment that people in them almost entirely eliminate their wants and needs to make sure they receive anything they can. There is often behavioral modeling happening, too. Those who were iced often ice other people when they're threatened. This wounding can also manifest itself in picking "big-personality" partners. A client I worked with often found herself attracted to powerful, high-achieving partners who would literally "suck all the air out" of any room they entered. Such people have a core wound—*I am not seen or heard*—and so they pick a partner who keeps them in this state of living out the expression of the core wound, once again pulling them toward the familiar state of smallness or invisibility. Playing this part, however, activates all the uncomfortable emotions associated with not being seen or heard. Every time this woman picked a big personality, the relationship inevitably failed when she started resenting her partner for the very reasons she had felt connected in the first place.

**Having a parent who vicariously lives through you or molds and shapes you.** When our parent-figures directly or indirectly express preferences about our beliefs, wants, and needs, it creates a lack of space for our authentic Self-expression. This can manifest itself in a variety of ways and often results in reliance on external guidance—from partners, friends, even mentor types—for input into or feedback on all of life's big and small decisions. These are the people who always need to talk things out—sometimes multiple times with multiple people—in order to figure out how they "feel." Because they have always been told what they feel, think, or should be, they have no connection to an intuitive guidance. Often, this leads to their constantly seeking a guru or guide or constantly "drinking the Kool-Aid" of new ideas or groups.

**Having a parent who does not model boundaries.** As children, we intuitively understood boundaries even though many of us were raised in homes where our parent-figures didn't have clear limits themselves. Some of our parent-figures unconsciously crossed our boundaries by telling us to do things we didn't feel comfortable with for the sake of being "polite" or "good." Those experiences overrode our intuition and innate limits, causing us to question our inner messages. In adulthood, we may find ourselves overriding our own needs in relationships and consistently allowing our limits to be crossed. Over time this denial of need can morph into anger or resentment—a concept known as contempt and shown in extensive studies by renowned couples therapist Dr. John Gottman[74] to be a known relationship killer. We feel resentment and wonder "Why do people take advantage of me?" or "Why don't people appreciate me?" which is a normal response to boundary violations. What we don't understand is that this behavior is related to our lifetime lack of setting boundaries or limits to the time, energy, and emotional resources we expend on others.

**Having a parent who is overly focused on appearance.** Many of us received both direct and indirect messages about appearance by parent-figures who focused on the way we looked physically (our weight, our hair style, our clothing) or even how the family unit was perceived by others within the community. As adults, we can develop a habit of comparing ourselves to others to see if we measure up on superficial levels, not understanding that emotional wellness goes far deeper than surface appearance. This reliance on external appearance leads us to be overly focused on the image of ourselves that we present externally. We may even deny or intentionally hide painful or difficult issues we are experiencing in order to maintain the appearance of being "perfect." Social media, which enables us to post pretty photos and captions, can exacerbate this, even though many of us are suffering deeply behind the facade.

**Having a parent who cannot regulate their emotions.** When we see our parent-figures coping with their emotions by exploding or withdrawing, we are left feeling emotionally overwhelmed. By adulthood, we lack adaptive emotional coping skills and overall emotional resilience. Many of us model the same emotional reactivity or inhibition that was expressed by our parent-figures. Some of us may find our emotions exploding out of us as we yell at others or storm around the house slamming doors. Others may deal with their big emotions by detaching. This might look like someone who is avoidant or conflict averse. On the more extreme end, these are the people who engage in dissociation. Some use external aids to create that state, numbing themselves with drugs and alcohol, distracting themselves with social media, sedating themselves with food. The bond itself may even be the numbing agent, and when we are preoccupied with a relationship, we don't have to ask ourselves if something deeper is making us unhappy.

With these general archetypes in mind, pay attention to how your body feels around the people in your life. Our relationships are a guidance system that enables us to determine the state of our mental wellness. Take a moment to write down the names of some of the people you have the closest relationships with. Underneath the names, write down how you feel most often when interacting with them. Do you feel tense, anxious? Or do you feel free, safe? This will begin to give you an awareness of some of the relationship patterns you learned through your experiences in childhood.

## THE TRAUMA BOND TRAP

More often than not, each individual in a relationship is dealing with the aftereffects of their unique childhood traumas while, at the same time, both are trying to live, love, and thrive together. No one ever said this relationship stuff was easy.

One of my clients, a practicing therapist, came to me for help with her seesawing interplay with her husband. As with any trauma bond, there are aspects of their bond that are highly unique and others that are more generalizable. Joshua and Shira's relationship shows how the personal can often be universal.

Joshua and Shira are active members of the Orthodox Jewish community. Family, ritual, and tradition are essential to both of them. Other than these shared values, the two could not have been cut from more different cloth. Shira's parent-figures both had special needs and were largely unable to care for her, leaving that responsibility to members of the extended family—namely, grandmothers and aunts. It was never hidden from Shira that her parent-figures had special needs and on the deepest level she longed for a bond they were unable to provide. That emotional abandonment left her feeling perpetually unloved. To cope, she became a people pleaser, always seeking out external validation that she was worthy of love.

Joshua, by contrast, came from a family with eight brothers and sisters. His mother struggled to regulate her emotions and was very egocentric. Her needs came before any of her children's, and as the oldest boy, Joshua believed that he had to keep his mother stable to survive. The best way to do that, he learned over time, was to remain quiet and smother his own emotional world. As you have probably already guessed, that resulted in dissociation. His family environment, combined with the cultural messages that men should not be emotional, pushed Joshua to find his "love" in the outside world through achievement and success. He studied medicine, was accepted to one of the best medical schools in the country, and eventually became a surgeon.

When Shira came to me, Joshua had been experiencing physical pains that left him feeling fragile and frustrated and at times made his work as a physician incredibly difficult. The physical pain exacerbated all the issues that had been ongoing in the relationship since its inception. He was unemotional, keeping himself at a distance during times of stress and conflict, which opened up Shira's abandonment wounds, making her feel desperate, fearful, and needy. When Joshua came home after a hard day, feeling depleted, he would detach and shut down. Sensing a lack of connection, Shira would act out.

"What's wrong? Are you mad at me?" The chase for affection would begin.

Then it would grow into accusations: "You don't love me! You're having an affair!"

Panic-stricken and deeply alone, Shira would physically *chase* Joshua, calling him fifty times in a row, showing up at his practice, confronting family members about his behavior. The only way she felt she could truly feel safe was to reduce the perceived space between them.

As an attempt to regain safety for himself, Joshua withheld his emotions even further, feeling Shira's attempts for closeness as threatening, similar to how he felt when his mother's emotions overtook his own. Shira and Joshua's relationship is a classic example of approach/withdrawal patterning: as he withholds his love, she feels abandoned and understandably deeply hurt, and begins to move closer to him in order to regain her own felt emotional safety. The closer she comes, the more he pulls away, the greater her anxiety grows. Neither partner's needs are being met, and each partner grows upset with the other. This is the essence of the trauma bond dynamic. When needs are consistently unmet, resentment soon follows. Resentment is a relationship killer.

## AUTHENTIC LOVE

Just because you are participating in trauma bonds, it doesn't mean that your relationship is doomed—far from it. Trauma bonds are teachers, outlining the relationship patterns we've always carried and the areas that we can begin to work on changing. Luckily, there is nothing determined about these patterns. Like everything else we've learned so far, once you are aware of them, the process of change can begin.

I wouldn't say that Joshua and Shira have fully healed their trauma bonds, though I will say that they both agreed to do the work on both themselves and their relationship accepting the role that their childhoods have had on it. When the push-pull trauma bond trap emerges, Shira has learned ways to compassionately cope with her understandable emotional reactivity and engaging in breathwork and meditation to try to separate herself from her instinctual urges to react. Meanwhile, Joshua has learned to express himself when he starts to emotionally detach, beginning to tell his wife "I'm feeling myself pull away" or "I'm feeling overwhelmed by this situation." It might not sound like a lot to an outsider, and for Shira, just hearing her partner verbalize the experience of his inner world helped her feel more emotionally connected, deactivating her nervous system from the understandable threat of abandonment. When she hears him express himself, she gets the connection she craves, allowing her to then feel just safe enough to practice giving him the space he needs emotionally.

Lolly and I also started out in a trauma bond. We connected in the aftermath of my divorce after I had finally decided I was ready to date casually again. I was instantly drawn to her self-confidence. She seemed extremely self-assured, and that energy was intensely attractive.

Even the most secure-appearing people have wounds. Lolly has her own history of trauma, as she dealt with a heightened emotional childhood environment, like Joshua did. To cope, she assumed avoidant attachment, which attaches a lot of fear to romantic bonds—

essentially *I'm scared you'll leave me; I'm scared you'll stay*. One day she would be engaged and passionate; the next day, when conflict arose, she'd flee. Of course, that activated the hell out of me emotionally, and it also kept me bound to her, as the roller coaster of our early relationship so closely mirrored the stress and chaos of my childhood. When things were bad, I would feel all those emotions storm through me and ride the wave of anxiety until things were good again, at which point I was waiting for the other shoe to drop. Before either of us knew it, wc began to collude in various ways to make sure things went south. It was a stress train we were both addicted to. Neither of us aware of our dynamics.

Lolly always wanted to be an agent of change. She never wanted to stagnate and believed that relationships should constantly evolve in order to thrive. She wanted to grow and expand, as opposed to being comfortable with the status quo. I had been looking to grow myself, learning from my newly gained awareness about my past relationship patterns.

Meeting Lolly coincided with a period in my life when, now living in my home city of Philly, I was spending more time with my family. Given the frequency with which I was seeing them, many of the patterns of the past were coming to the surface—whether or not I wanted to actively admit it. Once Lolly began to spend more time with all of us, she gently began to share her observations. She noticed that in the lead-up to seeing my family, I would grow anxious and withdrawn, and then afterward, I would remain in a heightened emotional state, ready to fight, and remain on edge for days. That would put her on edge, too, as I discharged my emotional energy onto her.

I didn't see it at first. In fact, I was actively hostile to these observations in the beginning. Over time, with a deeper awareness and access to self-truth, I began to see all those now-obvious conditioned responses. She helped me see the light. Instead of pushing me away or punishing me, she became an instigator of positive change.

Our desire for growth extended out further as we dove deeper into *the work*. We both committed to showing up every day and doing *the work* together. We went to bed earlier. We worked out. We did our morning routines. We journaled. We changed our nutrition and detoxed our chemical-ridden bodies. In the beginning, all of that awareness and change was emotional. We would sometimes lie on the floor and cry—it was that overwhelming. It was overwhelming together. Our togetherness made the healing journey all the more transformative. Even on days when I really did not want to, I *chose* to show up because *she* was. Over time, I began to show because I wanted to for *myself*.

For a relationship to thrive, it can't be used as a means to fill the voids or wounds caused by a parent-figure. A healthy relationship provides space for mutual evolution. This is the essence of authentic love, when two people allow each other the freedom and support to be fully seen, heard, and Self expressed. Authentic love doesn't feel like an emotional roller coaster; it feels like peace and an inner knowing that you are both choosing to show up from a place of mutual respect and admiration. Authentic love feels safe. It's rooted in the awareness that the other person is not property, not something to be owned, and that your partner is not your parent-figure, not someone who can fix or heal you.

This is not the "rom-com" depiction of love. Authentic love doesn't always feel "good" or even romantic. The cycles of emotional addiction that we commonly associate with romance aren't activated, so it doesn't have the charge of excitement born of fear of abandonment or withdrawal of love and support. It is a grounded state. You do not need to perform in a certain way or hide parts of yourself to receive love. You will still feel bored or unsettled. You will still find yourself attracted to other people and may even mourn the loss of the single life. Conscious relationships aren't fairy tales. There's no "You complete me." There's no smile and *poof!*—living happily ever after. Like everything else you have encountered so far, authentic love requires *work*. The path forward is to become aware of the role of self-betrayal in your trauma bonds and the role that you can play in honoring your own needs.

## DO THE WORK: IDENTIFY YOUR TRAUMA BONDS

To gain an awareness of how your childhood wounds or suppressed feelings continue to affect you and your relationships in adulthood, take some time reflecting and writing using the following prompts for all that apply. Remember to look back to the journaling exercise you completed in chapter 3, taking note of the childhood wounds you experienced.

### HAVING A PARENT-FIGURE WHO DENIES YOUR REALITY

Reflect upon and write about how you react when you perceive someone denying your thoughts, feelings, or experiences. Spend some time witnessing yourself and exploring what kinds of experiences activate these feelings, and note your reactions. Use this journal prompt:

Today when [insert an experience in which you feel your reality is denied], I feel ________________ and I react by ________________.

### HAVING A PARENT-FIGURE WHO DOES NOT SEE OR HEAR YOU

Witness the experiences that continue to result in you feeling unacknowledged. Note the ways you attempt to be seen or heard in adulthood. For example, do you find yourself desperately trying to make others see or hear you, or do you have a deep underlying sense of being generally unacknowledged? Do you find yourself playing roles in your relationships in order to receive validation? Do you hide some thoughts, feelings, or parts of yourself that you feel others will not approve of? How do you react to feeling unacknowledged in adulthood? Use this journal prompt:

Today when [insert an experience in which you feel unseen and unheard], I feel ________________ and I react by ________________.

## HAVING A PARENT-FIGURE WHO VICARIOUSLY LIVES THROUGH YOU OR MOLDS AND SHAPES YOU

Witness the moments, relationships, or experiences in which you find yourself going through certain motions without a real passion or personal purpose behind them. Do you have feelings of shame, confusion, or lack of fulfillment? These often reflect living outside our true nature and purpose. Spend some time noting the different ways you continue to make choices based on external factors, such as the expressed wishes of others, received accolades, or imagined fears (e.g., *They'll stop loving me if I change*).

Notice how you continue to receive, rely on, and change based on messages you receive from others about who you are (or aren't). Note the many ways you continue to express only the parts of yourself you deem acceptable as well as repress the parts of yourself you deem unacceptable based on these messages. Don't worry if you are not yet sure of who you actually are, as many of us don't know because from a young age we've been told who we are.

Use these journal prompts:

Today I continue to make daily choices based more on external factors/live for others in the following ways: ____________

Today I continue to receive the following messages that shape my current behaviors: ____________

## HAVING A PARENT-FIGURE WHO DOES NOT MODEL BOUNDARIES

Spend some time witnessing—not judging or critiquing—yourself in relationships with others (friends, family, romantic partners). The following journal prompts will enable you to gain awareness of your boundaries in those relationships. You might not have any boundaries at all, I know at one time I didn't. As we become more aware, we can make new choices about the boundaries we have and how we respond to the boundaries of other people. Remember, this is a *practice*; it will take time to become comfortable with and confident in speaking your limits.

Do you feel free to say "no," or do you have guilt about or fear of doing so? __________

Do you feel free to declare your limits and your true feelings about situations? __________

Do you unconsciously attempt to force people to take on your viewpoints or opinions? __________

### HAVING A PARENT-FIGURE WHO IS OVERLY FOCUSED ON APPEARANCE

Spend some time witnessing—again, not judging or critiquing—your relationship with your physical appearance. How you feel about yourself physically is reflected in your relationship with both yourself and others. Most of your narratives about your physical appearance are unconscious, so becoming aware of them will enable you to understand your current narratives and create new ones. As you go through these prompts, remember to be kind and compassionate with yourself. You are not judging here. Your goal is to stay objective and curious.

How do I speak to myself about my body?

______________________

How do I speak to my friends about my body?

____________________

How often do I compare myself to other people physically?

___________

How do I speak about other people's physical appearance?

____________

**HAVING A PARENT-FIGURE WHO CANNOT REGULATE THEIR EMOTIONS**

Spend some time witnessing how you regulate your own emotions now in adulthood. Witness the ways you see yourself experiencing and coping with your emotions. Specifically, spend some time noticing the many ways you continue to deny certain emotions in your daily life or generally in many areas of your life. Do you always attempt to be positive or the life of the party? Do you feel unable to communicate what you're feeling to friends and partners? Do you hide some emotions and fully express others? Reflect using the following journal prompts:

When you have a strong emotional experience, how do you respond? __________

Do you have a coping strategy when you feel stress from your emotions? What is it? _____________

When you have a strong emotional experience, how do you communicate with those around you? _____________

After having a strong emotional experience, do you practice self-care, or do you find yourself shaming yourself for your responses?

______________

Today I continue to deny my emotions in the following ways:

_____________

# 10

# Boundaries

My client Susan was raised in a "typical" middle-class home where the mantra was "Family is everything"—similar to my own. Early on her healing journey, Susan idealized her family, overcompensating by speaking only about the wide support and love her parents provided. As far as her own struggles with feeling lost and unfulfilled went, she would say, "I don't know why I'm like this. I had everything I ever wanted." Her parents had a stable marriage. They showed up to every school event. They both showered her with affection.

Susan particularly idealized her mother, engaging in patterns of near hero worship. When she first heard about inner child work she dismissed it, calling it "woo-woo nonsense." Susan's fear of her own traumas resulted in an overcompensated admiration with no room for anything even remotely uncomfortable when discussing her past. As she continued to witness herself more honestly, a more critical portrait emerged. Her mother could often be overbearing and controlling. There was a lot of unconscious molding and shaping going on in her childhood, and her mother wanted Susan to live the life that she herself could never have. The dynamic seemed to intensify once Susan left the codependent nest. Her mother called several times a day, using guilt as a weapon if Susan did not pick up or return her calls fast enough to satisfy her.

What really bothered Susan was how often her mother arrived at her home unannounced; she would just show up and expect Susan to drop everything for her. That made Susan feel desperately angry and sparked memories of her childhood, when her mother would barge into her room and read her diaries. Yet Susan never complained—not even when that more obvious transgression occurred. Susan, who fit the inner child archetype of the caretaker, always tried to appease her mother. She took on the maternal role in life, offering all others the patience and boundless love that had not been present in her own mother/child dynamic.

Interestingly, Susan began her healing journey after years of feeling desperately unable to connect with others. She often thought of and described herself as a "doormat" for her friends. She was a mere sounding board for all of the stresses and issues of those around her (something I refer to as emotional dumping, which we will talk about later in this chapter). One friend in particular took advantage of her compliance and patience by calling her during every perceived catastrophe in her romantic relationship, which was especially chaotic. This friend had no qualms about calling in the middle of the night to vent. Even though Susan thought that was inappropriate, she always picked up. The mere idea of rejecting her friend's phone call made her feel physically ill and filled her with a sense of guilt and shame. *Her friend needed her.*

Susan was always the "good friend," "the nice one," "the one who is always there." That was her narrative, and she stuck to it. She kept picking up the phone. She kept lending her time and emotional resources to others who did not reciprocate. She kept showing up to her draining relationships, all along feeling that the interactions were one-sided, unfair, even shallow. *Did any of her friends truly know anything about her?* She felt invisible. She often cried during our sessions. "Will I ever find someone who truly cares about me?" she asked.

Over time, as Susan's relationship with her mother continued to cause her stress, she became aware that her mother made her feel unsafe. She didn't feel free to express her real feelings, as she consistently ignored her own desires so she could instead cater to her mother's wishes. She didn't *want* to visit her mother as often as she did, yet she did so out of guilt, shame, and fear, just as she always picked up the phone when her neediest friends called. She found her identity in pleasing others, and since she had no boundaries in place to protect her, she became so *in service to others*, that she lost all connection with her authentic Self.

## ENMESHMENT

When many of us are introduced to the idea of boundaries it is often a startling revelation. Boundaries, the clear limits that separate you (your thoughts, beliefs, needs, emotions, and physical and emotional spaces) from others, are necessary in order for you to be able to develop and maintain authentic relationships. The ability to set clear limits and keep them over time is critical to our overall wellness.

A lack of boundaries in childhood often manifests itself as a similar difficulty setting boundaries in adulthood. If we didn't have the space to express our separateness—separate emotions, separate opinions, separate realities—in childhood, or if we were engaged in family "groupthink" (*We do this, not that. We don't like those people. We are this kind of family.*), we often weren't given the chance to express our authentic Selves. Some parent-figures, as a result of their own lived experiences and related emotional wounding, unconsciously view their child as a means to get their own needs met (this may involve confiding in the child or treating the child as a "best friend").

In this dynamic, emotional lines blur because no one in the family has the space to develop autonomy or express their authentic Self fully. This is called enmeshment. In the enmeshed state, there is a complete lack of separateness. Parent-figures are overly invested in their children's lives; emotional activation spread across the whole family; spending time away from other family members is actively discouraged or even punished. Though there may be almost constant contact (mostly because being out of contact brings out fear and emotional reactivity in everyone). The parent-figures fear not being able to control the child, and the child fears being ostracized from the family unit. There isn't a true connection, a uniting of souls, because no one is truly ever fully themselves. Often those engaging in enmeshed patterns will feel a false sense of closeness and intimacy with their family unit. The sharing of heightened emotions bonds the group together, and the lack of boundaries enforces a shared reality. There is no authentic connection because true closeness, as you will come to find, involves mutual sharing with clear boundaries and the freedom for separate realities to exist at the same time.

As we saw with Susan, enmeshed childhood wounds shape the way we engage with others into adulthood (i.e., they are trauma bonds) as we follow external, not internal, guidance systems. Because we don't have a secure relationship with ourselves and have actively denied our own needs, we don't know what our needs are, let alone how to communicate them clearly. Instead, we look to others to draw our limits. Susan is a classic example of the enmeshed child grown up: she is a people pleaser, in many ways a martyr, who sacrifices her emotional, psychological, and spiritual well-being without asking for anything in return, because that was what was required of her to receive love in childhood. Over time, feelings of worthlessness, joylessness, and depression often emerge. Over time, as our core needs continue to be consistently unmet, we may grow angry and resentful. All of this is intertwined with the guilt and fear of abandonment, keeping us emotionally addicted and stuck in a vicious cycle.

True closeness, as we will find, involves mutual sharing together with the implementation of clear boundaries. Once we learn how to establish boundaries, there is space for us to be as we really are with others as they really are.

## AN INTRODUCTION TO BOUNDARIES

Boundaries embody every aspect of *the work* we've learned so far. I hate to identify one concept as "most important," though I truly hope that if anything sticks with you while reading this book, it's this chapter. Boundaries protect you. They keep you physically balanced. They help you connect to your intuitive Self and are critical to experiencing authentic love.

Boundaries provide a necessary foundation for every relationship you have—most importantly the one you have with yourself. They are the retaining walls that protect you from what feels inappropriate, unacceptable, inauthentic, or just plain not desired. When boundaries are in place, we feel safer to express our authentic wants and needs, we are better able to regulate our autonomic nervous system response (living more fully in that social engagement zone because we have established limits that cultivate safety), and we rid ourselves of the resentment that comes along with denying our essential needs. Boundaries are essential—and they're also scary as hell, especially if we come from an enmeshed family dynamic where boundaries were nonexistent or constantly trespassed upon.

Most of us have never learned how to say "no." As a result, we say "yes" to too much and fulfill too many demands until we hit a breaking point where we "put our foot down." Afterward, we often feel guilt and shame about our sudden about-face. So we apologize, wave away our own needs, or overexplain. If you see yourself in any of these practices, there is a high likelihood that you would benefit from some new boundaries in your life.

The first barrier to boundary work is the notion of "niceness"—a character trait that needs a reassessment. In his book *Not Nice: Stop People Pleasing, Staying Silent & Feeling Guilty . . . and Start Speaking Up, Saying No, Asking Boldly, and Unapologetically Being Yourself*, self-confidence expert Dr. Aziz Gazipura argued that niceness is based on the following inaccurate formula: "If I please others . . . then others will like me, love me, shower me with approval and everything else

I want."[75] He referred to this phenomenon as "the niceness cage"—wherein the compulsion to be valued locks us in a trap of our own making. The reality is that being "not nice" (i.e., being true to your authentic Self) enables us to assert our own value. It's not about being mean or arrogant or inconsiderate; it's about knowing what you want, what your limits are, and then communicating that. Learning to say "no" and not being so compliant all the time is an important part of reclaiming yourself. Learning to say "no" is often the kindest thing you can do for yourself and those you love.

Though many of us struggle with permeable or nonexistent boundaries, quite a few of us exist on the other extreme: we create too-rigid boundaries. We don't allow for any interconnectedness, walling ourselves off with moats of emotional withdrawal to stay separate from others. We uphold strict rules of conduct and behavior for those who do make it past the wall. If a boundary was repeatedly violated in childhood by a primary attachment figure, we may continue to feel unsafe in most other relationships. For some, the wall we build is a form of protection after living in an enmeshed childhood experience. When we withdraw out of self-preservation, we make free and spontaneous connections with other humans impossible, keeping us and others more controlled and therefore—or so we assume—safer. In doing so, we repress our intuitive voice and end up in the same lonely, inauthentic place as those who live with no boundaries at all.

Spend some time witnessing different aspects of your life and use this self-diagnostic tool to help you identify where your boundaries fall within the three categories "rigid," "loose," and "flexible."

### RIGID

- Has few intimate/close relationships
- Has a chronic fear of rejection
- Overall, has difficulty asking for help
- Is fiercely private

### LOOSE

- Engages in compulsive people pleasing
- Defines self-worth by the opinions of others
- Has a general inability to say "no"
- Consistently overshares private information
- Is a chronic fixer/helper/saver/rescuer

### FLEXIBLE

- Is aware of and values own thoughts, opinions, and beliefs
- Knows how to communicate needs to others
- Shares personal information appropriately
- Is consistently able to say "no" when needed and accepts others' doing the same
- Is able to regulate emotions, allowing others to express themselves

With all kinds of boundaries, it's key to understand this: the boundary is not for others, it's for *you*. It is not an ultimatum to make another person behave a certain way. An ultimatum is a statement that assigns a consequence to someone else's behavior as a means of trying to effect a change in it. A boundary, rather, is a personal limit that is expressed so that your need will directly be met. It is an action we take for ourselves regardless of how the other person reacts. That the other person may change in some way is a secondary gain. An important aspect of setting boundaries is allowing others to have their own limits and boundaries and respecting and honoring theirs while you maintain your own.

When our needs aren't being met or are being actively infringed upon, we cannot point a finger at another person and say, "*You* have to change." A better question to ask is: *What do I need to do to make sure that my needs are better met?*

## TYPES OF BOUNDARIES

Since boundaries apply to the wide array of the human experience—of body, mind, and soul—there is a need for different boundaries to reflect that range.

The first is a *physical boundary*. Loose physical boundaries can result in a hyperfocus on image—seeing your worth in how you look, what your body can do, how others view you sexually. On the other end of the spectrum, you can almost become bodiless—a floating mind without any connection to your body and wholly disconnected from your physical needs. If we have too-rigid physical boundaries in place, we may feel overwhelmed by our bodies and want to restrain or confine our sensations, denying our needs and sexual desires as acts of repression.

Honoring your body's wants and needs can look like outlining your personal space and describing your preferred level of physical contact. It can include setting boundaries around what you will and will not discuss (your comfort with verbal commentary on your body or sexuality, for example). It may also include the awareness and execution of your own self-care needs, such as your required number of hours for sleep, what you eat, how you move your body.

The second type of boundary is a *resource boundary*. When we are too free with our resources, we are always "on call," much as Susan was with her friends. Those with too few resource boundaries in place are endlessly giving and generous to a fault, which makes for unequal, draining exchanges with friends, partners, and family members. When we give and give, it's typically out of a belief that the more selfless we are, the more love we will receive, and that our time should be given away freely. This is not an accurate reflection of reality; time is one of the most precious of our resources. Yet most of the people I've encountered who struggle with resource boundaries can't say "no" when asked to devote time or energy to things they don't really care about.

There is also the flip side to this: those who have too-rigid boundaries around their resources. Having a rigid resource boundary around time can involve adhering to a predetermined schedule every day (going to the gym at a certain time is a common one) no matter what the external situation or their internal state may be. Even in the face of a family emergency, those with rigid resource boundaries will engage in their "scheduled" activity no matter how dire the circumstances around them are. I used to have this rigidness around planning; I would even painstakingly plan my TV consumption. Ultimately, a lack of flexibility around how we expend our resources can be confining and doesn't serve the varying needs of the authentic Self.

Then there is the *mental/emotional boundary*, one that is often crossed in families with enmeshment issues. When we have loose mental/emotional boundaries, there is often a feeling that we are responsible for the mental/emotional states around us and an internalized need to "save" others or keep everyone happy. It is impossible to always make another human happy, so this boundarylessness is often detrimental to our own resources and exhausting. Always meeting the needs of others is an unattainable goal and ultimately results in a neglect of our own needs.

In an enmeshed family, we also develop loose mental/emotional boundaries, which result in a tendency to engage in groupthink. This happens when there is a group conceptualization of our thoughts and beliefs, which is particularly salient in religious households, where it's "understood" that everyone will follow the same practices and beliefs. The message, both direct and indirect, received by all family members is one of conformity accompanied by a fear of being ostracized for noncompliance.

In those of us with too-rigid mental/emotional boundaries, there is often a complete lack of interest in anyone else's worldview. If we are stubborn and adamant about our own beliefs or emotions, we remain separate from the people around us, making true connection impossible. With our guard always up, there is no space for a meeting of minds or souls. We become an island. Such extreme rigidness is uncommon, I should add, but is seen in lesser degrees in small acts, like when we insist that we get exactly half of something even when we do not actually want the thing in any way.

Mental/emotional boundaries enable us to separate ourselves and our emotional world, while allowing others to have their own separate emotional world. With boundaries in place, we can more easily access our intuitive voice and better regulate our emotional states. In this place of emotional safety, we feel more comfortable sharing our thoughts, opinions, and beliefs with others. We don't feel compelled to please or agree with others all the time.

## EMOTIONAL DUMPING AND OVERSHARING

Emotional oversharing is an issue that comes up a lot in my SelfHealers community. Many of us were never allowed to keep things to ourselves, especially if we had intrusive and enmeshed parent-figures who modeled oversharing, demanded full disclosure, or shared an overwhelming amount of information when it was inappropriate at our developmental stage. I hear so many stories of "best friendship" in the mother/daughter dynamic that began with the sharing of inappropriate information at too young an age. Olivia, a SelfHealer who struggles with a compulsion to overshare, says that this dynamic with her mother started when she was only six and her mother told her about having sent a friend to remove her father from a strip club. It was too much information too soon. Her mother's boundarylessness shaped Olivia's boundary use with others, and she noticed she often found herself oversharing in times of stress or discomfort. She described herself as an "air filler" who would just talk and talk if she felt any discomfort in the other person. It was an automatic reaction, and sometimes she would say things that she would later regret.

It is beneficial for us to put up boundaries around our internal world. We then allow moments of quiet in conversations without rushing to fill the silence with our own stream of consciousness. There are things that we can decide to keep private. When we have proper boundaries in place, we have a choice about when and to whom we direct our emotional energy. Choice is pivotal; it's the understanding that your thoughts, feelings, and beliefs are your own and you can decide if you want to share them with everyone or with no one.

Another common outcome of mental/emotional and resource boundarylessness is emotional dumping, the spilling of emotional issues onto a person without being empathetic to *their* emotional state. I'm sure you can think of at least one person in your life who does this (maybe it's you). Some people call it "venting," though that's not accurate. Venting has positive associations; it revolves around one singular topic, helps with stress release, and is often geared toward a productive outcome. Emotional dumping, by contrast, involves the airing of negative, circular, and obsessive thoughts. People who are prone to emotional dumping are often caught in the loop of emotional addiction; their heightened emotional state reinforces the behavior, even when it is not reinforced by those around them. It is a human instinct and often emotionally helpful to share with others and reach out to others for help and guidance. Emotional dumping is not about reaching out for help; it is a repetitive and obsessive coping strategy that leaves no room for anyone else's needs, let alone guidance. Emotional dumping is a coping skill born of boundarylessness on both sides: the emotional dumper has loose mental/emotional boundaries, and the people on the receiving end (if they find themselves in this situation regularly) also don't have sufficient boundaries to end it.

Sometimes people emotionally dump in an attempt to escape an emotion that they don't believe they can bear alone. However, it can be harmful to unload negative emotional energy on another human. There can be times when emotional dumping feels like a punishment, as when someone consistently dumps doom and gloom even when learning good news about another person. Like when you tell a friend about a job promotion or a recent vacation and they immediately steer the conversation back to their problems at home or even your issues with your spouse. Though it may feel aggressive and even weaponized, it's not necessarily intentional. Often emotional dumpers feel comfortable, or in familiar homeostasis, only when discussing topics that allow themselves to feel depressed. When faced with the unfamiliar positive, they turn the conversation back to the more distressing baseline where their entire system feels at home.

Emotional dumping need not be one-sided. A relationship can be built around emotional dumping as the main form of connection. An example of mutual emotional dumping is when a relationship revolves around a central shared conflict. Two people might bond over their bitter divorces and share detail after detail of the horrible things about their partners, even if their marriages ended years before. The two people are locked in an emotionally addictive cycle of autonomic activation.

## HOW TO SET BOUNDARIES

The first step in using boundaries is to define them—to examine your life and notice where boundaries are lacking. If you don't have boundaries, it can be hard to decide where to set them. This is totally normal. Look at the people and events in your life. When you think about having brunch with a college friend, how do you feel? Does your chest tighten? Is there a feeling of resentment leading up to it? How about during the meeting? Do you feel expansive, spacious, and nourished, or do you feel depleted, constricted, and limited? How about afterward? Do you want to see her again soon, or are you already wondering how you can dodge her next call?

Boundaries keep us connected to our intuitive voice. (That tightness in your chest is a big clue!) It is important to tune in to how you feel to use boundaries. Remember we are not in the thinking mind when we're witnessing how we feel; instead, we are noticing how something or someone registers in our body.

Once you start noticing your bodily sensations, assess where your current boundaries are lacking. What do you need to shift or change to make you feel safe and secure in your relationships? This assessment is for *you*. If you come from patterns of enmeshment there will be a pull to imagine the effect on the other person (*How will Janet feel if I cancel our plans?*). The goal is to reclaim your own energy and ask what will make *you* feel happier, safer, and more comfortable. Spend a few days looking over your relationships, and identify and list your most commonly crossed boundaries. This will give you a road map of where to start setting your boundaries.

Here are a few examples of crossed boundaries by type:

**Physical:** Your mother makes jokes about other women's weight.

**Change needed:** You want her to stop.

**Mental/Emotional:** A friend often emotionally dumps about her ex-boyfriend.

**Change needed:** You want a more reciprocal relationship.

**Resource:** A coworker insists on taking his meal with you on every lunch break.

**Change needed:** You want some time alone.

Now that you've located the areas where boundaries would be helpful and what you'd like to accomplish with them, it's time to determine how to begin to practice setting them. Obviously, how you proceed will vary based on what you hope to accomplish, and the first step is communicating your boundary. When you communicate clearly, you set yourself (and your relationship) up for successful change.

Setting an intention for yourself gives you the space and opportunity to identify your "why": *I'm doing this because of x or y*, for example, *because I want the relationship to survive, because I care about our friendship.* While this does not need to be articulated to the other person it is helpful for it to be fully clear to you. If you would like to articulate your "why" to the other person, this may sound like "I really care about you, and I will have to make some changes in the way we communicate."

When you state your boundary, it is helpful to use objective language as much as possible. You want to focus on *facts*. "If a phone call occurs in the middle of the night while I'm sleeping, it will go unanswered." It's best to avoid "you" language as much as possible, as it can activate the defensiveness of the other person's ego. Try to be confident and respectful, as hard as this may be. Remind yourself you are doing nothing wrong. You are respecting yourself and your relationship. To help you get started, I've included an example of a boundary-setting template that can be adapted to fit your needs:

> "I am making some changes so that [*insert your intention for your new boundary*] and hope you can understand that this is important to me. I imagine [*insert your understanding of their behavior*]. When you [*insert problematic behavior*], I often feel [*insert your feelings*], and I understand that is something you may not be aware of. In the future, [*insert what you would or would not like to happen again*]. If [*insert original problematic behavior*] happens again, I will [*insert how you will respond differently to meet your own needs*]."

Keep in mind that timing is key. It is helpful to communicate a boundary at a time when both parties are as emotionally settled as possible. When we're activated, we're in no state to receive anything challenging. (Remember, even our middle ear muscles close off when our vagus nerve is fired up.) To the best of your ability, try to find a time that's as emotionally neutral as possible for both people to share your new boundary.

As you begin to think about creating new boundaries, it is helpful to focus on how you will continue to respond differently in the future, instead of becoming consumed with how the other person will feel. Many boundaries are erased before they're even articulated—we start envisioning how our boundaries will hurt others or how they will fire back and hurt us. We beat ourselves up. We tell ourselves that we're ungrateful or selfish, what I call the "feel-bads." Without doing the holistic work that comes beforehand—rebalancing our dysregulated nervous system, acknowledging the wounds of our inner child, and understanding our trauma bond patterns—these "feel-bads" can easily prevent us from taking concerted action that would ultimately help maintain and strengthen our bonds.

Sometimes it's not realistic to have an active conversation about the boundary, and you can communicate your new limit without having a preemptive conversation (this is especially relevant in less intimate relations, such as having lunch with a coworker). Here are some prompts to establish a boundary with a mere sentence:

"I wish I could; now isn't a good time."

"I'm not comfortable with that."

"This isn't doable for me."

"Wow, thanks for the offer/invite, though that isn't something I can do right now."

"I will have to get back to you on that."

For me, setting boundaries started professionally. It felt safer for me to say "no" via an email to a stranger than to my partner or family members. I started setting time boundaries around how much emotional energy I would expend on certain activities (such as scrolling through social media) or with certain people.

Especially if you are new to boundary setting, I suggest you start small. Practice on the periphery or in less stressful emotional entanglements, such as having lunch with a coworker. These are great places to begin to practice boundary setting. Because there's not as much history or baggage associated with more casual relationships, they're great places to flex your boundary-making muscles and get used to saying "no." The more you practice, the better you'll get. Over time you will learn that boundary setting will go one of two ways: the other person will be offended—or won't. Imagine all the worst-case scenarios. Are they really that bad? In action, trust me, they often aren't.

The discomfort we face while setting boundaries will save us years of anger and resentment. The relationship that emerges after a boundary is set might not look anything like the way it did before, and it will be stronger, more honest, and ultimately more sustainable. Boundaries are essential to all healthy relationships. Think of them as an act of service.

The third step may seem simple, though it's often the hardest one: maintain your new boundary. Once you've set a boundary, it's important to remain present and calm, resisting the urge to defend or overexplain yourself, regardless of the reaction you are receiving from the other person(s). You may feel stress as a result of someone's reaction, or the reaction from a greater unit (your family, work, etc.). It's very important that once you set a boundary, you keep it set.

When we begin to change how we show up in relationships, it is helpful to remember that the longer the relationship has existed, the more expectations have been enacted and solidified over time. It can be helpful to accept the fact that the other person's expectations of you will be disrupted, sometimes abruptly (from their perspective). On top of this, the receiver of a new boundary, especially one with abandonment wounds, will likely react defensively or even offensively.

Much of this maintenance involves quieting an inner voice (those "feel-bads") that sneaks up on us, telling us that *I have no right to set boundaries. I am being selfish or rude or mean.* As you set your boundary and keep it in place, you might encounter confusion, pushback, snarky remarks ("You've changed" is a common one), or even rage. At the same time, you'll likely feel fear, doubt, and a pull to return to the familiar (that pesky homeostatic impulse at work). Once you've decided to start honoring and keeping yourself and feel a bit safer, don't look back. There is no going back to old patterns if you truly need and want change. If you put up a boundary and take it down when someone freaks out, all you are doing is reinforcing that person's ability to walk all over your limits with their behavior. It's classic negative reinforcement: they'll continue that behavior anytime they're faced with opposition in your relationship. *If I scream and yell enough, everything will go back to normal.*

## EXPECTATION AND COMPASSION

The mother who expects you to listen to her gossip, the colleague who expects you to have lunch with them every day, the friend who expects you to pick up the phone when she wants to emotionally dump—all of these people will likely be disappointed, upset, or angry when their expectations (and their perceived needs) go unmet. That's okay.

Instead of expectation, what you've given them is a choice. They can choose to continue engaging in that behavior and be faced with a boundary (often the removal of your presence or support), or they can choose to respect your boundary and continue their relationship with you in a new way. This is what is empowering about setting boundaries: you are giving them a choice, too.

Remember, expectations run both ways. Often the internal work around boundaries involves navigating our own expectations and acknowledging what certain people are and aren't capable of. It's important to accept that many people will not change, at least not right away, and some might never change. It can sometimes be helpful to use your past experiences to form your expectations around another person's response to a boundary. If you have a mother who has historically been unapologetically intrusive, you might choose to engage in some level of compromise; it's likely that Mom is going to keep doing what she does. In this case, it can be helpful to determine your absolute limits, using them as no-compromise areas for yourself. You may also find it helpful to shift your internal expectation that others change more completely and become more flexible in response to their limitations, abilities, and level of consciousness. In a circumstance where flexibility is impossible for us, we may have to take ourselves completely out of the interaction or relationship, which means forming the most extreme kind of boundary: discontinuing contact.

As we begin to practice the tools of SelfHealing, gaining more understanding of our own repeated patterns, we similarly begin to see others from a bird's-eye view. When we do so, we often find that compassion emerges for other people in our relationships, even those with whom we may have chosen to cut contact. I'll return to the example above about the mother who often makes mean-spirited jokes about other women's weight. The fellow SelfHealer, Zoe, whose mother does this, believed for a very long time that it was meant to cut her down, as she has often struggled with her weight. After beginning her own healing journey, she took a step back when I asked her, "What is it about heavier women that makes your mom so reactive?"

A light bulb flashed behind Zoe's eyes. "The woman who my father left her for is a heavier person." A few moments passed. "My mom has a core abandonment wound that was activated by my father's infidelities. But the wound is truly the abandonment she felt as a child when her father died suddenly."

Aha! Suddenly those jokes weren't about cutting her daughter down; they were the expressions of a deeply wounded child dealing with the loss of a parent-figure. Even though Zoe still refused to participate in her mother's comments (she set a new boundary and ended any and all conversations when her mother started to discuss weight), she now felt sympathy for her mother and love for the inner child inside her who felt so unlovable, so worthless, that she needed to disparage others to feel better about herself. When we understand other people's limitations, when we see pain and fear where we once saw cruelty, this is healing.

## THE ULTIMATE BOUNDARY

Boundary work came into my life organically. It wasn't as if I decided *Now that I've worked on my body and mind, it's time to do "people work."*

Instead, as I started to explore my past and present selves, my need for self-protection became apparent.

I started the process on the periphery by witnessing my inner experiences around my friends and colleagues. *I don't really ever feel excited when this person texts me.* Or *I feel drained after I have lunch with that person.* I started to spend less and less time within several of those relationships. I noticed the effect of my boundarylessness on others. With one friend, I routinely emotionally dumped, just chewed her ear off about the latest drama or issue in my life. That uncomfortable awareness hit me in the face: I knew hardly as much about her as she knew about me. It didn't feel great to see myself as I truly was, yet it was instrumental in saving our relationship; today we continue to be friends, as I've actively worked on changing our interpersonal dynamic.

The unfolding of my boundary journey eventually led me to my enmeshed family unit. It took time, and I became ready to pose the question *Can I create a relationship structure that is healthy with my family?*

It started with food. In a big Italian family, meals are the primary source of bonding and an expression of love. There's guilt if you don't take a second helping and disapproving looks if you decline a particular meal when you're being careful about what you're putting into your body. As Lolly and I began to drastically change our nutrition, I decided to set a new boundary for myself around food and my family: I wouldn't eat anything I didn't want to eat. If there was pushback, I would remain steadfast. I wouldn't expect anyone else to change their habits or make special meals for me, and I would honor my new personal choice.

Then I began practicing time limit boundaries, using similar techniques from my professional life. I set a timer for myself on holidays: *I'll spend two hours with my family on Christmas Eve, and I won't go to Christmas Day dinner.* When my parents called to invite me, I made a conscious effort to take a minute or two before calling them back.

The texts and calls inevitably rolled in: "Are you okay? Are you okay?"

"I'm okay," I would respond. "I just need some space."

A couple of days later, the frantic calls and texts would start up again. In response, I set a boundary that I wouldn't call or text back until I actively wanted to. That was the start of separating myself from the enmeshment of my family by validating my own reality. I could have my own wants, needs, and desires, and they didn't have to match theirs.

I then negotiated a boundary with my sister, which was harder because I'm closest with her. Our boundary surrounded our interactions, which all revolved around my mother: her medication management, her doctor visits, her mental health. I decided to first put a limit on how available I was for doctor's appointments. Then I put a boundary into place on the phone—no more hour-long chats about Mom. None of those steps was easy. Delivering that new (and unexpected) message of "no" jolted my inner child, whose patterns and conditioning around enmeshment are so bound up with my core identity. The voices in my head gave me all the reasons why I should let that boundary go: *You're a bad daughter/sister/aunt.* I knew that I was working on preserving our relationship and without my intervention things would remain exactly as they were.

At that time, my family didn't see any need to change anything at all. I was told that I was selfish. My sister shrieked, "You can't do this to me!" My mother guilted me; my father reprimanded me. When I confided in my sister some of my realizations about how emotionally estranged I'd always felt from our mom, she shared those thoughts with the rest of the family, severing the bond of trust and connection between us. I stopped confiding in her about anything.

It got more and more difficult to remain committed to both my own healing and my family at the same time. I began asking myself *What is the cost to my own healing in managing these relationships?* Eventually, I came to the conclusion that the cost was too great. I was energetically drained, unfulfilled, and resentful. I decided to set the ultimate boundary: a complete separation. It was a decision for my inner child, showing her that, yes, I could take time and space away and could make choices that were good for me, even at the "expense" of others. For the first time ever, I authentically showed up for myself, while learning how to show up authentically for others, too.

That boundary—one born of extremely painful deliberation—completely reoriented my life. This would push me to find my community, a new family of sorts, and would also put me onto the path to finding my calling, my true spiritual path in life.

---

## DO THE WORK: CREATE A NEW BOUNDARY

**Step 1. Define the boundary.** Take a look at the following list of the different types of boundaries available to you in all of your relationships. Spend some time witnessing yourself in these different kinds of relationships. For example, many of us have friends, family members, colleagues, and/or romantic partners with whom we regularly interact. Exploring your relational patterns with them will help you get a good idea of the most consistent boundaries (or lack thereof) you see in each of these relationship types.

- **Physical boundaries:**
  - The amount of personal space, physical contact, etc., that is most comfortable for you and your preferred timing for physical contact
  - Your overall comfort with verbal comments on your appearance, sexuality, etc.
  - Your overall comfort with sharing your personal space (apartment, bedroom, office, etc.) with others (including friends, partners, colleagues, etc.), sharing personal digital passwords, etc.

- **Mental/emotional boundaries:**
  - Your overall comfort with sharing your personal thoughts, opinions, and beliefs with others without changing them to match those of another or insisting that others change to match yours
  - Your ability to choose which personal thoughts, opinions, and beliefs you share with others without feeling it necessary to overshare or attempting to insist that they overshare
- **Resource boundaries:**
  - Your ability to exercise choice around where and how your time is spent, avoiding any tendency toward people pleasing, etc. and to allow others to have a similar choice
  - Your ability to negate personal responsibility for others' emotions, avoiding the tendency to play the role of "fixer" or to make others responsible for your emotions
  - Your ability to limit the amount of time spent on venting problems on the part of either person

Take some time to identify your most commonly crossed boundaries in each of these areas. Not sure? That's okay; many of us have never heard of boundaries before, so it's hard to know if we are setting them at all. If this is you, you will want to take some time to explore your own boundaries (or lack thereof) in all areas of your life. You may tend to place and hold similar boundaries across most of your relationships, lacking certain boundary types entirely. Or you may find variations across different relationship types. You may be able to set boundaries around your time at work and with friends though not with romantic partners, becoming unable to say "no" consistently to a certain family member or romantic partner's requests for time or favors.

It will be helpful to begin to identify the changes you would like to see in this area. To help you do so, you may want to use the following prompts:

My physical self feels uncomfortable/unsafe when

__________________________.

To create space for my physical self to feel more comfortable/safe, I

__________________________.

Examples:

My physical self feels uncomfortable/unsafe when my coworker (uncle, friend, etc.) consistently makes jokes about my appearance.

To create space for my physical self to feel more comfortable/safe, I no longer want to be around people who make those types of jokes.

My mental/emotional self feels uncomfortable/unsafe when

__________________________.

To create space for my mental/emotional self to feel more comfortable/safe, I __________________________.

Examples:

My mental/emotional self feels uncomfortable/unsafe when my family member (friend, partner, etc.) constantly comments disapprovingly about my new health choices.

To create space for my mental/emotional self to feel more comfortable/safe, I no longer care to hear about, argue about, or defend my personal health choices.

My resources feel uncomfortable/unsafe when

__________________________.

To create space for my resources to feel more comfortable/safe, I

__________________________.

Examples:

My resources feel uncomfortable/unsafe when my friend calls me at all hours to emotionally dump about her relationship issues.

To create space for my resources to feel more comfortable/safe, I am no longer able to take calls at certain times and I will actively choose when I take part in emotional dumping.

**Step 2. Set boundary.** Communicating a new boundary takes practice. The more clearly you communicate your new boundary, the greater the likelihood of successful change.

Here is some helpful language you can begin to practice using to communicate your new boundary to others:

> "I am making some changes so that [*insert your intention for your new boundary*] and hope you can understand that this is important to me. I imagine [*insert your understanding of their behavior*]. When you [*insert the problematic behavior*], I often feel [*insert your feelings*], and I understand this is something you may not be aware of. In the future, [*insert what you would or would not like to happen again*]. If [*insert original problematic behavior*] happens again, I will [*insert how you will respond differently to meet your own need*]."

Examples:

> "I am making some changes so that we can maintain our relationship as I care about you and hope you can understand that this is important to me. I imagine you may be uncomfortable with my new food choices. When you consistently comment on what I am or am not eating, I often feel uncomfortable eating around you, and I understand this is something you may not be aware of. In the future, I would like to avoid talking about food or food choices altogether. If commenting on my food choices happens again, I will remove myself from our conversation or the activity we are engaging in."

"I am making some changes so that we can maintain our relationship as I care about you and hope you can understand that this is important to me. I imagine you may be unhappy in your relationship and want to be heard. When you consistently call me to vent, I often feel emotionally depleted, and I understand this is something you may not be aware of. In the future, I may not be able to always be available when you feel you want to vent. If calling me for each relationship issue you're having happens again, I will not always be able to support you at that exact time."

Feel free to use this prompt, filling in the blanks with details appropriate to your desired new boundary. You may find that this new language feels weird at first. That's totally normal. Remember, given our subconscious mind, most of us feel uncomfortable with unfamiliar things. Practice will help you gain comfort with this new communication style. This practice may involve rehearsing these scripts alone, which will help you gain confidence before you communicate them to others.

"I am making some changes so that [____________], and I hope you can understand that this is important to me. I imagine [____________]. When you [____________], I often feel [____________], and I understand this is something you may not be aware of. In the future, [____________]. If [____________] happens again, I will [____________]."

## TIPS

- Timing is important! Communication is best made at a time when neither party is emotionally reactive. *Trying to communicate a new boundary when you're in the middle of a conflict is not helpful. Find an emotionally neutral time.* Don't forget the deep belly breaths you learned in chapter 5; they can help calm any nervous system reaction you may be experiencing and will help bring your body back to calm.

- When communicating, try to focus on how *you* will begin to respond differently in the future instead of focusing on the other person's reaction or change.
- Communicate in as confident, assertive, and respectful a manner as possible. At first this may be difficult, because it's new (and scary for most of us), and practice will make it easier.
- Planning ahead and practicing are critical. Start out by communicating new boundaries in relationships where the stakes are low. This will help you gain experience for more difficult interactions.
- If applicable, be open to compromise. Remember you also want to work to honor others' boundaries so may find yourself open to modifying your initial request. Know what is and isn't negotiable for you. For example, you might be open to using your resources in supporting someone emotionally and might not be open to compromise around your physical boundaries, and that is okay.

**Step 3. Maintain the boundary.** Once you've communicated your new boundary, it is very important for you to hold it. What this means is *not going back to your older patterns*. For many of us, this is the hardest part—we're not sure we have a right to set boundaries. We may feel that it's selfish, rude, or mean to do so or find ourselves feeling bad about any reaction by the other person. For a lot of people who have core attachment wounds around abandonment (and many of us do!), your explanation of your new boundary may open those wounds. They may feel wounded and may even lash out in response. You may experience emotional reactivity, confusion, pushback, and/or snarky comments by others (*You've changed. Are you holier than thou now?*).

Or you may catch a case of the "feel-bads" (shame, guilt, selfishness), creating a strong impulse to go back to your old patterns. Remember, this is all a normal part of change.

Creating boundaries is some of the hardest work that you'll encounter on your healing journey. It's also probably one of the most important steps in reclaiming a connection to your authentic wants and needs, while honoring and respecting those you love. This is what *the work* is all about: making space to allow each of us to be seen, heard, and authentically expressed.

# 11

# Reparenting

Despite the popular perception, awakenings often aren't instantaneous. Though dramatic flashes of insight are the stuff of legends (and Hollywood), they are usually not reflective of real life. Though we may have an *aha!* moment that hits us like a lightning bolt, most awakenings emerge from an accumulation of insights over time.

Psychologist Dr. Steve Taylor studies the phenomenon he terms "awakenings"[76]—you can call them flashes of insight, realizations, or whatever else you like. After his own spiritual awakening sparked his research interest, he found that these experiences typically have three common elements: they often emerge from a state of inner turmoil; they often occur in a natural setting; and they often connect us to some kind of spiritual (in the most expansive sense of the word) practice. Awakenings open us to the reality that we are more than simple creations of flesh, that we have a soul or spirit, that we desire connection to something greater than our individual selves. Awakenings show us that who we *think* we are isn't necessarily who we *are*.

Often, we gain these insights through suffering, living through confusion and sorrow on our way to finally becoming conscious. An awakening is a rebirth of the Self that involves tearing down parts of who you were when you lived in an unconscious, autopilot state of existence. Even if we've primed our bodies in all the right ways, the jolt of opening our eyes to a whole new world is painful. Being conscious in an unconscious world is uncomfortable as hell. It's telling that brain scans have shown that during and after spiritual awakenings, the same neural pathways light up as are active in depression, which researchers called "two sides of the same coin."[77] The critical difference is that people who are engaged in consistent spiritual practices activate and even expand the size of their prefrontal cortex—the site of the conscious mind—while those who struggle with depression and negative thoughts decrease activity in the same area.

My awakening unfolded in phases. It occurred during a time of extreme physical and emotional stress when I was imbalanced in body, mind, and soul. It was a crisis of the Self. Life began to feel intolerable, old and new struggles compounding around me so that I had no choice but to address those that had gotten so far out of hand that they were my "normal." It's highly likely that if I had sought outside help again at this time, I would have been diagnosed with depression or anxiety, as I had been in the past. Instead I was intuitively drawn inward to self-witnessing that showed me how disengaged I had been. For the first time ever, I began to view these signs as messengers, not as something to repress or avoid.

I remember the time in my late twenties, years before I embarked on the journey of SelfHealing, when I complained to a friend about feeling pulled in two separate directions—by my wife at that time and by my family—about where I would spend my holidays. My friend looked at me and innocently asked, "Well, what do *you* want?"

I almost fell off my chair. *I had no idea what I wanted.*

Years later, during my self-imposed period of isolation after cutting ties with my family, removing myself from people and places that I no longer felt energetically served me, and generally becoming less available to others, feelings of disconnection began to haunt me again, though this time they did not come from my old habit of dissociating. I felt as though I had abandoned most everyone I had known from my past and imagined that some might now hate me. I was lonely, terribly lonely. I thought to myself *Will I ever find my people?*

I didn't know it at the time, but I was in the midst of a spiritual transformation. *A spiritual transformation!* Those words coming from the brain of a data-obsessed psychologist who considered herself at the very least an agnostic. My god was science. I shunned the idea of spirituality; it just wasn't part of my awareness at the time.

Before I could fully connect with others, I had to understand my own emotional, physical, and spiritual needs and, for the first time in my life, work on meeting them. It's a painful process—a shedding of old skin, becoming aware of yourself in a way you've never been before. You have to see yourself to love yourself—and you have to love yourself in order to give yourself what you weren't able to get from others.

## AN INTRODUCTION TO REPARENTING

Children's healthy development is dependent on their intrinsic needs being met. When we are in a state of dependence, we rely on our parent-figures and the family unit as a whole to provide us with physical, emotional, and spiritual nourishment. We deeply desire to be seen, heard, and authentically expressed (to simply just be us!). When we experience our parent-figures engage in supportive behaviors, we learn that it's safe to express our needs and reach out to other people for help. Most parent-figures never learned how to meet their own needs, let alone another person's, passing on their own unresolved traumas and conditioned coping strategies. Even well-intentioned parent-figures don't always give us what serves us. Meeting all of someone's varied and unique needs all the time is almost impossible.

That said, if we lived with an emotionally immature parent-figure, our needs were likely routinely unmet or dismissed. Emotional immaturity results from a lack of emotional resilience, the ability to process emotions, communicate boundaries, and return our nervous system to balance. An emotionally immature parent-figure may throw tantrums, acting selfishly or defensively, and often the whole family unit ends up revolving around their moods. Like psychotherapist

Lindsay Gibson wrote in one of my favorite books on the subject, *Adult Children of Emotionally Immature Parents: How to Heal from Distant, Rejecting, or Self-Involved Parents*, understanding your parent-figures' level of emotional maturity (or lack thereof) "frees us from emotional loneliness as we realize that their negativity wasn't about us, but about them."[78]

I've repeatedly observed the various outcomes of living with emotionally immature parent-figures—parent-figures who can't identify their own needs, who betray themselves to receive love and validation, who live in a state of resentment because they believe others should "just know" what they need. Their adult children often live from that protected and familiar space of their ego (with all of its stories) and often have an intense need to be "right," rejecting other people's opinions and making others feel just as small and insignificant as they once did. Others create avatars of themselves—always wearing a mask—fearful that they may scare people away if they show their true face. Some avoid any type of intimacy, and some cling to it desperately. The manifestations run the gamut, but the way we heal these wounds is to give ourselves all the things we didn't get as children. The way we move forward is to have the awareness that we can become the wise parent to ourselves that we did not have as a child. This is a process called reparenting, and it enables you to relearn how to meet the unmet needs of your inner child through daily, dedicated, and conscious action.

Concepts similar to reparenting have existed in the psychodynamic field for decades. They have emerged from the mainstream therapy model that a secure relationship with a therapist can provide a grounding for healthier relationships in life. Psychoanalysis is built upon this framework with the concept of transference, or the "transfer" of feelings from our childhood onto a therapist, being an integral part of the therapeutic process. Though it may be incredibly helpful to have that support—if we have the means, access, and privilege to do so, of course—no one can figure out and know your wants and needs and how to meet them better than you. No one but you can, and will have to, show up each and every day to take care of those ever-changing needs. These are efforts that must come from you, and in the process of harnessing your own power, you will create a deeper, more authentic connection to your Self.

It's our responsibility to teach ourselves the tools to meet our own needs. When we reparent, we begin by learning how to identify our physical, emotional, and spiritual needs and then we practice noticing the conditioned way we've gone about attempting to get those needs met. Many of us may find that in adulthood, we often embody the *critical* inner parent, denying our reality, rejecting our needs, and choosing the perceived needs of those around us over our own. Guilt and shame replace our intuitive voice.

The reparenting process looks different for everyone. Generally, we want to quiet our inner critic and embrace self-respect and compassion. With the help of the *wise* inner parent, you can learn how to validate your reality and feelings by witnessing them, rather than instinctually judging or ignoring them. Your wise inner parent cultivates acceptance while honoring the needs of your inner child—to be seen, heard, and valued for the authentic parts of yourself. *You* become the priority.

To develop your wise inner parent, you will want to learn how to trust yourself (maybe for the first time in your life). You can begin to rebuild this lost trust by setting small promises to yourself to engage in daily acts of self-care, and following through with those intentions. It will be helpful to begin a new habit of speaking kindly to yourself, as if you were dealing with a child in pain. Each day, you could begin to ask yourself the question *What can I do for myself in this moment?* The more you do this, the more it will become an automatic response to the world around you that will reconnect you to your intuition.

## THE FOUR PILLARS OF REPARENTING

Below I describe pillars to ground the work, though it is helpful to know that this process is different for everyone and does not have exact linear steps. We are constantly changing, transient creatures. Our needs change and evolve daily. Our ways of addressing those needs must evolve, too.

The *first pillar* of reparenting is emotional regulation, or the skill to successfully navigate our emotional states. Emotional regulation is our ability to cope with stress in a flexible, tolerant, and adaptive way. We've been working on this step throughout the book, especially when we discussed the role of the nervous system. The ways we can regulate our emotions are all practices you are likely well versed in by now: deep belly breathing to regulate our stress response, nonjudgmentally witnessing changes in our body's sensations, and noticing patterns in our ego-based narratives that are connected to those emotional activations. All the foundational work that came before has prepared you for this next process. Many of you may arrive at reparenting and realize you would benefit from engaging more consistently or deeply with the earlier regulatory bodywork. If you recognize yourself in this paragraph, I give you permission to put the book down, take a step away, and go back before continuing.

The *second pillar* is loving discipline. This pillar involves creating boundaries with ourselves that are maintained over time. We do this by making and keeping small promises and developing daily routines and habits. Discipline is an important part of the healing process and cultivating it helps us to show up for ourselves. Many of us were raised with shame-based perceptions of discipline—it involved punishment for being "bad" and we may have felt judged or rejected. It's the reverse of self-betrayal. We have chosen to make a new habit, and by proving to ourselves that we are worth showing up for, we build a sense of inner reliability and resilience. This instills a deep sense of confidence that touches other aspects of our lives. The act of loving discipline cultivates routine with compassion and flexibility.

Your promise can be small—such as SelfHealer Ally's drinking a glass of water on a regular basis—or big, such as learning how to say "no" to things that don't serve you on your journey. I've seen so many other helpful examples from the SelfHealer community: floss your teeth every night, wash your face every evening, do a crossword puzzle every day. The key is to do something *every day*—do it consistently, and build up the trust that you will show up consistently for yourself.

Many parents I've spoken with say they set their alarm clock for an hour before their children wake up so that they can get a head start on the day. They put their phone on airplane mode and do one thing for themselves before they shift their attention to the needs of everyone else. This one thing can be cooking breakfast, going for a walk, reading a book, working out, or just relaxing. As one SelfHealer wrote, "Nobody can take away this hour from you."

I want to emphasize that this act of daily discipline should be a loving one. Many people have created too-rigid boundaries around what they allow themselves. Military-style discipline, which leaves no room for flexibility and the inevitable mistake, can result in destructive patterns that do not express the true wants and needs of our authentic Selves. There will be days when we want to lie in bed all day, drink some wine, indulge in some pie, or take a break from washing our face. That's fine. If we've developed confidence over time, we know that we can take a break and the ritual will always be there to return to when we so choose. We will not fall apart if we take a day to rest.

The *third pillar* goes hand in hand with loving discipline: self-care. The phrase itself has gotten a bad rep in recent memory, as it's been commodified and used as an example of self-indulgence. True self-care—supporting your needs and valuing your worth—is not indulgent at all, and it's fundamental to holistic wellness. Self-care is the act of learning to identify and care for your physical and emotional wants and needs, especially those that were denied in childhood.

There are so many ways to incorporate acts of self-care into our day: meditating for five minutes (or longer), moving our bodies, journaling, spending time in nature, spending time alone, allowing the sun to kiss our skin, connecting intimately with a person we love. I believe that one of the most critical aspects of self-care is developing good sleep hygiene; getting quality sleep makes us happier and cognitively stronger and even lengthens our lives. Go to bed a half hour earlier. Turn off your phone two hours before bed. Stop drinking caffeine after 1:00 p.m. Try one or all of these things, and see how much better you feel in your body and mind.

The *fourth pillar*, one of the ultimate goals of *the work*, is to rediscover our childlike sense of wonder. This state is made up of a combination of creativity and imagination, joy and spontaneity, and, of course, playfulness.

Psychiatrist Stuart Brown, author of *Play: How It Shapes the Brain, Opens the Imagination, and Invigorates the Soul*, called play a "public necessity" after he studied the lack of play in the childhoods of young men who went on to commit homicidal acts. He's since studied the role of play in the lives of thousands of people and has found that a life lived without play contributes to the development of depression, chronic stress-related illnesses, and even criminal behavior. "A lack of play should be treated like malnutrition," he wrote, "it's a health risk to your body and mind."[79]

The reality is that most of us were raised in homes where childlike wonder was not valued or even tolerated, so creativity was not fostered. How many of us were told to put away our paintbrushes because "artists don't make money"? How many of us had parent-figures who ignored or suppressed their own creative endeavors in favor of more practical pursuits? How many of us were punished for unstructured playing when we were supposed to be "working"? I don't have one memory of my mother playing with me as a child. Not one. That's sad for me, of course—and sad for her, too.

As adults, it's crucial for us to prioritize the things in our lives that bring us joy in themselves, not because of any secondary gains (money, success, adoration). We can help reengage our sense of childlike wonder by streaming our favorite music and dancing or singing freely. We can do something off the cuff, be impulsive, follow our passions. We can try something new that we've always wanted to do just because we want to and without needing to perfect it: learn how to sew, study a new language, take surfing lessons. It can involve getting your hands dirty in the garden with your plants, complimenting a stranger on their outfit, or reconnecting with old friends. All of these examples share one essential component: doing something for the enjoyment of it, not for any external reward.

## DEALING WITH LONELINESS, DISAPPOINTMENT, AND ANGER

Reparenting is hard, consistent work. It's one of the deepest agents of change and takes time and a lot of fine-tuning, as our needs change every day—every moment, really. Reparenting is a practice—it is highly individualistic work that requires us to constantly identify our evolving needs and coping strategies. I warn you: there may be fallout. I've received emails from several SelfHealers who have shared their struggles with parent-figures, family members, and even friends who actively resisted their decision to embark on the reparenting process. One of the most striking emails was from a SelfHealer's mother, who wrote to reprimand me for "brainwashing" her child into severing contact with her when she started the reparenting process. How could I blame her for directing her anger somewhere outside the family unit? She spent a whole lifetime living in the conditioned patterns that her daughter was now actively changing. It was not only normal but probably felt safer to place blame on an outsider rather than looking at how the intergenerationally transmitted patterns played a role in her daughter's decision.

It's not just the judgment of outsiders that we will face but also the judgment that comes from within. Loneliness is a theme that comes up throughout the healing journey but especially during the reparenting process. Reparenting forces us to come into close contact with our authentic Self, and if we don't have a strong bond there, it can feel unnerving. It might make you feel insecure, lonelier than you were when you began. It might even seem irritating or counterproductive to engage with yourself so openly. You can't deeply engage with reparenting until you truly become conscious of yourself.

One realization many SelfHealers have while reparenting is that they've been living with unexpressed anger. Opening our eyes to the ways we were let down, rejected, or traumatized in our past can awaken latent feelings of anger and sometimes even rage. Some of us may want to point a finger at or blame our parent-figures for our suffering. Some of us may want our parent-figures to swoop in and "kiss it all better," as we hoped they would do in childhood. At the very least, many of us want our pain to be acknowledged. Those of us who are problem solvers often wish for a concrete resolution. In fact, many SelfHealers go back to their parent-figures and demand to be heard or ask for an apology.

Some may be willing to have this kind of dialogue. I've spoken to many SelfHealers who have improved and deepened their relationships with their parent-figures after having painful and honest conversations with them. If you feel this is a step helpful for you on your reparenting journey—to speak your truth—then go ahead and do it. The primary goal in this communication would not be to change the other person's experience, it would be to express your own reality. There is a deep intrinsic value in expressing how we feel and how we view the past. If you can find this value and you're able to tolerate and hold space for whatever reaction may come, you are ready to take part in a dialogue. If you're going in with the expectation that your parent-figures will apologize, validate your feelings, or affirm your experience, I would suggest holding off on having this conversation until you feel more tolerant of the uncertainty of the outcome. Your inner healing is the priority. Often, parent-figures are not as open to these conversations as many of us would hope. This makes perfect sense; our parent-figures have lived in a conditioned state for their whole lives. Decades of learned behavior do not just evaporate when you point them out. There will undoubtedly be confusion. Sometimes these conversations may be more hurtful than they are productive. There might even be anger directed back at you.

All of this is to say that it's natural to unearth anger and it's easy to let that anger start to consume you. It's important to allow the anger in, be in it, and, yes, communicate it if you choose—and it's helpful to do so without expecting that an outside party will validate your reality or experiences. The only person who can do that for you is *you*. Your reality is valid because you've experienced it, not because someone or something external has said so.

I think it's time for me to remind the readers with children to take a deep breath. Parent-figures often enter the reparenting process with a huge dose of fear and guilt. They can't help but think of all the ways they will fail (or already have failed) their own kids.

"How can we make sure we don't do this to our children?" is a question I'm asked almost every day.

Let's get this out of the way: you can't.

Parenting is difficult and incredibly emotionally activating. Being present and attuned to oneself enough to be present and attuned to another in order to identify and meet their needs is a tall order. The reality is this: You're going to make mistakes. You're going to fall short. You're going to mess up in some way or another. It's not only okay, it's actually beneficial in the long term. Experiencing some stress helps children build resilience, which is a key component of emotional maturity. We will discuss this in more detail shortly.

## HEEDING THE CALL OF THE WEST

Even though the origins of my awakening were very uncomfortable, they afforded me an opportunity to shift my entire existence. When I finally distanced myself from my family, giving myself the space to exist without being *in relation to* my family, I started to truly understand the varied needs that I had been denying or suppressing. As someone who is codependent, my needs were always defined by others (and many times I even believed I didn't have any needs). I had to create space for myself to gain entry into my separate being and see myself as independent of my family. In the wake of the fear and devastation, I met myself. I found out for the first time what I really needed.

There have been only three times in my life when I honored my needs even though it meant that others would be hurt by my decision.

The first time was in college, when I decided to quit playing softball because it was no longer making me happy. I did that even though I knew that my parents, my mom in particular, would be disappointed and that I might be letting my team down. I did it for *me*. The second time was when I finally ended my marriage after years of disconnection. There was a part of me that would have gone on forever, but another part decided *This isn't working for me. I need to make a change.*

The third time was when Lolly and I decided to move to California. Moving out west was something I wanted to do, though dismissed as even a possibility because I knew that it would upset my family. After I cut my ties with them, I was no longer bound by the invisible chains that held me to the East Coast, a place that I knew intuitively was no longer serving me. Just a decade ago, if you told me I would be living thousands of miles from Philadelphia and New York City, I would have laughed in your face. I was addicted to the emotional activation of the city environment—the chaos, the noise, the bright lights, and the vacant-faced crowds were a direct reflection of my inner world. Former friends interpreted my transition as evidence of an early midlife crisis: I dropped my whole life—a private practice, a family, my friends, my past—and moved across the country to start a new life. When I began to speak my emerging new truth to some of those closest to me, I'd at times be met with raised eyebrows, intrusive questions, and even hostility.

When Lolly and I visited California, we both knew that it was the place for us. More balanced internally, I became drawn to what naturally instills balance in my body: nature itself, the sun's warmth, a place where I can breathe freely and move my body. When we finally decided to act, it was a symbolic extension of the reparenting process. I acknowledged my needs. I listened to my desires. I allowed myself to fulfill them. I felt the intuitive *ping* of my inner guidance system and this time I listened.

The move wasn't easy. Transitions are hard. No matter how perfect the situation is, you are still disrupting your homeostasis and at the minimum it feels uncomfortable. We are creatures of habit, and when we can't engage in our usual patterns, we feel thrown off, vulnerable, even hostile to change. Anytime we are faced with an allostatic life event—a job change, a move, a death, a birth, a divorce—it forces us out of our safety zone and into the great unknown, a naturally disquieting place.

When I decided that California was my destiny, it meant closing down the private practice that I worked so hard to build and saying good-bye to many of my clients, whom I had grown attached to. I had to find new virtual ways to engage with some relationships I cherished. It also meant that my decision to put a hard stop to my contact with my family now was *real*. I was physically separating myself from my trauma bonds, and it felt freeing and terrifying at the same time. I now had the skills and practices to deal with the discomfort and uncertainty. I could finally tap into my intuitive trust in myself—and that felt amazing. Though I still struggled with loneliness and many doubts about my future, I felt more in alignment than ever before. My sleep quality improved; my digestion quickened and the stagnation in my gut loosened; my lungs seemed to expand to take in the clean air; I felt lighter in my soul; my mood lifted. The more my spirit seemed to speak through my body, the more I realized I craved joy. And, I realized, I was worthy of it.

One day, while working on this book, I took a walk to clear my head. As I ambled along the beach in my new neighborhood, taking in the sensations of the world around me, I started practicing kind messages of support and love: *What can I do for myself in this moment?* Just as that question crossed my mind, the Mumford & Sons song "There Will Be Time" came on in my earbuds. I turned up the volume, swallowed up by the percussive beat, the swell of the keyboards, and the mingling of the vocal harmonies.

*So open up my eyes to a new light . . .*
*And indeed there would be time*

Their words were prophetic. I stood there seeing finally with the open eyes of consciousness, learning how to connect to my innermost wants and needs, and for the first time truly trusting in the infinite possibilities of the choices we are gifted in any given moment of time.

I turned it up louder. I started to bob my head and sway my hips.

This was totally out of character for me. I have long disliked dancing. I have come to realize that my aversion came from a childhood ballet class when I caught a glimpse of myself in the mirror and noticed how much bigger my belly was than those of the rest of the girls in class. From that point on, I began to feel more and more uncomfortable and constricted in my own skin, my own body. After only a short time, I no longer danced in public and eventually ended up watching others doing so, who could be so free, with nothing short of disdain. Yet here I was, over three decades later, out in the open in a strange new world, and I was swaying to the music. Before long, I was raising my hands up to the sky and jumping around. I was dancing. Full on. For anyone and everyone to see.

Letting go of the fear of what others think, the conditioned state of judgment, and all the pain of our wounded inner child is all part of the joyful side of the reparenting process. Dancing on the beach was my radical act of self-acceptance, an intrinsic step forward in my healing journey.

## DO THE WORK: DEVELOP A REPARENTING MENU

Spend a few moments exploring which of the four pillars of reparenting you might work on first. A great way to begin is to ask yourself "What am I needing most right now?"

- **Emotional regulation.** As children, many of us were not taught the value or practice of being emotionally aware. As adults, it's crucial to our healing that we develop this practice. You can begin cultivating emotional regulation by:
    - Practicing deep belly breathing

- Witnessing the sensations that different emotions activate in your body
- Noticing what causes you to feel emotionally activated
- Allowing emotional responses *without judgment*; allowing any and all emotions to pass through you while simply witnessing them

Using the examples just provided (if needed), journal or list what you can give to (or create for) yourself right now in this area of emotional regulation. (Over time, you may discover new ways to cultivate this new daily habit.) ______________________________________
______________________

- **Loving discipline.** As children, many of us were not taught simple, helpful, supportive habits and rituals. As an adult, you can begin to cultivate this loving discipline by:
  - Keeping small promises to yourself each day
  - Developing daily rituals and routines
  - Saying "no" to things that do not serve you
  - Holding boundaries even when you are uncomfortable doing so
  - Disconnecting and spending time in self-reflection
  - Clearly stating your needs in objective (nonjudgmental) language

Using the examples just provided (if needed), journal or list what you can give to (or create for) yourself right now in this area of loving discipline. (Over time, you may discover new ways to cultivate this new daily habit.) ______________________________________
______________________

- **Self-care.** As children, many of us were not taught the value of things such as high-quality sleep, movement, nutrition, and connection to nature. As an adult, you can cultivate this self-care by:
  - Going to bed a bit earlier
  - Cooking and/or eating a home-cooked meal
  - Meditating for five minutes (or longer)
  - Moving your body for five minutes (or longer)
  - Journaling
  - Spending time in and connecting to nature
  - Allowing the sun to touch your skin
  - Connecting with someone you love

Using the examples just provided (if needed), journal or list what you can give to (or create for) yourself right now in this area of self-care. (Over time, you may discover new ways to cultivate this new daily habit.) ______________________________

______________________________

- **Childlike wonder: creativity plus imagination; joy and spontaneity plus playfulness.** As children, many of us were not taught the value of taking joy in spontaneity, creativity, play, and pure presence. As adults, it's crucial to remember to play, to connect with and develop hobbies we enjoy. You can cultivate this joy by:
  - Dancing or singing freely
  - Doing something unplanned
  - Finding a new hobby or interest

- Listening to your favorite music
- Complimenting a stranger
- Doing something you loved doing as a child
- Connecting with friends and loved ones

Using the examples just provided (if needed), journal or list what you can give to (or create for) yourself right now in this area of childlike wonder. (Over time, you may discover new ways to cultivate this new daily habit.) ________________________________________

________________________________________________________

# 12

# Emotional Maturity

Emotional maturity has nothing to do with numerical age. Some of us hit maturity levels that exceed those of our parent-figures before we hit puberty—and some emerge from the womb more mature than our parent-figures. (I'm only half kidding.)

Emotional immaturity is far more common and revolves around the inability to *tolerate*. Those who are emotionally immature have trouble tolerating their own emotions; they cope with anger by slamming a door or with disappointment by deploying the silent treatment. Emotionally immature people are so uncomfortable with their emotions that they typically lash out and become defensive or completely shut down whenever they experience one.

This may manifest as a father who screams "Stop being dramatic!" when a child's emotions run counter to his own. It may be a friend who completely shuts down and goes into silent treatment mode after a disagreement. This behavior is often the result of the inability to witness another person's discomfort, an inability to tolerate the mere existence of different emotions. Other people's perspectives can feel threatening, and fear of them breeds intolerance.

The psychotherapist Lindsay Gibson described emotional immaturity (with a focus on parenting) as the "lack of emotional responsiveness necessary to meet children's emotional needs."[80] The outcome for children of emotionally immature parent-figures is loneliness, which is "a vague and private experience . . . you might call it a feeling of emptiness or being alone in the world."[81]

I related to this feeling of emptiness deeply, having never felt fully able to appreciate, let alone enjoy, my experiences. For most of my life, I struggled to access a "soul laugh"—embodying the pure enjoyment of life. *How could I know what made me happy if I didn't know what I really needed?*

This feeling of emptiness, I believe, comes from a continued disconnection from our authentic Self. Years of conditioned living, unable to truly meet our physical, emotional, and spiritual needs, is often coupled with a fear of being misunderstood. Those of us raised in homes where free self-expression was not supported may find ourselves overly focused on what others think or feel about us. This was a common experience for many of us, and I believe it is one reason why social anxiety is such an epidemic today. We see social anxiety and an overfocus on appearance playing out in the new virtual arena of social media that many of us engage with daily—our obsession with "views" and "likes" being driven largely by our unmet need to be seen and heard. Most of us spend loads of mental energy trying to be *understood*. Our fear of being misunderstood drives our body's physiological reaction, propelling us into a stress response in which cyclical thought patterns and egoic stories drive our behavior. This fear binds our sense of identity with the perceived approval or disapproval of others. As social creatures whose evolution was based on community and acceptance, rejection from our herd could have dire, even fatal, outcomes. Our fear of ostracization continues today, even if the stakes are lower. The evolutionary drive toward social acceptance makes it impossible for us to connect with the people around us when we are in a fear state. It makes us reactive and irrational. It makes us scared of doing something silly, like dancing to our favorite song in public.

For many SelfHealers, it is not our understanding of ourselves that pains us but our increased understanding of others. As we become more consciously aware of our conditioned way of living, we become equally aware of the often cyclical patterns of those around us. This is, of course, why so many of us find visiting "home" so difficult. Visiting our families provides us with a view into our own habits and patterns as well as our deeper inner wounds, at the same time activating many of those wounds. Some of us even have an emotional response similar to what is described in popular literature as "survivor's guilt," the feeling of being "the one that got away." These feelings may make some of us hesitant to share details about our growth and achievements with those we "left behind." Or we may find ourselves feeling terrible about evolving out of our old roles and want our loved ones to follow in our path of transformation so that our relationships with them can remain intact. Many of us truly care for our loved ones, and want them to "see that change is needed" so they can then heal. This is a wonderful aspiration, and the reality is that not everyone may be on the same path. Healing, as you now know, takes daily commitment and has to be *chosen*. When our loved ones are not choosing the same path as we are, it is helpful to stop fighting the reality of what is freeing up some of our energy to practice accepting all of our feelings about that reality.

One of the major achievements of emotional maturity is learning how to be at peace with these misunderstandings or with being misunderstood. This will help you to continue to live your life as your most authentic Self—no matter what the fallout may be—when your opinions, beliefs, and realities are *valid*—not in relation to anyone else, just because you have them. We might not like all parts of who we are, and yet they exist and must be acknowledged. When our core sense of self is so variable and dependent, so open to outside influence, even what we *think* others believe about us can shape the way we see ourselves. There is no place for maturity in a state of boundarylessness.

Most of us never learned how to navigate our emotional worlds and have little emotional resilience; we are unable to rebound when things inevitably don't go our way. When you are authentically you, you will encounter judgment and criticism. You will also disappoint others. These are just facts of life—a part of being a dynamic, individualized human. It does not mean that you are inherently wrong or right. As you mature emotionally, you will create more and more space for people who may not look, sound, act, or think like you. Learning how to tolerate differences—even outright contrasts—is a hallmark of emotional maturity.

## THE NINETY-SECOND RULE

Emotional maturity allows us to accept *all of our emotions*, even the uglier ones we don't want to admit we harbor. The fundamental aspect of emotional maturity is the ability to be aware of and regulate our emotions in order to allow others to express themselves. Or simply the ability to tolerate all of our emotions without losing control, which is at the core of all the work we are doing.

Believe it or not, there is a "ninety-second rule" of emotions:[82] as physiological events, they last for only a minute and a half. Then they come to an end. Our body *wants* to return to homeostasis. When stress occurs, our body's cortisol spikes and our internal anxiety circuit is activated, and when the stress is perceived to be handled, a countering system will bring our body back into balance. This, of course, can happen only if our mind doesn't get in the way.

Few of us have the ability to allow our emotions to be purely physiological. Most of us bring them up to our mental world and start spinning stories, ruminating, and engaging in circular thoughts, which brings us back into the feedback loop of emotional addiction. Suddenly a ninety-second irritation grows into days of irritability, anger, or even years of grudge keeping and resentment. For those of us who are dissociated and don't allow ourselves to *feel* what we're feeling, sensations can't properly pass through us, remaining trapped as we keep ourselves a safe distance away.

When you replay distressing thoughts, you activate your nervous system response as if you're experiencing the distressing event over and over. Your body can't tell the difference between what was in the past and what is happening in the present—it's all threatening. Distressing emotions often feel as though they last longer and are more intense than positive emotions are. Studies have even shown that during moments of emotional intensity, our sense of time is skewed—sometimes seemingly running faster and sometimes slowing down to a snail's pace.

There's an upside to this phenomenon: we can use the power of our conscious mind to create another, more positive "reality." As I began to reconnect more and more with my body, learning the variations among feelings, I discovered the difference between stress and excitement. Anytime I felt activated, I thought that I was experiencing stress and would shut down or lose control. As I started to witness myself, I found that I often confused excitement for stress. Now when I feel the instinctual pull to label what I'm feeling as *anxiety*, I can take a second, look at it from a different angle, and, when applicable, reframe it into something a bit more helpful, such as *excitement*, when appropriate. The butterflies in my stomach that appear just before I launch an Instagram post on a topic I'm passionate about aren't necessarily stress, they're physical manifestations of my enthusiasm and excitement. Stepping away from instinctive reactivity gives us the ability to sever the mind-body activation circuit and just exist with our body's sensations. When we resist the habit of creating a story about where our emotions came from, we shorten our body's often prolonged physiological reactions. In doing so, we can come to experience the truth that they will pass.

Witnessing the changing sensations of our emotions helps us learn how to differentiate among them so that we can understand the different messages our bodies are sending us. When we are conscious and practicing objective witnessing of our bodies' ever changing sensations—the muscle tension, the hormonal dips, the nervous system activations—we gain access to the wisdom of our bodies. We can then begin to use this information to communicate our more fully realized internal state with others.

## COPING WITH EMOTIONAL MATURITY

We don't just want to label our emotions; our goal is to return to homeostatic balance as quickly as possible. Stress is an inevitable part of life. Emotional maturity allows us the opportunity to choose how to respond to the external world. This then helps us to travel back up the polyvagal ladder and return to the safe baseline of social engagement, where we feel safe and secure with ourselves and within our connections with others. So many of us continue to cycle through the older, conditioned coping habits we learned in childhood that often do not always serve our authentic Selves. So how can we discover and meet our needs in emotionally mature ways?

Soothing is the preferred way to deal with discomfort. The soothing methods we developed as children were adaptive in response to our environment. Put simply, we coped with our past environments and experiences the best way our circumstances would allow. As adults, many of us greatly benefit when we update the ways we attend to our emotional needs with the new information from our lives now. Instead of instinctually falling back into the coping strategies of our childhood, proactive soothing methods involve making a conscious choice. Soothing occurs when we act with agency and proactivity, meeting a problem head-on, which often feels very satisfying. After you've named and nonjudgmentally labeled your emotions, you will want to find a way to neutralize your reactions.

Soothing is not necessarily intuitive, especially if we were not modeled appropriate ways of dealing with adversity. At the beginning of my journey of developing emotional maturity, I was totally lost about how to make myself feel better when I felt angry or agitated. The only ways I was modeled were icing and yelling. Seeing evidence of those now-unwanted habits in my adult self, I tried various new things. Some worked; some made me feel worse. I realized that when I'm angry or agitated—another feeling I've historically confused with anxiety—I benefit from moving my body. Anything that I experience as stagnating feels counterproductive. That means that when I'm feeling challenged, I take a walk. I do the dishes. I get my body moving any way I can to discharge the physiological energy associated with my feelings. When I try to ease my feelings by relaxing—reading a book (my favorite hobby) or taking a bath—it actually puts me more on edge. The opposite may be true for you, and you'll know only by trying it out when you are energetically activated.

The less obviously satisfying and arguably equally important coping strategy is to increase our ability to tolerate distress. We never want to feel that we are dependent on one thing to soothe us (like an adult version of a pacifier). We want to develop as much flexibility as possible to bob and weave in response to adversity. We might not always be able to take a walk or draw a bath when we're feeling emotionally activated. Given certain circumstances, many of us find ourselves faced with having to endure our distress. In our earliest years, we relied on others to help us tolerate or soothe our different discomforts. As we age, it is helpful to learn how to tolerate the natural range and diversity in our emotional experiences.

The challenge for so many of us is to honor the emotions that come up in our body. It is often helpful to witness the stories that play out in our mind: note that they're happening, be present, and try not to judge. Enduring requires an inner trust that soothing methods do not; we have to have faith in ourselves that we will get through this. It creates a sense of confidence that enables us to face the challenges thrown at us without needing anything outside ourselves to take away our "feel-bads."

As you begin to cultivate emotional tolerance, understand that your inner resources are far from limitless. If you are absolutely exhausted and try to push yourself despite your limited resources, you'll likely fall back on more familiar coping strategies (e.g., lashing out, withdrawing, social media scrolling). Set yourself up to succeed by acknowledging your resource levels. If you feel overwhelmed, take yourself out of a situation before you feel emotional activation. If you're stressed and tired, stay home instead of testing the limits of your emotional resources to cope. Give yourself permission to say "no" when it serves you. Emotional maturity is understanding your own emotional boundaries and communicating them to others without fear or shame.

Coping (soothing but especially enduring) teaches us that we can tolerate discomfort. We previously surrounded ourselves with distractions because on some level we believed that we could not deal with distressing situations. Every time you widen your window of tolerance, you teach yourself that *yes, I can get through this*. So often we hear about throwing ourselves into the emotional deep end and sinking or swimming, concepts that are problematic for the nervous system. Instead, I encourage you to work on opening that window little by little until it's thrown wide open—and once it's open, you will find a deep reservoir of tolerance for the entirety of your internal and external world.

## A NOTE FOR PARENTS

Just as you can cultivate emotional maturity in yourself, there are ways you can help cultivate it in children. As a parent-figure, the best thing you can do for your child is to devote time and energy to making sure that *you* are taken care of. When you honor your body, learn how to harness the power of your nervous system response, access your authentic Self, and model emotional regulation and flexibility, your child internalizes it all through co-regulation. Staying in a balanced and self-expressed state will help your child deal with their own moments of dysregulation, using you as a secure base to help return to safety.

Once you've begun to cultivate your own emotional maturity, you can start to devote some of your internal resources to helping your children deal with their emotions. You can encourage self-care and loving discipline in their lives by making sure they're moving their body, getting alone time, getting enough sleep, and so on. At the same time, when stress does come, you can help them make sense of it in the same way that you do—by identifying sensations in their body. Ask them what their body does. *My face feels hot when Samantha makes fun of me. My heart races when I have to share my toys with Timmy.* Help them name the emotion that might correspond to those bodily sensations (shame, anger, jealousy) and allow them to try different ways to actively soothe those sensations. Remember, these will not always be the same as the ways you find helpful; think of this process as an opportunity to learn about your children as unique humans.

Realistically, there will be times when a child will be stressed by something happening outside the home and you will not be there to help them cope. Learning how to endure is a key lesson for parent-figures to model. You don't know what's in your child's future. And although none of us wants to imagine distressing things happening to any loved one, we cannot necessarily keep those things from happening. When we model stress tolerance, or the ability to sit through difficult feelings and let them pass, our children will develop the internal reserve that will go on to sustain them in their childhood world and well into their adulthood.

If you haven't realized it by now, the overarching key as parent-figures is to be okay with being imperfect. I realize that allowing imperfection isn't easy for many of us, especially those of us whose childhood wounds drive people-pleasing or high-achieving habits. I can hardly stand it when Lolly or anyone I love is disappointed in me. I hate the feeling of being seen at my less than shiniest—or as simply unable to support them as they need me to in any given moment for whatever reason. With disappointment being part of being human, parent-figures can rest assured that the traumas experienced in childhood will not be debilitating if a space of authentic love is created and internalized by the child. If parent-figures can cultivate the ability to hear and accept the differing realities of their own children, they will grant them permission to question and express the views and experiences of their authentic Self to the rest of the world. With that safety and security, children will begin to reflect that honesty and security right back—a relationship of authentic Self expression co-created and co-experienced by parent-figure and child. This reciprocal authentic expression is the core of the secure attachment style we encountered earlier. When you come from a place of security and safety, you are freer to navigate the world around you, make mistakes, and get back up when you fall. This builds up our internal resources and helps foster resilience as we navigate all the hardships that life inevitably brings.

As you cultivate more and more grace toward and acceptance of your own imperfections, you may find yourself extending a similar compassion to your own parent-figures (as hard as that may be for some of us) and other loved ones. Yes, coming to accept that they are fallible beings can be frustrating, even rage inducing. Over time, as we continue to dig more and more to try to understand their conditioning and life circumstances, we can begin to empathize without explaining the problems away. You can relate to their wounds and feel for their suffering while maintaining the boundaries that are necessary for *your* mental, physical, and emotional health. Emotional maturity is about combining softness and toughness when necessary—not only with the people around you (parent-figures, children, friends) but with yourself.

## MEDITATION AND MATURITY

The best phrase to describe John, one of the more emotionally immature SelfHealers I've encountered (this is not to disparage him; he totally agrees with that evaluation!), would be "larger than life." He's the kind of person who takes all the oxygen out of a room; the one who has to steer the conversation in a conference call; the "alpha male" who blows up if he thinks that his authority is being questioned by someone, especially if that someone is a woman. I can safely describe him as "emotionally stunted"—everything was always about him, an egocentric worldview similar to the one that an infant or toddler would have. When things didn't go his way, he'd yell or, when really angry, would go darkly and ominously silent. He worked in sales at a job he hated, but he derived all of his identity from hitting his monthly numbers—or, better yet, toppling them. Though he thrived at the office, he struggled with intimacy. He never felt comfortable enough to let his hair down and really just *be* with anyone, especially a romantic partner.

That was how he was before he started the healing journey. Once he began peeling back the layers of his reactivity, he found a soft, wounded core of childhood trauma. His narcissism was a front for his deep hurt. He began to share stories of his father, a man who would "blow up" especially when fueled by alcohol, though he could lose his cool anytime. Sometimes he would hit John with a belt. His mother, who had also experienced those scenes, would walk out of the room and later make excuses for his father's behavior. Tellingly, John felt angrier at his mother for not protecting him than at his father for abusing him.

People often seek out others with similar levels of emotional immaturity, and certainly that was the case for John. The women he found himself attracted to (and attracting) seemed passive and compliant. They allowed John to rant and rave and rarely intervened or questioned him—until a blowup moment when the relationship would dissolve and once again John would feel alone and unseen. It was his last breakup, which ended with his violently smashing a dozen glass plates onto the floor, that led him to his healing journey.

When he was first introduced to the concept of emotional immaturity, John felt embarrassed. He hated seeing how deeply those words applied to him. It was so jarring that he stopped engaging with the materials for a period of time. Becoming conscious can sometimes feel abrupt and uncomfortable. He eventually began to dive more deeply into meditative practice, inching up his daily meditation rituals from five minutes to ten to eventually twenty minutes a day. His boundaries, an area of his life that he never realized was not well defined, became a passion for him. He made lists of the people in his life and what his needs were in his relationships with them, and he began making efforts to change his own expectations about how others showed up in his relationships. When difficult feelings arose, he worked on sitting through the pain and irritation instead of externalizing it onto others.

Today John wouldn't dare to call himself "mature" (which I think is a sign of his growing maturity), and he has made incredible progress. He continues to struggle with reactivity—especially in situations that activate childhood trauma, where he feels judged or misunderstood—and now he has the tools to help him manage. When a difficult feeling such as anger comes up, he sees it as a physiological response not having any reflection on *who he is* and is better able to let the sensations pass through his body without acting on them. He still works in sales, but he is also a licensed meditation practitioner, which he says is his passion (his fourth reparenting pillar). He says that he works on his reactivity every day; it's part of his day-to-day existence.

## INNER EMOTIONAL MATURITY BEAMS OUTWARD

When we are faced with stressful situations that tax our resources, our emotional maturity is tested. John explains that he's consistently evaluating his responses, looking for clues of his immaturity peeking through the layers of coping and reparenting, ready to reemerge, which sometimes does happen despite his best efforts. To give us the best sense of when we are nearing the limits of our internal resources to cope with stress or what throws us over the edge, self-accountability check-ins can be helpful. When life becomes stressful or after we have had a moment of stress-induced reactivity, it can be helpful to touch base with the events that impacted our experiences. Some questions that can help us get a firm hold on our reactivity before we are taken over by it include:

- What can I learn about myself from what happened?
- What patterns brought me here?
- How can I embrace discomfort and grow from it?
- How can I learn how to accept criticism without making it absolute truth?
- How can I forgive myself and others?

The more we learn self-accountability, the stronger our faith in our Self will grow. This allows for failure. It allows for flexibility and forgiveness when we inevitably fall off the path. When we have self-trust, we know that the path is still there waiting for us. This is the essence of self-accountability that leads to empowerment.

You, too, will fall off the wagon. There will be weeks when you are too tired to do anything. There will be times when you are tested and you react in ways that make you embarrassed. Whenever new stress enters your life in whatever form—you're dealing with a sick relative, you've just brought home a new baby, or you're going through a breakup—your tools might go straight out the window. We all have our moments of emotional immaturity. That's human. Our access to emotional maturity changes as we do, responding at different points to our environment, our hormonal state, whether we're hungry or tired. The goal is to empower yourself with the ability to make the best decision for your emotional state as the world shifts and changes around you.

Emotional maturity is not a goal to check off a list, like reaching the next level in a video game (now you're a fully realized human, you win!). It's not a magical state. The underlying message is not one of a state of enlightened beingness—it's one of work and self-forgiveness that will ultimately lead us to a greater togetherness.

## DO THE WORK: DEVELOP EMOTIONAL MATURITY AND RESILIENCE

**Step 1. Reconnect with and rediscover your emotions.** Emotions are events that happen in your body and are accompanied by shifts in your body's hormones, neurotransmitters, sensations, and energies. Each of you has individual ways your body responds to different emotions. In order to develop the ability to identify (and then ultimately soothe) your feelings, you will first want to get more connected with how your body responds to emotional events.

To do so, I encourage you to build a new daily habit of connecting with your own unique body. To help you with this process, use the following meditation script. (Those of you who would prefer an audio version can head to my website, https://yourholisticpsychologist.com.)

### BODY CONNECTION MEDITATION

Practicing this meditation throughout your day will help you stay connected to your body's ever-changing emotional state. To begin, find a quiet place and a comfortable position in which to sit or lie down for the next few minutes. To help you with this process, you may use the following guided script:

> Settling into the present moment, begin to turn your attention to yourself and your inner experience. If you feel comfortable, gently close your eyes or find a spot at which to gently gaze.
>
> Take a deep breath, bringing the air all the way down into your lungs . . . feel your belly inflate . . . spend an extra moment or two letting out a nice slow, long breath . . . and repeat . . . feel your lungs fill up, expanding with air . . . exhale nice and slow. [You can repeat this breathing as long as you would like, noticing your body sinking a little deeper into the meditation experience.]

When you feel ready, turn your attention to your physical body and all of the present sensations. Starting at the top of your head, scan your body, noticing if you feel tension, tightness, warmth, tingling, or lightness anywhere. Spend a moment or two on your head, neck, and shoulders, then move downward, noticing any and all sensations present in your arms and hands. Move a bit lower, noticing your chest area and stomach. Travel down your upper and lower legs, and end with your feet and toes. [Again, spend as much time as is comfortable on this body scan.]

Spend as much time reconnecting with any area you feel called to, and when you feel ready, return your attention to your breath, gradually expanding it to the environment around you and returning to the sights, sounds, and smells present in this moment.

---

## FSJ: EMOTIONAL BODY CHECK-IN

To help you with this process, you may want to use the following example (or create a similar one of your own):

**Today I am practicing** being conscious of my body's changing emotional state.

**I am grateful for** an opportunity to work on becoming more emotionally mature.

**Today, I am able to** connect with my body to help me understand my emotions.

**Change in this area allows me to feel** more connected to my emotional world.

**Today I am practicing when** I take moments throughout my day to check in with my body's sensations.

---

**Step 2. Help your body return to balance.** Now that you are becoming more aware of the changes in your body as a result of your emotions, you can begin to develop practices to help your body return to its baseline state. Remember, everyone is unique and will respond differently to the activities below. Take some time to explore the various ways you can soothe your emotions; it may take some experimenting with these activities to see which ones work best for you.

There are two main sets of coping tools we want to cultivate: soothing and enduring.

- **Soothing activities:**
    - *Taking a bath.* Soaking in warm water can help calm the body. (If you have Epsom salts available, throw some in if you'd like some added muscle relaxation.)
    - *Doing self-massage.* This can be as simple as rubbing or massaging your feet or lower legs. There are YouTube videos on different pressure points that can help relieve stress.
    - *Reading.* Catch up with that book or article you've been meaning to read.
    - *Listening to, playing, or writing music.* It's your choice!
    - *Snuggling.* This can be with anyone or anything, including your pet(s), your kids, your friends, your partner, or a comfy bed pillow.
    - *Moving* (if possible). Any kind will work!
    - *Expressing your emotions.* Try screaming into a pillow, in the shower, or outside in a large empty space (so as not to activate a neighbor's nervous system!).
    - *Writing.* Write a letter, a journal entry, a poem about what you're feeling. (Try not to use this time to write about the

activating event, or you will continue to activate your body's physiological reactions.)

- **Enduring activities:**
  - *Resting.* Yup, that's it, even if it means canceling plans.
  - *Grounding yourself.* Use your five senses to direct your attention to what you can see, smell, touch, taste, or hear in your environment. This will help bring you to a fuller presence in safety of the current moment.
  - *Engaging in breathwork.* This can be as simple as putting a hand on your belly and taking two or three deep breaths, feeling your lungs expand and contract and noticing any shifts in your body's energy. There are a ton of guided practices that can be found on YouTube or Spotify.
  - *Spending time outside in nature.* Bring your attention to the full experience of your external surroundings, and notice the different grounding and calming energies present.
  - *Meditating or praying.* This can include any activity or engagement with any spiritual- or religious-based practice of resonance.
  - *Reciting affirmations or mantras.* Repeat intentional statements quietly to yourself. Some examples are "You are safe," "You are in control," "You are at peace."
  - *Distracting yourself.* Redirect your attention to anything except your emotions. Yes, you read that correctly—you can choose how much attention you give your emotions as long as you aren't *always* distracting yourself from them!
  - *Getting support.* Reach out to someone with whom you feel safe. Having someone available to you who can actively listen to your thoughts and feelings can be really helpful.

When you are aware that you want someone to listen actively (as opposed to offering advice, as many well-meaning friends do), it is helpful to express that before you begin to share. Also remember that this is different from venting or emotional dumping, in which you simply relive the activating event over and over again, often getting stuck in this cycle.

# 13

# Interdependence

You are never "done" with your development of emotional maturity. It's an evolving, everyday process of self-awareness and acceptance. There will be times of growth, and there will be setbacks that will test the progress you've made. In fact, as I was writing this very chapter, I was tested.

It had been a rough week. I was tired, overworked, and feeling depleted when I saw a stranger aggressively criticizing me online. I felt so demoralized, as though I was one comment away from crying. I wanted to pack up my things and run away from the life that I had built because I hated being misunderstood so grossly.

I brooded instead. I sat on my couch, scrolling through Instagram for other transgressions that would rile me up and rip me apart from the inside, piling on more hurt.

"Get up, let's go," Lolly urged. "Let's go to the beach."

It wasn't just a reason for me to get out of the house and stop my pity party, it was a special day at Venice Beach, a unique opportunity to see the waves alight with the neon created by the bioluminescence of an evening algae bloom. Even still, I declined her suggestion.

She went to the beach and left me to stew. As I wallowed in self-pity, I grew angrier and angrier. My outraged ego created a story: *How dare she leave me like she always does when times get hard? This is an affront!* Even though I had told her to leave, my mind created a story in which she was the betrayer and I was the one betrayed. I witnessed myself enough by now to realize that this ego story was a projection from the inner child wound I had long struggled with, my core belief that *I am not considered.* That led to a darker place: *I'm so pathetic. Lolly can't even stand to be around me.* My mind began to orbit around one thought: *I'm alone. I'm alone. I'm alone.*

I could view all of that internal dialogue, yet I couldn't yet summon up the energy to get myself out of the circular thinking. Instead, I let my inner child sulk for a few more minutes. Then I lifted my head and started to apply the tools that I had been honing (and have shared with you). I began with my breath, becoming aware of the air moving into and out of my lungs. I witnessed. I named the physiological responses in my body: the jolt of agitation, the gut-sinking feeling of disappointment, the electricity of outrage that came from the hits of social media negativity. I started to name the feelings associated with the sensations: anger, fear, sadness. As I gave them names, narratives began to creep around them, crowding my consciousness. When my ego began plucking up examples to prove how worthless I am, I leaned back into my conscious mind, witnessing without judgment, letting the feelings come and go.

With my conscious mind in control, I asked myself: *What can I do for myself in this moment? How can I cope with these "feel-bads"?* I walked over to the sink to tidy up and do some dishes and began to tell myself a counterstory: *I am worthy. I am loved. I am not alone, even if I am physically alone at this moment.* As I immersed my hands into the warm, soapy water and focused my attentional muscles on the physical act of doing, my emotional energy discharged outward and left me enough room to witness my emotional state for what it was: *I'm tired, I'm working too much, and I let someone else's criticism of my work cause a full-body emotional meltdown. I don't want to be here sulking. I want to be with my partner looking at something beautiful.*

I decided that either I could stay stuck, trying to wash out my feelings, or I could remove myself from the instinctual pull toward the familiar and do what I promised myself I would do that day: see those amazing blue waves. I made the choice to leave my cocoon of self-loathing.

When I reached the beach, I spotted Lolly staring out at the impossibly blue sea. She was flanked by dozens of others taking in the majestic gift that Mother Nature had given us. I joined Lolly, and together we gazed off into the brilliant, almost supernatural sea without saying a word.

I was still a wounded child, still hurting and feeling misunderstood, but I was not alone, imprisoned by my own thoughts and feelings. Standing on the beach would have been impossible if I allowed the narrative to swallow me up. None of that beauty would have reached me.

That moment on the beach was about so much more than my own emotional maturity; it was about my emotional state in relation to others—especially those I love the most. This is the ultimate goal of *the work*—from setting boundaries to meeting our inner child to reparenting ourselves—all of this work leads us to a state of honest togetherness.

As we change our mind and brain and access our authentic self, we create joy, creativity, empathy, acceptance, collaboration, and eventually oneness with our greater community. Dr. Steve Taylor from two chapters ago found similar increases in love and compassion, deep knowing, and inner calmness in all of the awakenings he studied. These elements are the essence of what is called interdependence, a state of authenticity and connectedness that is the ultimate testament to the power of holistic healing. *The work* so far has been leading us up to this moment, to the ability to embody oneness, taking us back, back, back to a state of pure awareness and connectedness with all that is. We are literally transforming our mind and body and returning to our purest soul expression. We find the divine in ourselves, which extends to the world around us.

## FINDING THE SELFHEALER COMMUNITY

I haven't yet shared a central piece of the puzzle in my healing journey: finding my community. This is the goal of the interdependent self. Community is a very mutable concept; some people find it in their online social network, some in their immediate neighborhood, others in their interests, churches, school system, or hobbies. I found mine during that lonely period of self-exploration when there were few people I felt could relate to my new awareness. I felt so alone, as though Lolly and I were the sole people awake in a slumbering world. As I created boundaries when learning how to reparent, I ended relationships that were not serving me, which meant cutting ties with some people I once considered part of my core community. I started to make choices that went against the societal grain—no more happy-hour drinks, no more overtaxing myself by creating plans, no more late nights that messed with my sleep and morning routine.

I had come so far. And I was so proud. My intuitive voice urged me to connect with others and the greater world around me. It wasn't fulfilling to remain cut off from everyone. I needed to find my people, share my insights, and learn from others. That's when Lolly suggested that I start posting about my experience online. At the time, I was still in Philadelphia, working as a therapist who came from the mainstream model, and I needed to keep my day job. My beliefs, I feared, would not only alienate me from many of my colleagues but also might push away some of my more traditional clients, and I still needed to put food on the table. Yet there was inauthenticity in my Self-expression. My desire for connection was the major impetus to posting about my journey on Instagram, as I looked for others who might be able to understand the language of SelfHealing and relate to this new world of holistic wellness. I started The Holistic Psychologist in 2018, and the response was almost immediate. So many other people were just as hungry for connection and were living with very similar experiences and knowings. Armies of people were ready and willing to engage in this deep work. The word spread, and another intention emerged: to build a safe and secure community that would foster the greatest possible space for healing. The numbers kept climbing. Each person who joined the ranks of SelfHealers confirmed my faith in the message, giving me the confidence to devote myself fully to affirming the concepts of Holistic Psychology.

As I embraced the teacher role, sharing information as I was incorporating it into my own life, the community expanded and kept giving and giving. It was the conscious co-creation of a new community of fellow souls on a similar journey back to their true essence. People from all over the world shared their tools and practices. The more I shared, the more other people joined in and offered their own healing experiences. The more I adapted and evolved, the more the community reflected that growth, like co-regulation on a grand scale. This interpersonal social media exchange has been the most profoundly rewarding interaction of my life. I've found my people—and in doing so have found the power of my voice, my mission, my higher purpose, my interdependent self.

## THE POWER OF COMMUNITY

Research shows that three out of every five Americans feel alone.[83] I would argue that that number is artificially low because people are ashamed to admit being lonely. Admitting that we feel alone makes us vulnerable and seems to expose some core deficiency: *I am unloved because I am unlovable.* This resonates deep in my bones, as I'm sure it does for many other people.

We all emerged from tribal living. Our ancestors, no matter where they were from, lived in groups for safety, division of labor, stress reduction, and support in all aspects of life. Whether we consider ourselves to be individualistic or collectivistic, every single person needs other persons to thrive. Our bodies and brains were built for connection.

Connection is inherent in the human condition; without it, we cannot survive. That is why researchers have found that today's epidemic of loneliness is in fact an urgent public health issue. Loneliness increases the rates of autoimmune diseases and chronic illnesses in many of the same ways that trauma does. Dr. Vivek Murthy, the surgeon general of the United States under Presidents Obama and Biden, wrote in his book *Together: The Healing Power of Human Connection in a Sometimes Lonely World* that loneliness is "associated with an increased risk of heart disease, dementia, depression, anxiety, sleep disturbances, and even premature death."[84] Clearly, lack of connection does not only hurt us psychologically.

Relationships that are "ambivalent" (those in which our bond is emotionally conflicted) have been shown to have the same detrimental effects on our mental and physical health as being alone. More than half of all married couples view their spouses ambivalently, according to journalist Lydia Denworth's book *Friendship: The Evolution, Biology, and Extraordinary Power of Life's Fundamental Bond*. In my view, these ambivalent relationships are often trauma bonds and not based in authenticity. How can they be? If you are tapped into your wants and needs, how can you choose to spend your life with someone you don't really like? So many of our relationships, even our closest ones, don't serve our authentic Selves because we are not connected with our intuition.

Luckily, those of us with supportive partnerships, friendships, and community see the opposite effects on our well-being: we are happier and healthier and live longer. This is not something that is up to chance. You can make concerted efforts to find your community, even if it is not directly outside your front door. Studies have shown us that internet connections can be just as meaningful as real-life ones.[85] Get out there and find your people. Trust me, they are there.

## AUTHENTIC FRIENDSHIP

Interdependence, a two-way state of authentic connection, is the act of being separate together. Only when I am a unified whole will I be able to connect authentically with others in ways that serve *both of our spiritual, emotional, and physical needs*. Not all relationships, of course, serve us in all the same ways, and not every relationship is equally reciprocal. Once we've expressed our needs and openly established our boundaries, we can enter an arena where we feel secure. When we have trust in our inner world, knowing that we have the tools to face the assorted trials that life will bring, we can reflect that trust and security out into our community. The way we are to ourselves informs the way we are to others and the reverse. It's all interconnected.

To experience authentic relationships, you need to work on being one with your own authenticity. It's only then that you will feel and respond to that *ping* from your intuition telling you *This is someone you should connect to*. I'm sure you've been there. Sometimes it takes just a glance and you know: *This person is meant to be in my life.* It's a fluttering in your soul telling you that you were meant to cross paths with this human.

That happened to me after I had done years of work on reconnecting with myself—I was a few years into doing *the work*. I felt much more in alignment, and as I began to spread my messages of healing, I felt confident enough in my own inner resources to know that though my message might not resonate with everyone, it would reach the people it was meant to reach.

That was when I met Jenna, who arrived early to the SelfHealers community. Even over the internet, I felt our connection and always resonated with her comments. That *ping* of intuition was calling out through the digital interface.

After the first free public inner child meditation at Venice Beach—the first event as the Holistic Psychologist that I wrote about in the book's preface— a line formed around me. I greeted everyone, feeling overwhelmed by the outpouring of gratitude. A few hours later as the end of the line came into sight I spotted one woman who waited until the very end and was smiling at me while holding her hands over her heart. Out of the sea of faces I gazed upon that day, there was that *ping, ping, ping* again. Even before she said a word, I felt a rush of familiarity, as though I had always known her, as though our souls were already in deep communion.

"I'm Jenna," she said.

I couldn't believe it. My intuition pointed to her out of a crowd of thousands. We chatted, both exhilarated to make the in-person connection. She almost spontaneously handed me her oracle cards, a deck of beautiful illustrations. The generosity of the gift—really the giving of an intimate part of herself—meant so much to me. I kept it with me during every life change that followed. It was one of the few items that I took with me during my move from Philadelphia to California a year later.

A few months after the meditation, Lolly and I launched the Self-Healers Circle, a virtual community that would provide access to the framework and daily tools for self-guided healing. The first day of the launch was wild: within an hour, six thousand people signed up and our system crashed. Two days in, I was entering a nervous breakdown, realizing that I was in way over my head. The need was too great. We weren't equipped to handle it all on our own.

Right as I was about to bury my head in the sand and call it quits, out of nowhere, Jenna messaged, saying that she was following a strong inner pull to reach out. "I'm committed to this movement. We know a new world is possible and we are co-creating it. My soul is called to this. I'm here to support you and the future of this movement. Let's have a conversation." It was as if the universe was winking at the three of us, nodding and saying *Yes, I will continue to put the right people on your path when you are in a place of being open to them.*

Jenna became the first person to join our team a day later. She has since become integral to every single working piece of the holistic wellness movement. I can say without a doubt that for this serendipitous connection to happen, we both needed to have tapped into our intuitive voices. When you stand in alignment, you will attract people who are similarly attuned.

## THE COLLECTIVE "WE"

As we now know, we enter the world in a state of pure sponginess. Learning how to survive and navigate the unknown, we accumulate our egoic separateness of being and learn how to define ourselves in relation to others. *We are this, not that. We like these things, not those things.* This separation emerges as a narrative that defines "us" versus "them," the "outside" versus the "inside." For those of us who grew up in codependent families (like me), this comparison narrative, with *us* safely on the inside and *them* on the outside, is an especially ingrained part of our core identities.

As we heal, we go back to the connection to the authentic Self that characterized us in our infancy. Many of us can't even think about returning to that state of vulnerability because our ego is so sensitive, so focused on trying to keep us safe and secure, that the story of who we are is bound to the opposition of the "other." In this state, we often do not feel safe enough to access the collective "we" or the interconnectedness of all humans. The process of peeling back the layers of our psyche, learning about our conditioning, separating from our beliefs, and witnessing our bodily states enables us to appreciate our similarity not only with those we love but with our communities and the world at large.

When we all begin to tap into that collective mentality, we begin to evolve to an altruistic, reciprocal society. Altruism seems opposite to the "survival of the fittest" evolutionary drive, yet in reality it has been essential to the endurance of the human species.

In tribal days, allowing for the unique expression of each individual enabled the needs of the greater community to be met. Each puzzle piece had a function. When we are part of the collective We, the needs of one are the needs of all.

We can participate in this expression of collective unity only when our nervous system is open and receptive to connection. This means we have to be in a calm, balanced state to be able to connect with and care for others. When we're in the happy place of our social engagement mode and in a stable, comfortable environment, our perceived stress levels go down, our vagus nerve shifts us into our desired resting state, and we are in a prime state of joyful expression, spontaneity, healing, and connection. To achieve a sense of true unity, our bodies must feel fully safe.

As we learned in previous chapters, our physiology communicates this level of safety to others through the process of co-regulation. Our internal state is often mirrored by those around us, making our inner worlds contagious; when we feel safe, others feel safe, too. The trouble is that the reverse is also true. This is the key reason why it's been impossible for many of us to connect. As the large majority of us are living with a dysregulated nervous system, we find ourselves literally unable to feel safe enough to connect with others. This in turn results in our feeling lonelier, sicker, and less able to deal with the stresses of life. Over time this vicious cycle continues, sending us on a quick descent toward disconnection and illnesses of all kinds. It's the worst kind of catch-22. We are trapped in fight, flight, or freeze responses that make it physiologically impossible to form authentic bonds. This state is reflected back to those around us, who can't help but internalize it, contributing to our global epidemic of loneliness and disconnection. This inability to connect with others applies not only to our immediate family units and friendships but to the greater collective. None of us is alone in our struggle. You aren't just a cog in a wheel. Your internal state shapes those around you, for better or for worse.

When we feel safe and secure, we feel comfortable enough to express our internal state, even if it is dysregulated or negative, knowing that we can return to baseline with the help of our community. Those who never fight or disagree are actually locked in a dysregulated system that is artificially hampering their stress. Achieving intimacy requires expressing your authentic Self (as shadowy as it can often be) without fear of being misunderstood or facing reproach or retribution. When we are in a safe space of mutual respect, we can express our divergences without fear and still return to homeostasis. This knowledge—

that we have a core resting state within reach—gives us the flexibility to tolerate discomfort. These cycles of experience with moments of dysregulation leading to moments of co-regulation help all of us develop a core belief and trust in these internal resources.

It is important to note that sick or dysregulated systems make this return to safety near impossible for many BIPOC because safety and balance was never there in the first place. These individuals continue to find themselves trapped in a system that's been imbalanced from its conception and is now long overdue for the change absolutely necessary to create safe and secure communities for us all.

All of us deserve to have the opportunity to develop the elasticity to metabolize the changing stresses of life and return to a safe home. When we foster our supportive connections while engaging consciously with our inner world, everyone benefits. It's the essence of reciprocity. That essence binds all of humanity. There is no "us," and there is no "them."

By breaking down these barriers between us as individuals, we can become receptive to connecting with things that transcend our human comprehension. This may take the form of communing with your chosen God or your ancestors, experiencing the birth of your child, spending time in nature, or getting lost in an art form that particularly moves you. It's an experience of oneness on a grand scale that can also be appreciated in even the smallest moments, inspiring the indescribable and sublime feeling of awe.[86] Researchers have found that this sensation stems from an evolutionary response to uncertainty. It encouraged our ancestors to connect with others as they experienced and tried to make sense of the many mysteries of life. When we experienced an eclipse, for example, our communal awe bound us together in our appreciation of life's beauty and terror helping us to ultimately feel safer.

The only way to open ourselves up to awe is to open our mind's eye to the people and the greater world around us. The truth of our existence is in the unique soul that resides in the core of each of us. In the words of Chief Black Elk of the Oglala Sioux Nation, "The first peace, which is most important, is that which comes from the souls of people when they realize their relationship, their Oneness, with the universe and all its powers, and when they realize that at the center of the universe dwells the Great Spirit, and that this center is really everywhere, it is within each of us."[87]

At the beginning of this book, I suggested that transcendent experiences rarely occur within the stereotypical context of the divine—on a mountaintop or next to a babbling brook. Spiritual evolution can be a messy business. Once you do the work of healing the body, mind, and soul and regain the ability to connect with the greater universe, transcendence in its multitude of forms becomes accessible to you. Once you peel back the window dressings of your ego and connect to the purest, most authentic part of yourself, once you reach out to your community in an open state of open receptiveness—awakenings will come. It is in these moments that true enlightenment and healing are possible.

As you heal yourself, you heal the world around you.

---

## DO THE WORK: ASSESS YOUR INTERDEPENDENT RELATIONSHIPS

For many of you, especially if you're like me and come from co-dependent conditioning, developing interdependent relationships takes time. You can get started by taking the following steps.

**Step 1. Assess your current interdependence (or lack thereof).** To gain awareness, take some time to witness your current level of interdependence by assessing yourself in the following areas.

Are you comfortable establishing and maintaining clear boundaries in all relationships? Or do you need to spend some time identifying and setting some new ones? _______________

Can you hold space for open communication and for emotional processing for yourself and others? Or do you need to spend some time identifying your own emotions and becoming aware of when you need to take a break before communicating? ______________

Do you feel free to speak your truth and reality even when they don't align with those of others? Or do you still feel fear, shame, or guilt about how you imagine people will react? ______________

Are you clear about your intentions when you act? Do you know what drives your choices? Are you able to identify what you may be seeking from your experiences and relationships? Or do you need more time to practice self-witnessing? ______________

Can you witness your ego (and shadow) without acting on every thought? Or do you need more practice exploring these aspects of your daily experience? ______________

**Step 2. Cultivate interdependence.** Using the list in step 1 to determine the areas you want to strengthen, begin to make new choices that will support your goal of achieving interdependence. Starting with one area, practice setting a daily intention to create change, using the following examples.

---

## FSJ: CREATING INTERDEPENDENCE

**Today I am practicing** creating interdependence in my relationships.

**I am grateful for an opportunity to** create more fulfilling relationships.

**Today, I am able to** express myself authentically and still feel connected to others.

**Change in this area allows me to feel** connected to my authentic Self and needs in all relationships.

**Today I am practicing when** I speak my truth to my partner about how I felt about our recent argument.

---

Thank you so much for having the courage, the open mind, and the faith it takes to go on this journey with me. Remember, this journey is ongoing, and it will evolve and change as you do. My intention is for you to embody the truth that healing is possible. As you begin to do *the work*, your life will be a powerful, living testament to that possibility. I will leave you with "A Day in the Life of Doing the Work," which of course is my practice for you to use as a loose guide. I want you to make your practice of *the work* uniquely yours. Take what resonates and leave what doesn't. You are your own best healer.

---

## A DAY IN THE LIFE OF DOING THE WORK

BALANCE YOUR BODY:

- Explore your body's physical needs by answering these questions:
    - Which foods help your body feel good, and which make your body feel not its best?
    - How much sleep (and at what times) helps your body feel more restored?
    - How much movement (and when) helps your body release stored emotions?
- Balance your nervous system by engaging in daily polyvagal work (such as breathwork, meditation, or yoga).

BALANCE YOUR MIND:

- Build in more moments of consciousness and self-witnessing daily.
- Identify your ego stories and shadow self, noticing how your self-narrative drives many emotional reactions and coping behaviors.
- Cultivate a daily relationship with your inner child and begin to reparent yourself cultivating your wise inner parent to help you identify and meet your unique physical, emotional, and spiritual needs.

RECONNECT WITH YOUR SOUL:

- Explore and reconnect with your deepest wants and passions. Practice expressing your authentic Self in all areas of your life.

# Epilogue
# The Pizza Box

When I started thinking about writing this book and gathering up all the meaningful moments in my professional and personal life that I wanted to share with you, there was so much I couldn't remember. My brain was still dealing with the fallout of early childhood trauma, and my body still grappled with nervous system responses that kept me disengaged and unable to access the past. There were many blank spots in my memory bank, and the one that irritated me the most was my inability to recall the exact wording of the quote that I encountered during my walk past the Rubin Museum of Art in New York City, the one that opened my mind to the concept of consciousness and sent me into a whole new way of being. No matter how hard I tried, no matter how many phrases I searched or how many exhibition catalogs I tracked down in search of that quote, it remained lost.

Meanwhile, my transition into a new life in California continued. As I started to develop a routine, I also witnessed myself reverting to old patterns in a response to feeling outside my element. I started to mourn my old life. Even though I knew that life was not serving my best self, the old Nicole still found it safe and familiar.

At the same time this personal turmoil was occurring, the Holistic Psychology message was spreading like wildfire around the world with more than two million people following my posts on social media and engaging with the work on levels that my mind just could not grasp. I felt elated—vindicated, really—and also overwhelmed. My inner child, so desperate to be seen and loved, began to quake under the pressure of so many eyes. I feared being misunderstood, and when I inevitably was misunderstood, I felt like a failure.

Then a global pandemic hit, and everything was thrown into stark relief. There was so much pain, suffering, and trauma. We were all in it together, locked up, energetically and physically struggling in a new world that made no sense. Stress raged. Like so many, I felt deeply uncommitted to my journey for the first time in years. That lack of commitment manifested itself in small ways; for example, I stopped cooking for myself, a daily act of self-care that I valued. I usually enjoy nourishing myself and those I love. During lockdown, I just couldn't muster up the energy to make myself a meal. One evening Lolly, Jenna, and I were scrolling through Postmates and decided to order pizza. We found a store that offered gluten-free crust. I had never ordered from that restaurant, nor had I even heard of it, so our decision was based solely on the online reviews.

The pizza box was left at our front door, and when I lifted the box to eye level, I noticed some cute lettering on the side of the box. Then I read the words and nearly dropped the box. There it was, delivered right to my front door: "'We don't remember days, we remember moments,' Cesare Pavese."

It was the quote I'd been searching for—the one that sent me off down the rabbit hole of self-exploration. Out of the millions—billions?—of quotable phrases out there in the world, that one came back to me like an echo, a reminder of how much I had grown. Flashes of the past came into my mind's eye: crying into my oatmeal, the apartment pool where I fainted for the first time, wheeling my toy car under the kitchen table of my childhood home. It was all there with me, all parts of who I am now, who I was then, and who I will one day become. I let the words sink in as I breathed in and out. Gratitude filled every cell of my being.

I can't say that the pizza box directly led me to the next step of my personal and spiritual growth, though it did help affirm my self-trust and awareness. I was once unwell, wounded, and unconscious. Now, despite the present hiccups, I was living this quote. I think it's plausible to say that that pizza box gave me the confidence to make another conscious choice: I decided it was time to reach back out to my family.

When I set that hard boundary to cut off contact with them, I had needed to do it to find out who I really was without my family's overwhelming presence. For the first time, I was able to view myself: I saw my strengths; I saw my vulnerabilities; I met my inner child; and I accepted my wounds. I enforced zero communication because I didn't trust myself. I knew that there was a slippery slope back into codependence. Those rigid boundaries helped me to connect to my authentic Self, which enabled me to finally be able to connect more honestly with others—and ultimately with all of you. It was the perfect state for an attempt at reconnection. It seemed like a now-or-never moment.

It started with a letter. I kept it short and simple, essentially saying *I am ready to reconnect if you, too, are ready and willing to work together to create a new relationship*. It was an acknowledgment that I was ready to open the door to communication. My family responded. They felt hesitant but willing to engage, letting me know that they too took the space as an opportunity to begin their own healing.

I don't know what this new relationship will look like. I'm allowing myself the flexibility of choice. I'm giving myself the gift of openness and curiosity to explore the possibilities of a relationship that emerges from my own inner Self-trust and Self-love, and I'm excited to see what it may or may not bring.

Every moment, we make a choice: we can live in the past, or we can look forward and envision a future that is different. Our tendency when we return to a system, regardless of how much work we do on our own, is to revert to old patterns. The temptation is to embrace the familiar subconscious conditioning. We can also decide to participate in the opening of an unfamiliar, uncertain door. I know now that if that path is not serving me well, I will know and can turn right around, close the door, and choose a new one to open.

As of this writing, we have all changed in our own ways. My sister has started her own SelfHealing journey, and I have transitioned from attending family therapy to rebuilding our relationships in day-to-day life. The other day, when my dad was away, I called my mom to help relieve the loneliness I knew that she was feeling. I didn't feel an obligation of having to help her feel better; I did it because I wanted to. And it felt good.

I am still balancing on the shaky bridge of wanting to support my family but doing so in a way that works for me. I'm still taking it moment by moment, still asking my intuition for guidance in every interaction. I now have faith that I will ultimately make the right choice for me.

This is what this work is all about: the empowerment of being able to choose. We can choose how we treat our body, how we show up in relationships, how we create our realities and envision our futures. Whatever path you take, as long as you've consciously chosen it and trust yourself in the process, whatever the outcomes, you will be ready. There are no road maps, no directions, no gurus, no sages. There are no checklists that will fix you or magical pills that will cure you.

I am a powerful creator of my world, and my energy and thoughts shape the world around me. Yes, there are things outside my control, and we do have power over the way we experience the world. We can change the way we take care of ourselves. We can change the way we interpret our surroundings and relate to the ones we love. We can change the way we connect to our Self and in doing so change the way we connect to the universe. There is always an opportunity to grow, evolve, and inspire, which trickles out into the collective. The point of this book is to return us to our authentic essence, our pure awareness, the embodiment of who we were before conditioning took hold. We want to reconnect with the collective We and in doing so access the deep well of Self-empowerment within us all.

None of us can see the future. We have our intuition, we have our Self-trust, and we have our emotions—information—that can help us make the best choices possible. This is what healing is about: developing choice and trust in the tools we use to truly live our impermanent life, no matter what may come.

# Acknowledgments

It's been the greatest honor to share this work and watch as our community of #SelfHealers grew to become a huge movement. Each of you are the living testament and your countless messages of healing from around the world allowed this book to be birthed. I am forever grateful for your support, and belief in these teachings. You allowed me to have the faith in myself to keep going. With every person who heals, comes a person inspired to do the same. You are all changing our collective future.

To Ally, who has walked alongside me to stand in truth. Your story reflects the infinite possibilities that live in each of us. It is a true honor to share this journey of empowerment with you.

To my parents, who I believe I chose, thank you. Your story, your love, and your own unresolved trauma was a catalyst for me to resolve my own. I teach this work for you and every generation before you that did not have the access this knowledge and lived within inherited shame. You taught me how to take responsibility and to return to who I actually am. Thank you for allowing me to remember.

To my mentors, who are mostly from afar, I appreciate you beyond words for stepping out of the paradigm and blazing the trail. I've come to learn that it can be a difficult, and lonely journey at times, and your wisdom opened portals within me I had never learned within traditional schooling. Your courage inspired my own. I speak my truths so that others may be inspired in the way you inspired me.

Thank you to my agent, Dado Derviskadic, who has been such a loving wise guide during the process of writing this book. When you first birthed and spoke the title, I had chills through my entire body.

You do your work because you want to make the world a better place, and it's an honor to work alongside of you.

Writing my first book could not have happened without the support of the team at Harper Wave. You saw my vision, and believed that the world should see it, too. Thank you, Karen, Julie, Yelena, Brian and the rest of the Harper team who helped birthed this work. Special thanks to each of our international publishers, especially Pippa Wright and her team at Orion Publishing Group, who believed this work should be translated in their native languages to help spread this universal message of SelfHealing.

I've incredibly blessed to have a team of conscious, beautiful humans. Each of you embody this work and help to co-create the space for this to exist in the collective.

To Jenna Weakland, whose soul walked many lifetimes to join my own in service of the greater collective. Thank you for listening to your own calling and for fearlessly showing up to assume your integral place in this movement. Your heart is pure love and a daily inspiration for my continued expansion. Words cannot express my endless gratitude.

To my partner in life and business, Lolly, thank you for seeing me. Thank you for challenging me in my evolution. Thank you for believing in me before I knew how. You have taught me a new version of love, one that offers a real and honest space from which I have been able to finally acknowledge all that is me. You held our vision with blind faith and continue to stand in truth beside me every single day. I promise to shine the light of this vision. Always.

Each of you are holding this book because you're ready. You're returning home to who you actually are. I fully believe in your limitless potential and continue to walk this journey with you. This book is dedicated to everyone who is called to become free. Shedding our protective layers in service of collective healing is the bravest journey a soul can take. I see each and honor every one of you.

# Notes


1. LePera, N. (2011). Relationships between boredom proneness, mindfulness, anxiety, depression, and substance use. *The New School Psychology Bulletin, 8*(2).
2. McCabe, G. (2008). Mind, body, emotions and spirit: Reaching to the ancestors for healing. *Counselling Psychology Quarterly, 2*(2), 143–152.
3. Schweitzer, A. (1993). *Reverence for life: Sermons, 1900–1919.* Irvington.
4. Mantri, S. (2008). Holistic medicine and the Western medical tradition. *AMA Journal of Ethics, 10*(3), 177–180.
5. Mehta, N. (2011). Mind-body dualism: A critique from a health perspective. *Mens Sana Monographs, 9*(1), 202–209.
6. Lipton, B. H. (2008). *The biology of belief: Unleashing the power of consciousness, matter & miracles.* Hay House.
7. Kankerkar, R. R., Stair, S. E., Bhatia-Dey, N., Mills, P. J., Chopra, D., & Csoka, A. B. (2017). Epigenetic mechanisms of integrative medicine. *Evidence-Based Complementary and Alternative Medicine*, Article 4365429.
8. Nestler, E. J., Peña, C. J., Kundakovic, M., Mitchell, A., & Akbarian, S. (2016). Epigenetic basis of mental illness. *The Neuroscientist, 22*(5), 447–463.
9. Jiang, S., Postovit, L., Cattaneo, A., Binder, E. B., & Aitchison, K. J. (2019). Epigenetic modifications in stress response genes associated with childhood trauma. *Frontiers in Psychiatry, 10*, Article 808.
10. Center for Substance Abuse Treatment. (2014). *Trauma-informed care in behavioral health services.* Substance Abuse and Mental Health Services Administration.
11. Lipton. *The biology of belief.*
12. Fuente-Fernández, R. de la, & Stoessel, A. J. (2002). The placebo effect in Parkinson's disease. *Trends in Neurosciences, 25*(6), 302–306.
13. Lu, C.-L., & Chang, F.-Y. (2011). Placebo effect in patients with irritable bowel syndrome. *Journal of Gastroenterology and Hepatology, 26*(s3), 116–118.
14. Peciña, M., Bohnert, A. S., Sikora, M., Avery, E. T., Langenecker, S. A., Mickey, B. J., & Zubieta, J. K. (2015). Association between placebo-activated

neural systems and antidepressant responses: Neurochemistry of placebo effects in major depression. *JAMA Psychiatry*, *72*(11), 1087–1094.

15. Ross, R., Gray, C. M., & Gill, J.M.R. (2015). Effects of an injected placebo on endurance running performance. *Medicine and Science in Sports and Exercise*, *47*(8), 1672–1681.
16. Lipton. *The biology of belief.*
17. Brogan, K., & Loberg, K. (2016). *A mind of your own: The truth about depression and how women can heal their bodies to reclaim their lives.* Harper Wave.
18. Meador, C. K. (1992). Hex death: Voodoo magic or persuasion? *Southern Medical Journal*, *85*(3), 244–247.
19. Holder, D. (2008, January 2). Health: Beware negative self-fulfilling prophecy. *The Seattle Times.* https://www.seattletimes.com/seattle-news/health/health-beware-negative-self-fulfilling-prophecy/.
20. Reeves, R. R., Ladner, M. E., Hart, R. H., & Burke, R. S. (2007). Nocebo effects with antidepressant clinical drug trial placebos. *General Hospital Psychiatry*, *29*(3), 275–277.
21. Kotchoubey, B. (2018). Human consciousness: Where is it from and what is it for. *Frontiers in Psychology*, *9*, Article 567.
22. Dispenza, J. (2013). *Breaking the habit of being yourself: How to lose your mind and create a new one.* Hay House.
23. van der Kolk, B. (2015). *The body keeps the score: Brain, mind, and body in the healing of trauma.* Penguin Books.
24. Langer, E. J. (2009). *Counterclockwise: Mindful health and the power of possibility.* Ballantine Books.
25. Cacioppo, J. T., Cacioppo, S., & Gollan, J. K. (2014). The negativity bias: Conceptualization, quantification, and individual differences. *Behavioral and Brain Sciences*, *37*(3), 309–310.
26. van der Hart, O., & Horst, R. (1989). The dissociation theory of Pierre Janet. *Journal of Traumatic Stress*, *2*(4), 397–412.
27. Bucci, M., Gutiérrez Wang, L., Koita, K., Purewal, S., Marques, S. S., & Burke Harris, N. (2015). *ACE–Q user guide for health professionals.* Center for Youth Wellness. https://centerforyouthwellness.org/wp-content/uploads/2018/06/CYW-ACE-Q-USer-Guide-copy.pdf.
28. Bruskas, D. (2013). Adverse childhood experiences and psychosocial well-being of women who were in foster care as children. *The Permanente Journal*, *17*(3), e131–e141.
29. van der Kolk. *The body keeps the score.*
30. Scaer, R. (2005). *The trauma spectrum: Hidden wounds and human resiliency.* W. W. Norton, 205.
31. Gibson, L. C. (2015). *Adult children of emotionally immature parents: How*

*to heal from distant, rejecting, or self-involved parents.* New Harbinger Publications, 7.

32. Dutheil, F., Aubert, C., Pereira, B., Dambrun, M., Moustafa, F., Mermillod, M., Baker, J. S., Trousselard, M., Lesage, F. X., & Navel, V. (2019). Suicide among physicians and health-care workers: a systematic review and meta-analysis. *PLOS ONE, 14*(12), e0226361. https://doi.org/10.1371/journal.pone.0226361.
33. Krill, P. R., Johnson, R., Albert, L. The prevalence of substance use and other mental health concerns among American attorneys. *Journal of Addiction Medicine 10*(1), January/February 2016, 46–52, doi: 10.1097/ADM.0000000000000182.
34. Dutheil, F., Aubert, C., Pereira, B., Dambrun, M., Moustafa, F., Mermillod, M., Baker, J. S., Trousselard, M., Lesage, F. X., & Navel, V. (2019). Suicide among physicians and health-care workers: a systematic review and meta-analysis. *PLOS ONE, 14*(12), e0226361. https://doi.org/10.1371/journal.pone.0226361.
35. Lazarus, R. S., & Folkman, S. (1984). *Stress, appraisal, and coping.* Springer.
36. Maté, G. (2003). *When the body says no: The cost of hidden stress.* Knopf Canada.
37. Punchard, N. A., Whelan, C. J., & Adcock, I. M. (2004). The Journal of Inflammation. *The Journal of Inflammation, 1*(1), 1.
38. van der Kolk. *The body keeps the score.*
39. Matheson, K., McQuaid, R. J., & Anisman, H. (2016). Group identity, discrimination, and well-being: Confluence of psychosocial and neurobiological factors. *Current Opinion in Psychology, 11*, 35–39.
40. Paradies, Y., Ben, J., Denson, N., Elias, A., Priest, N., Pieterse, A., Gupta A., Kelaher, M., & Gee, G. (2015). Racism as a determinant of health: A systematic review and meta-analysis. *PLOS ONE,* Article 10.1371. https://journals.plos.org/plosone/article?id=10.1371/journal.pone.0138511.
41. Goldsmith, R. E., Martin, C. G., & Smith, C. P. (2014). Systemic trauma. *Journal of Trauma & Dissociation, 15*(2), 117–132.
42. Paradies et al. Racism as a determinant of health.
43. Williams, D. R., & Mohammed, S. A. (2013). Racism and health I: Pathways and scientific evidence. *American Behavioral Scientist, 57*(8), 1152–1173.
44. Porges, S. (2017). *The Polyvagal Theory.* W. W. Norton & Company.
45. Center for Substance Abuse Treatment. *Trauma-informed care in behavioral health services.*
46. Håkansson, A., & Molin, G. (2011). Gut microbiota and inflammation. *Nutrients, 3*(6), 637–682.

47. Campbell-McBride, N. (2010). *Gut and psychology syndrome: Natural treatment for autism, dyspraxia, A.D.D., dyslexia, A.D.H.D., depression, schizophrenia*. Medinform Publishing.
48. Peirce, J. M., & Alviña, K. (2019). The role of inflammation and the gut microbiome in depression and anxiety. *Journal of Neuroscience Research*, *97*(10), 1223–1241.
49. Caspani, G., Kennedy, S. H., Foster, J. A., & Swann, J. R. (2019). Gut microbial metabolites in depression: Understanding the biochemical mechanisms. *Microbial Cell*, *6*(10), 454–481.
50. Zheng, P., Zeng, B., Liu, M., Chen, J., Pan, J., Han, Y., Liu, Y., Cheng, K., Zhou, C., Wang, H., Zhou, X., Gui, S., Perry, S. W., Wong, M.-L., Lincinio, J., Wei, H., & Xie, P. (2019). The gut microbiome from patients with schizophrenia modulates the glutamate-glutamine-GABA cycle and schizophrenia-relevant behaviors in mice. *Science Advances*, *5*(2), eeau8817.
51. Li, Q., Han, Y., Dy, A.B.C., & Hagerman, R. J. (2017). The gut microbiota and autism spectrum disorders. *Frontiers in Cellular Neuroscience*, *11*, Article 120.
52. de Cabo, R., & Mattson, M. P. (2019). Effects of intermittent fasting on health, aging, and disease. *The New England Journal of Medicine*, *381*(26), 2541–2551.
53. Mattson, M. P., Moehl, K., Ghena, N., Schmaedick, M., & Cheng, A. (2018). Intermittent metabolic switching, neuroplasticity and brain health. *Nature Reviews Neuroscience*, *19*(2), 63–80.
54. Watkins, E., & Serpell, L. (2016). The psychological effects of short-term fasting in healthy women. *Frontiers in Nutrition*, *3*(7), 27.
55. Walker, M. (2018). *Why We Sleep: The New Science of Sleep and Dreams*. Penguin.
56. Brown, R. P., & Gerbarg, P. L. (2009). Yoga breathing, meditation, and longevity. *Annals of the New York Academy of Sciences*, *1172*(1), 54–62.
57. Nestor, J. (2020) *Breath: The new science of a lost art*. Riverhead Books, 55.
58. Hof, W. (2011). *Becoming the Iceman: Pushing Past Perceived Limits*. Mill City Press, Inc.
59. Sullivan, M. B., Erb, M., Schmalzl, L., Moonaz, S., Noggle Taylor, J., & Porges, S. W. (2018). Yoga therapy and polyvagal theory: The convergence of traditional wisdom and contemporary neuroscience for self-regulation and resilience. *Frontiers in Human Neuroscience*, *12*, Article 67.
60. Kinser, P. A., Goehler, L. E., & Taylor, A. G. (2012). How might yoga help depression? A neurobiological perspective. *Explore*, 8(22), 118–126.
61. Loizzo, J. (2018, April 17). *Love's brain: A conversation with Stephen Porges.*

Nalanda Institute for Contemplative Science. https://nalandainstitute.org/2018/04/17/loves-brain-a-conversation-with-stephen-porges/.

62. Villemure, C., Čeko, M., Cotton, V. A., & Bushnell, M. C. (2014). Insular cortex mediates increased pain tolerance in yoga practitioners. *Cerebral Cortex, 24*(10), 2732–2740.
63. Porges, S. (2015). Play as a neural exercise: Insights from the polyvagal theory. https://www.legeforeningen.no/contentassets/6df47feea03643c5a878ee7b87a467d2/sissel-oritsland-vedlegg-til-presentasjon-porges-play-as-neural-exercise.pdf.
64. Porges, S. (2007). The polyvagal perspective. *Biological Psychology*, 74.
65. Neale, D., Clackson, K., Georgieva, S., Dedetas, H., Scarpate, M., Wass, S., & Leong, V. (2018). Toward a neuroscientific understanding of play: A dimensional coding framework for analyzing infant–adult play patterns. *Frontiers in Psychology*, *9*, Article 273.
66. Gillath, O., Karantzas, G. C., & Fraley, R. C. (2016). *Adult attachment: A concise introduction to theory and research.* Academic Press.
67. Bowlby, J. (1988). *A secure base: Parent-child attachment and healthy human development.* Basic Books.
68. Leblanc, É., Dégeilh, F., Daneault, V., Beauchamp, M. H., & Bernier, A. (2017). Attachment security in infancy: A study of prospective links to brain morphometry in late childhood. *Frontiers in Psychology*, *8*, Article 2141.
69. Bradshaw, J. (1992). *Homecoming: Reclaiming and championing your inner child.* Bantam.
70. Ibid.
71. Hazan, C., & Shaver, P. (1987). Romantic love conceptualized as an attachment process. *Journal of Personality and Social Psychology*, *52*(3), 511–524.
72. Carnes, P. J. (1997). *The betrayal bond: Breaking free of exploitive relationships.* HCI.
73. Ibid.
74. Gottman, J. M. (2015). *The seven principles for making marriage work: A practical guide from the country's foremost relationship expert.* Harmony.
75. Gazipura, A. (2017) *Not nice: Stop people pleasing, staying silent & feeling guilty . . . and start speaking up, saying no, asking boldly, and unapologetically being yourself.* Tonic Books.
76. Taylor, S. (2017). *The leap: The psychology of spiritual awakening.* New World Library.
77. Miller, L., Balodis, I. M., McClintock, C. H., Xu, J., Lacadie, C. M., Sinha, R., & Potenza, M. N. (2019). Neural correlates of personalized spiritual experiences. *Cerebral Cortex*, *29*(6), 2331–2338.

78. Gibson, L. C. (2015). *Adult children of emotionally immature parents: How to heal from distant, rejecting, or self-involved parents.* New Harbinger Publications.
79. Brown, S. (2010) Play: How it shapes the brain, opens the imagination, and invigorates the soul. Avery.
80. Gibson. *Adult children of emotionally immature parents.*
81. Ibid.
82. Taylor, J. B. (2009). *My stroke of insight: A brain scientist's personal journey.* Penguin Books.
83. Cigna. (2020, January 23). *Loneliness and the workplace: Cigna takes action to combat the rise of loneliness and improve mental wellness in America.* https://www.multivu.com/players/English/8670451-cigna-2020-loneliness-index/.
84. Murthy, V. H. (2020). *Together: The healing power of human connection in a sometimes lonely world.* Harper Wave.
85. Antheunis, M. L., Valkenburg, P. M., & Peter, J. (2012). The quality of online, offline, and mixed-mode friendships among users of a social networking site. *Cyberpsychology: Journal of Psychosocial Research on Cyberspace*, *6*(3), Article 6.
86. Gottlieb, S., Keltner, D., & Lombrozo, T. (2018). Awe as a scientific emotion. *Cognitive Science*, *42*(6), 1–14.
87. Brown, J. (1989). *The Sacred Pipe: Black Elk's account of the Seven Rites of the Oglala Sioux.* University of Oklahoma Press.

# Glossary of Holistic Psychology Terms

**ALLOSTASIS:** The physiological process of transitioning from a stress response state (fight or flight) back to homeostasis.

**ANALYTIC MIND:** The thinking part of the brain, located in the prefrontal cortex, which is engaged in problem solving and decision making.

**ATTACHMENT:** The relationship or bond between humans that is influenced by early childhood relationships with parent-figures.

**AUTHENTIC LOVE:** A safe space of mutual evolution between people that allows each person to be seen, heard, and authentically expressed.

**AUTONOMIC NERVOUS SYSTEM:** The part of the body's central nervous system that is involved in the regulation of involuntary functions such as heartbeat, breathing, and digestion.

**AUTOPILOT:** The state of living unconsciously and without awareness, running on conditioned patterns (habit).

**BEHAVIOR MODELING:** The act of demonstrating behavior to others through one's actions, choices, and interpersonal engagement.

**BELIEF:** A practiced thought grounded in lived experience. A belief is built up over years of thought patterns that create neural pathways and requires both interior and exterior validation to thrive.

**BOUNDARY:** A protective limit established between oneself and others with the goal of defining where one ends and another begins. Clear boundaries enable individuals to honor their own needs and support authentic relationships.

**CONDITIONING:** The coping mechanisms, habits, and core beliefs we inherited from parent-figures, authority figures, and the culture at large, beginning in early childhood.

**CONSCIOUSNESS:** The present state of awareness in which choice becomes possible.

**COPING STRATEGIES (ADAPTIVE AND MALADAPTIVE):** Actions we take as an attempt to return us to feelings of safety.

**CORE BELIEFS:** Our deepest perceptions about who we are that are ingrained in our subconscious before the age of seven based on our lived experiences.

**CO-REGULATION:** An interaction or exchange between people that allows for safety and security to process difficult and stressful emotional experiences, for example, when a child or infant is in a stressful situation and the mother uses a soothing tone of voice and/or holds the child while simultaneously acknowledging the child's distress.

**CORTISOL:** A stress hormone involved in the fight-or-flight response that activates the body to engage with or remove itself from a perceived threat.

**CRITICAL INNER PARENT:** The internalized voice of a parent-figure who denied one's reality as a child or who shamed or invalidated our needs, emotions, and thoughts.

**DISSOCIATION:** An adapted stress response in which a person is physically present and mentally detached, numb, or shut down due to an overwhelming of the nervous system.

**DISTRESS TOLERANCE (ENDURANCE):** The ability to feel and be with a difficult emotion, then return to a regulated state.

**DYSREGULATION:** A state of physiological imbalance in the nervous system.

**EGOCENTRIC STATE:** A developmental state of childhood in which there is an inability to understand a perspective or opinion outside one's own. In egocentric states things seem to happen *to us*, *because of us*. resulting in a false belief that another's behavior means something about who we are as a person.

**EGO CONSCIOUSNESS:** Complete identification with the ego, often resulting in reactivity, defensiveness, and shame.

**EMOTIONAL ADDICTION:** The unconscious drive of the subconscious mind toward familiar emotional states in which the body's nervous system and neurotransmitters are activating stress hormone responses.

**EMOTIONAL DUMPING:** The unloading of emotional issues onto another person without considering or being empathetic with that person's emotional state.

**EMOTIONAL IMMATURITY:** The inability to hold space for others' thoughts, opinions, feelings, or perspectives because of personal internal discomfort.

**EMOTIONAL MATURITY:** The ability to regulate one's emotions allowing for flexible thinking, open communication, and resilience in stressful experiences.

**EMOTIONAL REGULATION:** The ability to respond to stress in a flexible, tolerant, and adaptive way, allowing our nervous system to return to baseline.

**EMOTIONAL RESILIENCE:** The ability to be flexible and rebound quickly while processing a wide variety of emotional states.

**EMPOWERMENT CONSCIOUSNESS:** The understanding and acceptance of the ego that create a space of awareness. This space enables a person to make choices beyond knee-jerk ego reactivity.

**ENMESHMENT:** A relationship dynamic in which both a lack of boundaries and shared emotional states cause a lack of personal independence and autonomy.

**ENTERIC NERVOUS SYSTEM:** The part of the autonomic nervous system that governs all activities of the gut.

**FIGHT OR FLIGHT:** A nervous system response aimed at keeping us safe from perceived threat.

**FUTURE SELF JOURNALING:** A journaling tool used to support the conscious creation of new neural pathways and emotional states, leading to sustained behavioral change.

**HOLDING SPACE:** Being fully present and curious with someone, without judging or attempting to change them, as they express their emotions and experiences.

**HOLISTIC PSYCHOLOGY:** A practical healing philosophy that considers and addresses all parts of the person (mind, body, and soul), encourages the exploration of causes of symptoms rather than suppressing them, and acknowledges the interconnectedness of the universe.

**HOMEOSTATIC IMPULSE:** A psychological and biological pull toward the familiar, known as the habit self.

**HOMEOSTASIS:** The ability to maintain a relatively balanced internal and nervous system state regardless of the happenings in one's external environment.

**INNER CHILD:** An unconscious part of the mind in which we carry our unmet needs, our suppressed childhood emotions, our creativity, our intuition, and our ability to play.

**INNER CHILD WOUNDS:** The painful experiences carried into adulthood of not having our childhood physical, emotional, and spiritual needs (*to be seen, heard, and authentically expressed*) met.

**INTERDEPENDENCE:** A mutual supportive connectedness within a relationship that allows for boundaries, safety, autonomy, and full Self expression.

**INTUITION:** An internal knowing and inner insight that when listened to guides us toward our authentic path.

**INTUITIVE SELF:** The most authentic, spiritually connected Self that exists beyond conditioned patterns and conditioned responses.

**MONKEY MIND:** The constant stream of mental chatter that runs through the human mind.

**NEGATIVITY BIAS:** The brain's evolutionarily hardwired bias of prioritizing (and therefore valuing) negative information over positive information.

**NEUROPLASTICITY:** The ability of the brain to form new connections and pathways and to change and adapt the way its circuits are wired based on our experiences.

**NOCEBO EFFECT:** A scientifically documented phenomenon of when negative expectations of medical treatment or prognosis lead to negative results.

**NORMATIVE STRESS:** Predictable and expected stressful events that are universally common throughout one's life, for example, birth, marriage, and death.

**PARASYMPATHETIC NERVOUS SYSTEM:** A division of the autonomic nervous system (sometimes called the "rest and digest" system) that is responsible for conserving energy, lowering heart rate, and relaxing the muscles of the gastrointestinal tract.

**PLACEBO EFFECT:** A scientifically documented phenomenon in which an inert substance (such as a sugar pill) improves the symptoms of illness.

**POLYVAGAL THEORY:** A theory put forth by the psychiatrist Stephen Porges suggesting that the vagus nerve plays a central role in the central nervous system regulation that influences social connection, fear responses, and overall mental and emotional well-being.

**PREFRONTAL CORTEX:** The area of the brain that governs complex functions such as problem solving, decision making, future planning, and metacognition (*our ability to witness and think about our own thoughts*).

**PSYCHONEUROIMMUNOLOGY:** A branch of science dedicated to the study of the complex interplay among the mind, the nervous system, and the immune system.

**REPARENTING:** The practice of relearning how to meet the physical, emotional, and spiritual needs of the inner child through daily, dedicated action.

**RETICULAR ACTIVATING SYSTEM (RAS):** A bundle of nerves located on the brain stem that filters the onslaught of stimuli in the environment and plays a crucial role in maintaining behavior, arousal, consciousness, and motivation.

**SELF-BETRAYAL:** A learned coping mechanism from childhood in which parts of ourselves are denied in order that we may be seen, heard, and accepted by others.

**SHADOW SELF:** The "undesirable" parts of our self that are repressed or denied as a result of conditioning and shame.

**SOCIAL ENGAGEMENT MODE:** A nervous system state of regulation in which safety and security can be accessed in order to be open and receptive to connections with others.

**SOOTHING:** The act of neutralizing our emotional states, enabling a return to homeostasis.

**SPIRITUAL TRAUMA:** The consistent experience of not feeling seen, heard, or free to express oneself authentically, resulting in a disconnection from the authentic Self and causing suffering, loneliness, and internalized shame.

**SUBCONSCIOUS:** The deeply embedded part of the psyche that holds all of our memories, suppressed feelings, childhood wounds, and core beliefs.

**SURVIVAL BRAIN:** A nervous system state of hyperfocus on perceived threats that results in black-and-white thinking, panic, and emotional shortsightedness.

**SYMPATHETIC NERVOUS SYSTEM:** The part of the autonomic nervous system that governs the fight-or-flight response to perceived stress.

**TRAUMA:** Any experience where an individual lacks the ability to emotionally regulate or process and then release the event, causing dysregulation to the body's nervous system. Trauma impacts each person differently due to their own conditioning and modeled coping skills and cannot be qualified or measured.

**TRAUMA BONDING:** A conditioned pattern of relating to others in a way that mirrors or reenacts our earliest attachments with parent-figures. Trauma bonds typically contain dynamics of emotional abandonment, lack of boundaries, enmeshment, or avoidance and can happen in both romantic and platonic relationships.

**VAGAL TONE:** The ability of our nervous system to shift between sympathetic and parasympathetic activation in response to daily stress. Poor vagal tone results in misdirected responses and high sensitivity to perceived threats in our environment. This overactivates the body's responses and leads to reduced emotional and attentional regulation overall.

**WISE INNER PARENT:** A nurturing practice within reparenting of creating an internal narrative that witnesses ourselves without judgment. The wise inner parent is able to see, hear, validate, and honor all emotional states, behaviors, and reactions with loving awareness.

# Suggested Further Readings


## THE CONSCIOUS SELF

Hawk, Red. *Self Observation: The Awakening of Consciences: An Owner's Manual.* Hohm Press, 2009.

Singer, Michael A. *The Untethered Soul: The Journey Beyond Yourself.* New Harbinger Publications, 2007.

Tolle, Eckhart. *A New Earth: Awakening to Your Life's Purpose.* Penguin, 2008.

## THE NEW THEORY OF TRAUMA AND TRAUMA BODY

DeGruy, Joy. *Post Traumatic Slave Syndrome: America's Legacy of Enduring Injury and Healing.* Joy DeGruy Publications, 2005.

Levine, Peter A. *Waking the Tiger: Healing Trauma.* North Atlantic Books, 1997.

Maté, Gabor. *When the Body Says No: The Cost of Hidden Stress.* Knopf Canada, 2003.

Menakem, Resmaa. *My Grandmother's Hands: Racialized Trauma and the Pathway to Mending Our Hearts and Bodies.* Central Recovery Press, 2017.

Stanley, Elizabeth A. *Widen the Window: Training Your Brain and Body to Thrive During Stress and Recover from Trauma.* Avery, 2019.

van der Kolk, Bessel. *The Body Keeps the Score: Brain, Mind, and Body in the Healing of Trauma.* Penguin Books, 2015.

Wolynn, Mark. *It Didn't Start with You: How Inherited Family Trauma Shapes Who We Are and How to End the Cycle.* Penguin Life, 2017.

## MIND-BODY HEALING PRACTICES

Balaster, Cavin. *How to Feed a Brain: Nutrition for Optimal Brain Function and Repair.* Feed a Brain LLC, 2018.

Campbell-McBride, Natasha. *Gut and Psychology Syndrome: Natural Treatment for Autism, Dyspraxia, A.D.D., Dyslexia, A.D.H.D., Depression, Schizophrenia.* Medinform Publishing, 2010.

Kharrazian, Datis. *Why Isn't My Brain Working?: A Revolutionary Understanding of Brain Decline and Effective Strategies to Recover Your Brain's Health.* Elephant Press, 2013.

Mayer, Emeran. *The Mind-Gut Connection: How the Hidden Conversation Within Our Bodies Impacts Our Mood, Our Choices, and Our Overall Health.* Harper Wave, 2016.

McKeown, Patrick. *The Oxygen Advantage: Simple, Scientifically Proven Breathing Techniques to Help You Become Healthier, Slimmer, Faster, and Fitter.* William Morrow Paperbacks, 2016.

Walker, Matthew. *Why We Sleep: Unlocking the Power of Sleep and Dreams.* Scribner, 2017.

## THE POWER OF BELIEF

Braden, Gregg. *The Divine Matrix: Bridging Time, Space, Miracles, and Belief.* Hay House, 2008.

Chopra, Deepak, and Rudolph E. Tanzi. *Super Genes: Unlock the Astonishing Power of Your DNA for Optimum Health and Well-Being.* Harmony, 2017.

Dispenza, Joe. *Becoming Supernatural: How Common People Are Doing the Uncommon.* Hay House, 2017.

Dyer, Wayne W. *Change Your Thoughts—Change Your Life: Living the Wisdom of the Tao.* Hay House, 2007.

Lipton, Bruce H. *The Biology of Belief: Unleashing the Power of Consciousness, Matter & Miracles.* Hay House, 2008.

# Index

# About the Author

DR. NICOLE LePERA is a holistic psychologist. She received training in clinical psychology at Cornell University and The New School for Social Research. With her hugely popular Instagram account, @the.holistic.psychologist, Dr. LePera has continued to expand her reach through her free daily content and The SelfHealers Circle, sharing her tools for transformation with an ever-growing community of #SelfHealers. She lives in Los Angeles.